The Early
Intervention Workbook

The Early Intervention Workbook

Essential Practices for Quality Services

by

Lynda Cook Pletcher
Early Childhood Technical Assistance Center
Chapel Hill, North Carolina

and

Naomi O. Younggren
Department of Defense Army Early Intervention

·P·A·U·L·H·
BROOKES
PUBLISHING CO.®

Baltimore • London • Sydney

Paul H. Brookes Publishing Co.
Post Office Box 10624
Baltimore, Maryland 21285-0624
USA

www.brookespublishing.com

Typeset by Scribe Inc., Philadelphia, Pennsylvania.
Manufactured in the United States of America by
Versa Press, East Peoria, Illinois.

All examples in this book are composites or pseudonyms. Any similarity to actual individuals or circumstances is coincidental, and no implications should be inferred.

Library of Congress Cataloging-in-Publication Data

Pletcher, Lynda C.
    The early intervention workbook : essential practices for quality services / by Lynda Pletcher and Naomi Younggren.
       pages   cm
    Includes bibliographical references and index.
    ISBN 978-1-59857-224-7 (pbk. : alk. paper) — ISBN 1-59857-224-5 (pbk. : alk. paper)
    1. Children—Services for. 2. Children with disabilities—Services for. 3. Child welfare. 4. Family social work. I. Younggren, Naomi. II. Title.

    HV713.P566 2013
    362.71'6—dc23   2013017419

British Library Cataloguing in Publication data are available from the British Library.

2017   2016   2015   2014   2013

10   9   8   7   6   5   4   3   2   1

Contents

About the Authors

Lynda Cook Pletcher, M.Ed., is a Technical Assistance Specialist with the Early Childhood Technical Assistance (ECTA) Center (formerly NECTAC), which is funded by the U.S. Department of Education, where she has worked for 10 years. Her work has included providing technical assistance to states' birth to 5 early childhood special education systems, leading state strategic planning, addressing service delivery approaches for Part C agencies, review and revision of federal and state policies, and change and implementation of evidence-based practices at the provider level. Lynda's previous experiences, spanning 35 years in the fields of early childhood and early childhood special education, have included teaching in Head Start and child care centers, in the public school systems (kindergarten and third grade), and at the university level, as well as being an early intervention home visitor, part of grant administration, a training coordinator, an agency director, and a state director of the Individuals with Disabilities Education Act (IDEA) Part C Program. She has been a frequent national presenter on a wide range of topics pertinent to early childhood and the systems to support evidence-based practices.

Lynda has served on many local- and state-level advisory boards and state initiatives and was a federal appointee to the Federal Interagency Coordinating Council for IDEA Part C. She is currently a member of the Council for Exceptional Children (CEC) and was previously a member of the National Association for the Education of Young Children (NAEYC).

Naomi O. Younggren, Ph.D., is Comprehensive System of Personnel Development (CSPD) Coordinator for the Department of Defense Army Educational and Developmental Intervention Services (EDIS) Early Intervention Programs; an adjunct early childhood faculty member with Central Texas College—Europe; and an independent early childhood consultant focusing on early intervention, preschool processes, and recommended practices. Naomi's 30 years of experience in early childhood special education include being a direct provider working with children with disabilities and their families in early intervention and preschool programs, providing technical assistance, authoring early intervention handbooks and training materials, and serving in a program development and leadership capacity. Her primary areas of focus include authentic assessment, individualized family service plan (IFSP) and preschool individualized education program (IEP) development, natural environments and inclusion, family-centered practices, home visiting, service delivery models, adult learning, and applying the Child Outcomes Summary (COS) for measuring outcomes.

Foreword

What is early intervention for families with infants and toddlers who have, or are at risk for, developmental delays or disabilities? How should early intervention be provided to maximize child learning and development? While early intervention is a relatively young field compared to the larger disciplines in which it sits—early childhood development, special education, and public health—there are decades of research, policies, and practical guides to inform the work. However, there continue to be questions and uncertainty about what early intervention should *really* look like in order to meet its ultimate aim as a developmental promotion program focused on family supports. This struggle results in the need for ways to translate and specify what we currently know about "what it takes" for early intervention to be successful. These approaches can then be used to guide administrators and professionals as they implement programs and practices to more effectively enhance the lives of families and their young children.

The basic framework for early intervention has not changed since the flagship federal policies were instituted in 1986 as Part H of the Education for All Handicapped Children Act (PL 99-457) and its subsequent regulations. The emphasis on a child's natural environment; the role of the provider as assessor and consultant; and the importance of meeting families' concerns, priorities, and resulting outcomes is backed by the child development—and, more specifically, early childhood special education—knowledge base. The foundations of early intervention are situated in the undeniable importance of quality parent–child interaction (Mahoney, Boyce, Fewell, Spiker, & Wheeden, 1998); the critical components of exploration, scaffolding, and mastery motivation as how *all* infants and toddlers learn (National Research Council, 2000); the additive effects on child outcomes when professionals support families in using strategies that enhance their child's learning and development (Shonkoff & Hauser-Cram, 1987); and the larger context of positive family functioning that results in families having the time, focus, and knowledge to then positively mediate their child's learning opportunities (Trivette & Dunst, 2005). However, further research was needed to identify what practices and systems design should *actually* look like and what *specifically* early intervention professionals needed to do if aligned to this knowledge base.

The next generation of research began to define the unique practices, or critical components, of early intervention. Research refined natural environments from a place—such as home, child care, or community—to what happens in those places: the routine activities in a family's everyday life, including their development-promoting characteristics (Bruder, 2001; Dunst et al., 2001; Dunst, Hamby, Trivette, Raab, & Bruder, 2000). As described in Chapter 2 of *The Early Intervention Workbook*, the impact of how professionals provide supports, versus only what supports are provided, has been illustrated (Peterson, Luze, Eshbaugh, Jeon, & Ross Kantz, 2007; Trivette, Dunst, & Hamby, 2010). We continue to understand more about intervening where families will use development-promoting strategies, tailoring interventions to family priorities, and providing a level of support necessary for families to truly learn and utilize intervention strategies (Bernheimer & Keogh, 1995; Hebbeler, Mallik, & Taylor, 2010; Ketelaar, Vermeer, Helders, & Hart, 1998; Woods & Kashinath, 2007; Woods, Kashinath, & Goldstein, 2004).

Even with this research, there continued to be implementation issues, which resulted in the community of practice on *Services in Natural Environments*, whose work is the core of *The Early Intervention Workbook*. The resulting *Key Principles* and related materials are the closest the early intervention field has to a common set of nationally endorsed practices. They are used repeatedly in preservice and in-service professional development initiatives and guidance documents across the county. Yet, as the authors of *The Early Intervention Workbook* identify, early intervention systems, programs, and professionals continue to ask for additional specificity to drill down further into "what it means" for their work. This response is a clear acknowledgment of the complexity and sophistication of early intervention.

Now the field of early intervention is entering a new stage in its evolution. There is a recognition of the nuances of early intervention practice and the need to go deeper— embedding quality into policies, designing and redesigning responsive systems that facilitate and expect use of recommended practices, readying professionals to apply those practices, and generating research that informs this work within the realities of service provision. Early intervention leaders are looking to the field of implementation science (discussed in Chapter 10) to guide policies, practices, and systems aligned to this complexity. The authors of *The Early Intervention Workbook*, who both have "boots on the ground" experience as systems leaders and knowledge translators, are well poised to support this work.

Implementation science provides a framework for answering those multilayered "what it takes" and "what it means" questions by aligning how research is conducted, translated, and communicated, and how practices—including systems and program supports—are implemented to assure both fidelity to recommended practices and authenticity to early intervention practical work (Metz & Bartley, 2012; Fixsen, Naoom, Blasé, Friedman, & Wallace, 2005). Working from the *Key Principles* of the Community of Practice in *Services in Natural Environments*, implementation questions include the following:

- How are systems designed and services provided with flexibility in order to dynamically respond to changing family priorities and needs?

- How are systems' processes aligned with the overarching aim of early intervention as a family support program so that families understand and appreciate the rationale for this approach and professionals work from that lens?

- How are processes designed and services provided to focus early intervention work on infant-toddler developmental competencies and functional outcomes in the way young children live, learn, and grow?

- What mechanisms are in place for systems and professionals to be mutually responsible for each other? For example, what feedback procedures are available so practitioners can share systems, programmatic, and other barriers to implementing contemporary recommended practices? And how are practitioners supporting systems in finding ways to encourage those practices?

- What mechanisms are in place to assure that professionals—disciplinary practitioners, service coordinators, and administrators—have the expertise needed to fulfill their responsibilities in the early intervention system?

The Early Intervention Workbook provides a structure for beginning to answer some of these questions. Using interaction points throughout the chapters for reflection and consideration, as well as real-life "what ifs" (Chapter 7) and case studies (Chapter 9), the authors provide opportunities for early intervention teams and individuals to translate the *Key Principles* into real solutions to facilitate the use of these nationally endorsed practices.

The work of all involved in early intervention continues. What used to be innovative practices are now foundational. The *Key Principles* can be the basis for answering questions and providing certainty as to what early intervention *really* looks like. Current and emerging practitioners, researchers, administrators, policy makers, and professional development providers can then contribute to advancing the early intervention field from that common vision.

Bonnie Keilty, Ed.D.,
Co-owner and Cofounder,
B2K Solutions, Ltd.

REFERENCES

Bernheimer, L.P., and Keogh, B.K. (1995). Weaving interventions into the fabric of everyday life: An approach to family assessment. *Topics in Early Childhood Special Education, 15*(4), 415–433.

Bruder, M.B. (2001). Inclusion of infants and toddlers: Outcomes and ecology. In M.J. Guralnick (Ed.), *Early childhood inclusion: Focus on change* (pp. 203–229). Baltimore, MD: Paul H. Brookes Publishing Co.

Dunst, C.J., Bruder, M.B., Trivette, C.M., Hamby, D.W., Raab, M., & McLean, M. (2001). Characteristics and consequences of everyday natural learning opportunities. *Topics in Early Childhood Special Education, 21*(2), 68–92.

Dunst, C., Hamby, D., Trivette, C., Raab, M., & Bruder, M. (2000). Everyday family and community life and children's naturally occurring learning opportunities. *Journal of Early Intervention, 23*, 151–164.

Fixsen, D.L., Naoom, S.F., Blasé, K.A., Friedman, R.M., & Wallace, F. (2005). *Implementation research: A synthesis of the literature*. Tampa, FL: National Implementation Research Network, Louis de la Parte Florida Mental Health Institute, University of South Florida (FMHI Publication #231).

Hebbeler, K., Mallik, S., & Taylor, C. (2010). *An analysis of needs and service planning in the Texas early childhood intervention program* (SRI Project: P19478). Menlo Park, CA: SRI. Retrieved from: http://www.dars.state .tx.us/ecis/analysis_complete_report.pdf

Ketelaar, M., Vermeer, A., Helders, P., & Hart, H. (1998). Parental participation in intervention programs for children with cerebral palsy: A review of research. *Topics in Early Childhood Special Education, 18*(2), 107–117.

Mahoney, G., Boyce, G., Fewell, R., Spiker, D., & Wheeden, C. (1998). The relationship of parent–child interaction to the effectiveness of early intervention services for at-risk children and children with disabilities. *Topics in Early Childhood Special Education, 18*(1), 5–17.

Metz, A., & Bartley, L. (2012, March). Active implementation frameworks for program success: How to use implementation science to improve outcomes for children. *ZERO TO THREE*, 11–18.

Shonkoff, J.P., & Phillips, D.A. (Eds.). (2000). *From neurons to neighborhoods: The science of early childhood development*. Washington, DC: National Academy Press.

Peterson, G., Luze, G., Eshbaugh, E., Jeon, H., & Ross Kantz, K. (2007). Enhancing parent–child interactions through home visiting: Promising practice or unfulfilled promise? *Journal of Early Intervention, 29*(2), 119–140.

Shonkoff, J., & Hauser-Cram, P. (1987). Early intervention for disabled infants and their families: A quantitative analysis. *Pediatrics, 80*(5), 650–658.

Trivette, C., & Dunst, C. (2005). DEC recommended practices: Family-based practices (Introduction). In S. Sandall, M.L. Hemmeter, B.J. Smith, & M.E. McLean (Eds.), *DEC recommended practices: A comprehensive guide for practical application in early intervention/early childhood special education* (pp. 107–112). Missoula, MT: Division for Early Childhood.

Trivette, C., Dunst, C., & Hamby, D. (2010). Influences of family-systems intervention practices on parent–child interaction and child development. *Topics in Early Childhood Special Education, 30*(1), 3–19.

Woods, J., & Kashinath, S. (2007). Expanding opportunities for social communication into daily routines. *Early Childhood Services: An Interdisciplinary Journal of Effectiveness, 2*(1/2), 137–154.

Woods, J., Kashinath, S., & Goldstein, H. (2004). Effects of embedding caregiver-implemented teaching strategies in daily routines on children's communication outcomes. *Journal of Early Intervention, 26*(3) 175–193.

Acknowledgments

We dedicate this book to the many families who we have been privileged to work with over the years. You have taught us so much about what is truly important about helping you help your children and families. This book is also dedicated to the numerous providers we have been honored to work with and learn from. You have kept us grounded in the day-to-day work of early intervention. We also dedicate this book to the staff and devoted administrators of local, regional, and state systems that have led change in their service delivery systems; to the researchers, model developers, and national experts who have paved the way for high-quality early intervention services in natural environments; to the Community of Practice and workgroup members, for your visionary thoughts, ideas, and trust in us to write this book; and to Cathy and Sarah, for reading our multiple drafts and giving us valuable feedback.

INTRODUCTION

From Ideas to Publication

Responding to Needs in the Field

In 2006, at the National Early Childhood Office of Special Education Programs (OSEP) meeting, the idea of national Communities of Practice (CoP) as a way to improve results for young children and families was introduced. OSEP determined the work of one particular community, *Services in Natural Environments*, to focus on improving the number of children in each state who received early intervention services in their homes or other community settings where children of the same age without disabilities participated. This location of services was defined as the *natural environment* and is a requirement under the Individuals with Disabilities Education Improvement Act (IDEA) Statute and regulations. This CoP grew to include Part C coordinators, parents, personnel, development staff, direct service providers from a variety of disciplines, national technical assistance providers, and OSEP staff.

As the CoP got started, many state representatives reported that high numbers of children were already receiving services in natural environments, and although this certainly presented a challenge, the greater issue at hand was *how* those services were being provided. In response to this expressed need, the newly formed CoP needed to shift its focus from *where* to looking at the *quality* of services being provided. Early intervention state and program representatives expressed familiarity with several research-based models or approaches for proving early intervention services in natural environments through reading publications as well as attending national conference presentations and state trainings. Yet, there was a desire to learn more about how similar terminology—such as *family centered, relationship based, coaching, primary provider, transdisciplinary teaming, routines-based learning,* and associated practices—were applied in the different approaches. As states and local programs considered the different approaches, they had many questions: How are the approaches similar or different? Which approach is better for our state and local programs? Which ones will help our state the most? What is the research to support these approaches? What does implementation look like at a local level for providers and families?

This high degree of interest and amount of questions became a call to action for the group facilitators (Joicey Hurth, Grace Kelly, Lynda Pletcher, and Nora Thompson) of this newly formed CoP to help explain the similarities and differences of the approaches and to develop materials appropriate for national use to help providers provide *quality* services to families of infants and toddlers in natural environments.

Responding to this need, the CoP facilitators coordinated a national webinar series featuring experts who developed the approaches identified by the states. During the webinars, the experts discussed the key features and some practices used in their approach and the supporting principles and research behind their work. A culminating webinar in this series highlighted the commonalities, including the shared philosophical beliefs, related research, and aligned practices.

Following the webinar series, there continued to be an expressed need for further guidance and resources. In response, a smaller service delivery workgroup from the larger CoP was convened. This workgroup included the national experts, parents, state Part C coordinators, technical assistance providers, service providers, and an OSEP representative. Members included Susan Addision, Betsy Ayankoya, Mary Beth Bruder, Carl Dunst, Larry Edelman, Andy Gomm, Barbara Hanft, Cori Hill, Joicey Hurth, Grace Kelley, Anne Lucas, Robin McWilliam, Stephanie Moss, Lynda Pletcher, Dathan Rush, M'Lisa Shelden, Mary Steenberg, Judy Swett, Nora Thompson, Juliann Woods, and Naomi Younggren. These members discussed, debated, and made consensus decisions about evidence-based practices in serving young children and their families in natural environments, which resulted in an agreed-upon mission statement, a set of seven key principles, and an endorsement of practices that all participants supported.

1. "Agreed-Upon Mission and Key Principles for Providing Early Intervention Services in Natural Environments"
    http://ectacenter.org/~pdfs/topics/families/Finalmissionandprinciples3_11_08.pdf

2. "Seven Key Principles: Looks Like, Doesn't Look Like"
    http://ectacenter.org/~pdfs/topics/families/Principles_LooksLike_DoesntLook Like3_11_08.pdf

3. A set of key practices aligned with steps in the early intervention journey beginning at initial referral and culminating with transition
    http://ectacenter.org/~pdfs/topics/families/AgreedUponPractices_FinalDraft2 _01_08.pdf

These documents were shared nationally through conference calls and presentations, and individuals across early intervention systems found the publications useful and beneficial. By 2011, more than half the states were using the CoP's mission and key principle documents to define their state-wide system of early intervention. Many states also used the practices during training—but they wanted more. "Great start, but still not enough" was a common sentiment. They wanted a more in-depth look, curriculum and training materials, or even a book that providers could use to improve their practices in their work with children and families. Based on input and real-life experiences from the providers working to implement many of the key principles and practices, this workbook was developed by two of the original workgroup members of the CoP.

WHAT IS IN THIS BOOK

This is your workbook. It is designed for you to write in answers to questions, engage in reflection activities, and add comments meaningful to your day-to-day work. The book centers around the early intervention journey you and families share together. Although the book does not specifically endorse one particular approach or model, it draws on the common elements in various models and expands the work from the CoP key principles and practices. In doing so, the authors highlight the valued contributions of the national experts that have dramatically helped pave the way for high-quality early intervention services in natural environments.

Chapters 1, 2, and 3 provide an essential backdrop for understanding the endorsed mission of early intervention, foundational principles, research, and definitions of terms frequently used in describing evidence-based practices.

Chapters 4, 5, 6, 7, and 8 describe the steps of the early intervention journey: referral and intake, evaluation and assessment, individualized family service plan (IFSP) development, ongoing intervention, and transition. Each chapter begins with a family story that illustrates various aspects of the key principles and practices referenced in the chapter. These chapters include tip boxes, conversation starters, applicable federal regulations, and "Give It a Go" activities for you to apply what you are learning and doing as you partner with families in early intervention.

Chapter 9 is a case study that includes excerpts of one family's early intervention journey. It includes illustrations of recommended practices as well as questionable practices that are not supported by what you read in the previous chapters. Your task in this chapter is to identify the questionable practices and apply all that you have learned by defining recommended practice alternatives. Then use the latter part of the chapter to verify your responses.

The final chapter, Chapter 10, takes a greater systems perspective. It provides information and invites self-reflection about personal and systemic change—the necessary components to shift practices. The book concludes with a list of helpful resources that include other books and online materials that can be used in conjunction with this text as you continue your work with infants, toddlers, and their families.

WHO THIS BOOK IS WRITTEN FOR AND HOW IT CAN BE USED

It is our hope that this workbook will be read and used by current and future early intervention providers of all disciplines who want to reflect on what they currently believe and do and consider how they might enhance their future work. This workbook can be used in a number of ways. While helpful for individual providers and preservice professionals to read and use on their own, programs or teams may establish a learning community as a means for discovering new ways of working together for the benefit of children and families. It can be used to support preservice and in-service course work helping prepare new providers. State agencies responsible for early intervention may provide copies to their programs as a tool to support a desired change in the way services are organized and delivered, impacting all levels of the state system. And of course, we hope that parents and parent organizations will use the book to gain insight about what early intervention is intended to be and to help them work in true partnership with their providers.

As we reflect on the content of this book, we are reminded that the work continues to evolve as providers, programs, and greater systems strive to ensure that the highest quality of support and services are being provided to all the families of infants and toddlers with disabilities who embark on the early intervention journey.

Over the years, we have met and been influenced by many wonderful families, their darling children, dedicated colleagues, visionary leaders, ambitious researchers, tireless technical assistance providers, and university professors. In many ways, they have all helped to write this book. We share the common goal of wanting the best supports, services, and systems so that families, infants, and toddlers have the best possible outcomes not only during their short time with early intervention but throughout their lives. Thank you to all.

PART ONE

Getting Started

Foundational Knowledge

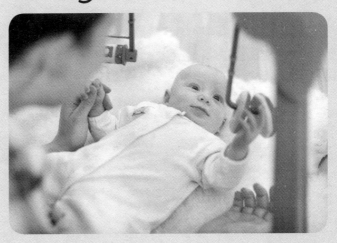

CHAPTER ONE

The Importance of Early Intervention

A Provider's Perspective

It is 7:30 a.m. Cyndi unlocks the state car and puts her purse, coffee cup, lunch bag, and laptop in the front seat and starts the engine. It is going to be a long day, as she has scheduled four home visits and one stop at a child care center. She thinks about the children and families she will see today as she pulls onto the interstate in a morning rain storm.

The first visit is with 7-month-old Zach and his family. Cyndi began working with the family immediately after Zach was discharged from the neonatal intensive care unit (NICU). He was a full-term infant, but things had gone terribly wrong at birth: He suffered a heart attack and a stroke minutes after the delivery. At discharge, his magnetic resonance imaging (MRI) showed that about one quarter of his brain had suffered a bleed, and no one was clear on what his prognosis would be. Amazingly, Zach has now been off seizure medication for 3 months, has had no seizures, and is demonstrating many age-expected skills. There is some concern about the low tone in his face and mouth, and one arm seems weaker than the other. The occupational therapist and physical therapist on Cyndi's team have made joint visits with Cyndi and have given her information and ideas. During the visit today, Cyndi will talk with Zach's mother about these ideas and get her input on how they might be incorporated into the family's day-to-day routines.

From Zach's, Cyndi heads to Christine's house. Christine is a 2-year-old girl with Down syndrome who began living with her 64-year-old grandmother ("Me-maw") after Social Services intervened. Christine has gained weight, her sleeping has improved, and her temper tantrums have decreased as Cyndi and Me-maw have taught her signs to help her express her wants and needs. However, Me-maw is exhausted most days and is interested in some type of daily preschool or child care for Christine. Cyndi spoke with the county respite program, and they are currently able to offer some help for 2 hours a few times a week. Cyndi hopes this will help Me-maw and allow her a little time to herself.

After lunch, Cyndi will see 32-month-old Jake and his mother, Mrs. Thomas, who called Cyndi yesterday to ask if they could meet at the family-owned restaurant where she works as a book keeper. Jake has been kicked out of child care again for biting and hitting, and his parents have no alternate child care for him. Jake's significant speech delay and his social and emotional difficulties make him an extremely difficult child to handle, even in the best of circumstances. On today's visit, Cyndi again needs to discuss transition because Jake is turning 3 in fewer than 4 months. She needs to discuss preschool special education services and the need to have a full evaluation conducted to assist with the transition process. This could be a difficult discussion as Jake's parents continue to feel Jake will outgrow his problems if teachers simply work with him better.

Cyndi has two children on her caseload that attend the Jack and Jill Early Learning Center and she stops in to consult with the teachers and join the class activities once each week for one or the other child. Corey, who attends the center from 7:00 a.m. to 5:30 p.m., is 18 months old and is experiencing significant global delays in development. The center staff has asked for some ideas to keep him motivated and engaged in activities. Cyndi also schedules a late visit to touch base with Corey's parents once a month when they pick him up at the center after work. They are not currently interested in home visits, saying they have too much on their plates and are happy with Cyndi's help through the learning center.

Because there is time before the visit to the McLearys, who get home at 5:30 p.m., Cyndi decides to go to the public library and catch up on record keeping and e-mail. The visit to the McLearys always includes the grandmother and sometimes the grandfather, who live next door and keep Jessica while her parents are at work. Jessica was born at 29 weeks, weighing 2 pounds. She spent almost 4 months in the NICU, where Cyndi began seeing the family and the tiny infant. Now, at 9 months, Jessica has received a diagnosis of cerebral palsy, which is affecting her left side.

Cyndi leaves the McLearys at 7:15 p.m. It has been a long visit with many new concerns raised by both Jessica's parents and her grandparents, and their expression of sadness about the recent diagnosis. Cyndi is very tired. She stops at the drive-in and gets another cup of coffee and a sandwich to eat while driving. As she eats, she reflects on her day and thinks about the visits she has scheduled for tomorrow.

Cyndi is the special instructor at a regional early intervention program located in a state that accepts federal dollars under IDEA Part C. She works with young children from birth to age 3 and their families. Her core team members are an occupational therapist (OT), a speech-language pathologist (SLP), a physical therapist (PT), and a social worker that supervises the team and helps out with service coordination. The team uses a transdisciplinary team-based approach with other members coming from other community services as needed. Some other professionals that Cyndi can include as part of a child's team are nutritionists, audiologists, nurses, psychologists, parent educators, and pediatricians or other medical personnel.

Each core team member can function as the primary contact and home visitor, referred to as a *primary service provider*, to a set number of families on the team case load. It is best for a family to have one primary person that makes the majority of visits to assist them in helping their child grow and develop. The core team members then consult with one another and with the family and make joint visits to families when needed. This method of working with families and young children has evolved over many years.

FROM YEARS PAST TO EARLY INTERVENTION TODAY

Attitudes and cultural beliefs about individuals with disabilities have varied over the ages. By the 19th century, the United States established training schools and institutions to provide care or treatment for these individuals, who were often described as feeble-minded, insane, or dumb. Families were encouraged to place their infant or young child in an institution right after birth with the assertion that such placement was best for society, the family, and even the young child. Over the years, attitudes have changed. In the past 3 decades, belief and practice have been that all individuals deserve help, support, and a chance to not only live with their families in the community but also receive education and quality care with all other children. Individuals with disabilities have the potential to become contributing members of their communities.

Crucial federal legislation established programs to provide needed resources to help young children with disabilities and their families. These programs helped young children remain with their families and paved the way for early intervention as we know it today. The early legislation facilitated a reshaping of attitudes, beliefs, and service systems.

In 1935, the Social Security Act Title V was established to provide funds for states to establish and pay for maternal and child health services and Crippled Children Services, as they were then called. Seventy years later, those early clinics are now called Child Health Specialty Clinics. Title V is the longest standing public health legislation in U.S. history and is a significant partner to state early intervention programs in both providing and funding services for infants and toddlers with disabilities.

In 1965, Medicaid (Title XIX) was established to provide health insurance coverage to low-income families and individuals with disabilities. In 1967, Medicaid's child health component was strengthened with the Early Periodic Screening and Diagnosis and Treatment program (EPSDT). This requires the state Medicaid plan to cover a very comprehensive set of services for children, including children with disabilities. State Medicaid programs continue to be a major source of funding for many early intervention services and are a significant partner for the state early intervention systems.

In 1965, legislation under the War on Poverty created the Head Start programs, establishing preschool services for the disadvantaged. This included the requirement that 10% of all children served have disabilities. Head Start expanded their services in 2000 to include an Early Head Start component, providing services to at-risk and high-risk infants and toddlers. Both Head Start and Early Head Start also have well-established family and health components for assisting families to help their children grow and develop. Young children with disabilities have opportunities to play and learn with same-age peers who do not have disabilities by participating in Early Head Start activities. After more than 40 years of research on the importance of early learning, it is now well known that the earliest experiences play a critical role in brain development (Shonkoff & Phillips, 2000). If young children, including those with disabilities, are to be successful in school and in the community and are to become productive adults, this development must be supported by healthy children and healthy parents living in supportive communities (National Scientific Council on the Developing Child, 2004).

In the mid-1960s, competitive federal funding grant opportunities were established to conduct research, develop and demonstrate practice models, and teach others about new practices through outreach efforts; all these efforts focused on young children with disabilities and their families. These efforts continue today as competitive federal grant opportunities and, over the years, have contributed toward the use of sound research to support evidence-based practices in early intervention (Gallagher, Danaher, & Clifford, 2009).

The year 1975 was the turning point for children with disabilities, with the celebrated signing of the Education for All Handicapped Children Act (PL 94-142) by by President Gerald Ford. This legislation was viewed as a civil rights act for all people with disabilities and the beginning of the end of institutional settings and training schools. Building off the importance of early health care, years of model projects, research, and the importance of early learning established by the Head Start program, the Education for All Handicapped Children Act was amended in 1986 to include a separate part of the legislation to assist states with establishing a comprehensive, interagency, multidisciplinary system of services and supports for families of infants and toddlers from birth to age 3 who had disabilities or conditions that had a high probability of resulting in later delays.

The original law has been amended several times. Cyndi and other early interventionists work under Part C of the bill now called IDEA 2004. IDEA Part C Early Intervention is also called the Infants and Toddlers with Disabilities program. Many states have chosen more consumer-friendly names to help identify their system of services, such as Sooner Start (Oklahoma), Babies Can't Wait (Georgia), Early Access (Iowa), and First Steps (Indiana), to emphasis that starting at the earliest point in a young child's life is paramount.

WHAT IS THE INTENT OF EARLY INTERVENTION PART C?

In section 1431(a) of the IDEA statute (2004), the following two purposes point out the dual focus of services and supports for infants and toddlers with disabilities and their families:

> Congress finds there is an urgent and substantial need: to enhance the development of infants and toddlers with disabilities, to minimize their potential for developmental delays and to recognize the significant brain development that occurs during the child's first three years; AND to enhance the capacity of families to meet the special needs of their infants and toddlers with disabilities.

In shaping this legislation, parents, professionals, and other advocates worked to ensure that crucial themes provided the foundation for the services and supports the law set out to provide. These themes included viewing infants and toddlers as whole individuals whose needs must be met by service strategies that cut across the traditional disciplines; appreciating that the development of infants and toddlers can best be understood and promoted within the context of family environments; and appreciating that early intervention is most effective when parents are respected and empowered as consumers and as active team members collaborating with professionals (RRCP-NECTAC-ITCA-OSEP Orientation Committee, 2009).

It is important to note that, although the federal regulations provide legal parameters for early intervention programs, there are differences from state to state and even within states. These differences can include who is eligible for services, which program or agency provides the services, how the services are organized and delivered, and who pays for the services.

WHAT EARLY INTERVENTION IS AND IS NOT

Early intervention was not intended to be a new and separate program. Rather, the intent of the law was to use federal dollars to assist in creating a better coordinated, interagency system building on what was already in place within each state. Cyndi, our early intervention provider, is very knowledgeable of children's development, disabilities, and early intervention practices. She understands that interventions with young children and family members must be based on explicit principles, validated practices, best available research, and relevant laws and regulations that can change over time. She also knows she cannot independently meet the needs of all the families on her caseload, nor can her early intervention program be the sole source of support for all families receiving services through local programs. As an early interventionist, Cyndi understands that she must partner with parents, early intervention providers, community agencies, and other support systems to effectively help the families with whom she works.

Cyndi works hard to respect each parent as the expert on his or her child and family and recognizes that, with the necessary supports and resources, all families can enhance their children's learning and development. Cyndi's team operates under that premise that each family's priorities, needs, and interests are addressed most appropriately by a primary provider who represents and receives team and community support. Accordingly, she does not work alone but, rather, is supported by her team, representing other disciplines who consult, coach, mentor, and teach her and the family when needed. Cyndi does not go into a home with her prescribed set of activities and therapeutic toys that she uses for an hour and then takes away when she leaves. She uses what is available to the family to help the child reach agreed-upon outcomes that are stated in the family's individualized family service plan (IFSP). The outcomes Cyndi works on with families are functional and based on children's and families' needs and priorities and have a focus on improving participation in meaningful activities.

Knowing that infants and toddlers learn best through everyday experiences and interactions with familiar people in familiar contexts, Cyndi helps families identify and enhance naturally occurring opportunities for learning. Cyndi's role with the family is not to fix them or their child: Her role is to help the family with the things they need and want assistance with. She sees her primary role as working with and supporting the family members and caregivers in a child's life and enhancing the family's competence and confidence in supporting their child's learning. When thinking about the time she spends with families, from initial contacts through the time they leave the program (called transition), Cyndi recognizes that her work must be dynamic and individualized to reflect each child's and family members' preferences, learning styles, and cultural beliefs.

In this description of Cyndi and her work as an early interventionist, many key principles and foundational concepts are identified. In the following chapter, we describe and explore these key principles and the many foundational beliefs and values that influence the day-to-day work and interactions with families and children.

In this first chapter you were introduced to Cyndi and learned about many principles she applies to her work as an early interventionist. In Give It a Go! 1.1, think about your level of agreement with the seven key principles developed by the national Workgroup on Principles and Practices in Natural Environments (2007). Rate yourself honestly using the 5-point scale. Then on the line beneath your personal response, use the scale again to rate how you feel your program agrees with these principles. As you go through this book, come back to Give It a Go! 1.1 and see if your level of comfort and agreement changes as you gain new insight into the meanings and practices these principles entail.

GIVE IT A GO! 1.1. SELF-REFLECTION

1. Infants and toddlers learn best through everyday experiences and interactions with familiar people in familiar contexts.

Self-Reflection:	5	4	3	2	1
	Strongly agree	Agree	Neutral	Disagree	Strongly disagree
Program Reflection:	5	4	3	2	1

2. All families, with the necessary supports and resources, can enhance their children's learning and development.

Self-Reflection:	5	4	3	2	1
	Strongly agree	Agree	Neutral	Disagree	Strongly disagree
Program Reflection:	5	4	3	2	1

3. The primary role of the service provider in early intervention is to work with and support the family members and caregivers in a child's life.

Self-Reflection:	5	4	3	2	1
	Strongly agree	Agree	Neutral	Disagree	Strongly disagree
Program Reflection:	5	4	3	2	1

4. The early intervention process, from initial contacts through transition, must be dynamic and individualized to reflect the child's and family members' preferences, learning styles, and cultural beliefs.

Self-Reflection:	5	4	3	2	1
	Strongly agree	Agree	Neutral	Disagree	Strongly disagree
Program Reflection:	5	4	3	2	1

5. IFSP outcomes must be functional and based on children's and families' needs and priorities.

Self-Reflection:	5	4	3	2	1
	Strongly agree	Agree	Neutral	Disagree	Strongly disagree
Program Reflection:	5	4	3	2	1

6. The family's priorities, needs, and interests are addressed most appropriately by a primary provider who represents and receives team and community support.

Self-Reflection:	5	4	3	2	1
	Strongly agree	Agree	Neutral	Disagree	Strongly disagree
Program Reflection:	5	4	3	2	1

7. Interventions with young children and family members must be based on explicit principles, validated practices, best available research, and relevant laws and regulations.

Self-Reflection:	5	4	3	2	1
	Strongly agree	Agree	Neutral	Disagree	Strongly disagree
Program Reflection:	5	4	3	2	1

CHAPTER TWO

Foundational Pillars of Early Intervention

In this chapter, we briefly explore five key concepts that over the past three decades have become the pillars that support early intervention practices today. These key concepts and supporting practices are based on years of research, application, and family input. They have also facilitated a major shift in how we define and deliver early intervention support and services. Knowing and understanding these key concepts is paramount for all early intervention providers, regardless of discipline, as they are essential for helping families and achieving the best possible outcomes for children and families. Many providers, though well trained in their disciplines, have narrow exposure to the theoretical or practical applications of these vital concepts. Although knowing about these concepts and understanding how they have an impact on practice is important, it is equally important to understand that these concepts and practices are heavily influenced by values and beliefs. What you as a provider and as an individual believe and value about children with disabilities, different types of families, children's learning, help giving, your role as a provider, and many other factors will influence your desire and ability to put these foundational concepts into practice.

In this chapter, we explore the origins, meanings, and impacts of these key concepts and share resources for you to learn more. These are the five key concepts:

1. Family-centered and relationship-based practices

2. Natural environments

3. Children's learning

4. Adult learning

5. Quality team practices

1. FAMILY-CENTERED PRACTICES

The term *family centered* embodies a set of interconnected beliefs and attitudes that guide the practices and behaviors of staff working with families (Pletcher & McBride, 2000). This term has been used since the early 1980s in nearly all help-giving fields with slightly different descriptions. Dunst and colleagues more recently defined the term *family centered* as "beliefs and practices that treat families with dignity and respect" (Dunst, Trivette, & Hamby, 2008, p. 1). The many descriptions and definitions of family centeredness draw from the core of

13

GIVE IT A GO! 2.1.

To get started, think about your actions and interactions with families in the context of early intervention visits. Make a list of behaviors you might use with families that would demonstrate your application of family-centered, relationship-based practices. As you read the next section, see how many of the things you listed are included and explained.

1. _____
2. _____
3. _____
4. _____
5. _____
6. _____
7. _____
8. _____
9. _____
10. _____

family systems theory, the ecology of human growth and development, and positive and proactive helping and empowerment principles. (Now complete Give It a Go! 2.1.)

Family systems theory grew out of the field of psychiatry. It reinforces how any person is part of the larger system in which they live and that the greater system influences the growth and development of the individual. Working with an individual in a family system requires an understanding of the family's entire system. Nicholas Hobbs and his colleagues (1984) proposed an intervention model aimed at strengthening the family system in which the goal was to identify needs, locate resources and supports for meeting those needs, and help link families with identified resources. By beginning with the identified needs of the family and moving to meeting those needs within the family's community, the family is better equipped to identify sources of support that can be used in the present and in the future.

Uri Bronfenbrenner, a cofounder of Head Start, theorized human development from an ecological framework. He accentuated consideration of all environmental tiers, the interactions among them, the influences on children, and a child's reciprocal

> Family-centered care assures the health and well-being of children and their families through a respectful family-professional partnership. It honors the strengths, cultures, traditions, and expertise that everyone brings to the relationship. Family-centered care is the standard of practice which results in high quality services.
>
> —National Center for Family-Centered Care, 1998

influence. Bronfenbrenner's (1979) organization of this complex interplay of environment and child has helped explain how children develop in the context of family and greater society. Children are not isolated beings; rather, they are part of the interconnected family interacting with others who surround the family and make up a network of formal and informal supports and entities. Societal factors in a community, such as poverty, the quality of child care and schools, access to jobs, and even the political climate, have an impact on the growing child. To truly intervene and help the child requires understanding the relationships of the family and the interactions within all levels of the environment. It could also mean intervening at a larger societal level, such as advocating for new jobs, better and more adequate health care, or higher-quality education programs for children to develop to their full capacities and become productive citizens. Family systems theory and Bronfenbrenner's ecological systems theory of human development guide early intervention in many ways, perhaps most apparently with their focus on supporting the family and enhancing its capacity to help children rather than focusing only on the child. This is a major reason why early intervention asks families about their networks of supports, their resources, and their strengths and priorities, as these are woven into the delivery of support and services.

Another influence on family-centered practices comes from the research and work of positive proactive helping and the relationship between the help giver and the help seeker. Few early intervention providers may think of themselves as help givers and the families they work with as help seekers. Yet ultimately this is the relationship that is developed. Help giving and help receiving are complex processes involving personal motivations, satisfaction, and experiences. There are times when a person giving help and a person receiving help feel good about the interactions. For example, when Cyndi helped Me-maw find respite care and enrolled Christine in preschool, Me-maw was so happy to finally have time to herself and to be less tired. There are other times when giving or receiving help may not feel quite right. For example, when Cyndi tried to make home visits to Corey's family, they were never available. (Now complete Give It a Go! 2.2.)

Intervention programs that place major emphasis on involving the parent directly in activities fostering the child's development are likely to have constructive impact at any age, but the earlier such activities are begun, and the longer they are continued, the greater the benefit to the child. One major problem still remains . . . [Many] families live under such oppressive circumstances that they are neither willing nor able to participate in the activities required by a parent intervention program. Inadequate health care, poor housing, lack of education, low income and the necessity for full-time work . . . rob parents of time and energy to spend with their children. (Bronfenbrenner, 1975, p. 465)

Work in the 1980s by DePaulo and colleagues (1983) and Dunst and colleagues (1988) led the field to understand that help giving has negative consequences when it

- Undermines a help seeker's sense of competence and control

- Fosters dependency

- Lessens the help seeker's self-esteem

GIVE IT A GO! 2.2.

Think of a time when someone helped you and it felt right or good. In the box, list the things that helper did or said and then list the words that describe how these actions made you feel. Now think of a time when someone helped you and it was not a positive experience. In the box, list the things the helper did and then describe how you felt.

Positive things the helper did or said	Negative things the helper did or said
How you felt	How you felt

As you review your completed table, reflect on what you wrote and how it relates to the concepts of family-centered help giving that are described in more detail later.

- Promotes a sense of indebtedness

- Is unsolicited

- Is incongruent with what is sought

- Is seen as needed by the help giver but not the help seeker

- Is provided in a way that does not require the help seeker to learn new competencies or use the skills he or she already has

On the other hand, someone who feels positive about the help received often reports feeling like he or she is listened to, treated with respect, not blamed, offered help that met an expressed need, given time, and treated kindly. Ultimately, the receiver of help should feel cared about, hopeful, in control of the situation, connected to others, and capable (Dunst, Trivette, & Johanson, 1994).

It is impossible to talk about positive proactive helping without talking about empowerment. In early intervention, a valued outcome is parent empowerment. A provider, however, does not empower the family; rather, when engaging in effective and positive helping, a provider creates opportunities for the family members to learn new skills, gain needed information, connect with necessary resources, become interdependent with the community, gain emotional support needed, learn to take responsibility, and believe in themselves to optimally care for their family. The following from the Barr and Cochran's (1992) *Networking Bulletin* article highlights empowering and contrary practices.

Considering these practices, you can see how empowerment is both a way of thinking and an approach to providing help. It can also be an outcome of an effective helping relationship. Yet only the person who receives the help can evaluate whether the help was truly beneficial and empowering.

Empowering practices	Contrary practices
Emphasizing family strengths	Emphasizing family weaknesses
Regarding families as basically good	Regarding families as basically bad
Partnering with families and promoting active participation	Doing for families and expecting little participation
Seeing families as resources	Seeing professionals as the only resource
Relying on families with support from services and professionals	Relying on experts or professional services
Regarding community supports as lasting resources	Regarding professional services as the lasting resource
Emphasizing prevention and promotion	Emphasizing crisis intervention

Source: Barr and Cochran (1992).

In the late 1980s, Carl Dunst and his colleagues at the Family Infant and Preschool Program in Morganton, North Carolina, put into practice a new model of working with young children and their families that was heavily influenced by the previously mentioned concepts. The ideas were first presented to the early intervention field in a book titled *Enabling and Empowering Families, Principles and Guidelines for Practice* (Dunst, Trivette, & Deal, 1988), which described the practices as family-centered help giving. The model included beliefs and helping practices that treated families with respect; were nonjudgmental, flexible, and individualized to each family and child; built upon the strengths and abilities that all families had; provided open and honest information and communication; and assisted families to be the key decision makers in all aspects of the services they were to receive. What providers and families established together were positive helping relationships and partnerships in which the provider engaged in help-giving behaviors that resulted in families feeling and displaying their competence and confidence in their own lives. This, in turn, had a direct and positive influence on their ability to help their child's growth and development. In addition to the use of the specific skills of positive help giving, this family-centered model emphasized providing help based on family-identified needs, concerns, and hopes; using specific family strengths, abilities, and capabilities to help meet their identified needs; and assisting in building and using networks of community support to mobilize resources to help meet the family-identified needs (Dunst, Johanson, Trivette, & Hamby, 1991; Pletcher, 1997).

> Empowerment: An interactive process through which people experience personal and social change enabling them to take actions to achieve influence over the organizations and institutions that affect their lives and the communities in which they live.
>
> —Whitmore & Kerans, 1988, p. 53

Family-centered practices have relational and participatory components (Wilson & Dunst, 2005). The relational component includes all the skills used by providers to build relationships with families, such as listening actively, showing compassion, respecting and valuing the other person, being nonjudgmental, offering help that matches what is desired, and believing that parents are capable and competent. The participatory component focuses on strengthening families by actively engaging them in decision making as well as understanding and treating families as the expert on their child and on their family. It also involves partnering with families to discover their priorities, collaboratively determining what help will be most meaningful, as well as helping families learn new skills, receive information, and access emotional support that meets their needs (Dunst & Trivette, 1994, 1996). It is the blending of these components that makes family-centered practices different from other approaches of working with families (Dunst et al., 1991). Research supports that the convergence of a provider's relational skills and family participation in priority setting and decision making must occur for achievement of optimal outcomes (Dunst & Trivette, 2005).

Family-centered beliefs and values continue to receive wide support and endorsement in the medical and early intervention fields. However, family surveys and reviews of practices indicate that the implementation of these beliefs and values has been a challenge for frontline providers, which may be due to a variety of factors including beliefs and attitudes of the providers, inadequate training and recourses for implementation, or inadequate reflective supervision and leadership (Bailey, Raspa, & Fox, 2012). While heartily endorsed in early intervention, the field still has a ways to go with implementation of these concepts and practices.

What does all this mean to you as a provider? It means that being an interventionist is more than simply being skillful in your discipline and being nice to families. It requires the full application of family-centered support and all that it encompasses. This is further reinforced in the early intervention legislation that specifies one of its goals as "enhancing the capacity of families to meet the special needs of their infants and toddlers with disabilities" (Title 20, U.S.C. § 1431 [a][4], 2004). Fully implemented, family-centered practices can achieve the purpose of present-day early intervention—to enhance the competence, confidence, and enjoyment of young children with disabilities (Dunst & Trivette, 2005; Hanft, Rush, & Shelden, 2004; Workgroup on Principles and Practices in Natural Environments, 2007).

Relationship-Based Practices

There are many similarities between the relationship-based approach and family-centered practices, as both approaches share common foundations. Many of the skills providers use with families and others to build positive relationships are similar to those described in family-centered proactive helping. Promoting child development through parent–provider and parent–child relationships is a major focus of relationship-based early intervention practices (Kelly & Barnard, 1999). Young children's development is affected by the everyday interactions and bonds they have with their parents and other immediate caregivers. Interactions with others and with the environment can be growth enhancing or growth inhibiting (Bronfenbrenner, 1992). For example, young children may be in an environment in which a parent or other caregiver is overwhelmed with daily life issues and may not be able to give time or expend personal energy in activities such holding, playing, or interacting with the child. This results in fewer opportunities for the child to experience adults as a source of nurture and learning.

On the other hand, a growth-enhancing environment is one in which the adult can and does respond to the needs of the infant quickly and responsively. They interpret what the infant needs, hold and provide comfort, and as the child begins to grow and develop, engage the child through conversation and activities that both enjoy doing together. Because learning takes place in the context of relationships, the quality of those relationships influences the quality of the child's learning opportunities (Norman-Murch, 1996). A child's early relationships are crucial as they, in turn, influence the way the child develops and maintains all other lifetime relationships (Vacca, 2001). Rather than just targeting the child for intervention services, the provider works to support and strengthen the parent–child relationship, helping the parent understand, interact, and enjoy his or her child in growth-enhancing ways.

Although a major focus in relationship-based practices is on the parent and child, another focus is on the parent–provider relationship. The essential behaviors identified in family-centered practices—such as seeing the parent as capable, using open and honest communication, respecting family priorities, displaying genuine caring, and being flexible—are the same behaviors that are needed to build a quality relationship with family members. Without building this essential parent–provider relationship, the provider will not be able to optimally promote the parent–child relationship.

Relationship-based practices also apply to provider-provider relationships and to work with others in the family's community. Without good relationships among team members and community partners, there are risks of families receiving conflicting information, including incongruent intervention strategies or an unnecessary duplication of services. Another important relationship is the provider-supervisor relationship. If you as a provider work in an environment in which you do not feel respected, listened to, encouraged, or supported, it becomes very difficult for you to practice relationship-building skills and behaviors with families or with colleagues.

> The essential features of the environment that influence children's development are their relationships with the important people in their lives—beginning with their parents and other family members and extending outward to include child care providers, teachers and coaches—within the places to which they are exposed—from playgrounds to libraries to schools to soccer leagues.
>
> —National Scientific Council on the Developing Child, 2004, p. 4

Respecting Culture

Truly applying family-centered and relationship-based practices requires being respectful of all individuals and their family culture. Cultural competence is defined

> A relationship-based organization is one in which quality relationships characterized by trust, support and growth exist among and between staff, parents and children: these relationships form the foundations for the work that's done. Relationships are valued, not as a touchy, feely nicety, but as a foundation for doing business.
>
> —Parlakian, 2001, p. 1

> as a set of values, behaviors, attitudes and practices within a system, organization, and program or among individuals and which enables them to work effectively across cultures; it refers to the ability to honor and respect the beliefs, language, interpersonal styles and behaviors of individuals and families receiving services as well as staff providing services. (Hagan, Shaw, & Duncan, 2008)

There are tangible aspects of cultures such as dress, food, and holiday celebrations as well as intangible aspects of culture such as beliefs and values, child-rearing practices, family interaction styles, and views about professionals and receiving help (Sanchez & Thorp, 2008).

Being family centered requires early intervention providers to momentarily relinquish their own cultural values and beliefs about child development and child rearing in order to fully understand the cultural values, beliefs, and child-rearing practices of others. Although individuals of similar cultures may have like customs, be cautious about stereotyping the ways of families based on generalized cultural practices. Recognize and understand child-rearing methods and unique cultural practices of the family to avoid making suggestions that may be in disagreement with family beliefs, values, and practices. For example, Western beliefs that toddlers need to feed themselves may not mesh with an Eastern belief that parents need to meet a toddler's caregiving need to be fed (Martini, 2002).

Families of different cultures may have different perceptions of disabilities and will consequently have different ideas about the type and degree of support needed (Zhang & Bennett, 2003; Lynch & Hanson, 2004). The early intervention emphasis on family involvement may be strange to families of different cultures. Some families may simply acquiesce to recommendations made by professionals, as they are not comfortable with their right to question those professionals or to contribute their own ideas (Zhang & Bennett, 2003). Remember that cultural diversity is part of life in the United States and that what is comfortable for you may be uncomfortable for a family and vice versa. When working with culturally and linguistically diverse families, it is necessary to develop an anchored understanding of their values, beliefs, and concerns to effectively partner with them (Barrera & Corso, 2002). Differing values, beliefs, and expectations could potentially become conflicts among providers and family members and get in the way of quality relationships. For example, not understanding culturally based differences and expectations in child-rearing practices such as feeding, playing, toileting, and discipline can cause confusion between a parent and an interventionist's expectations. Taking the time to understand family concerns, desires, and beliefs from the family's perspective is critical to ensure an anchored understanding. Before reading Section 2, complete Give It a Go! 2.3.

2. NATURAL ENVIRONMENTS

The word *natural* refers to things that are typical, expected, or accepted by an individual. What feels natural to one person may not feel natural to another. The *environment* refers to

GIVE IT A GO! 2.3.

Write a definition for the word *natural*.

_____
_____
_____

Write a definition for the word *environment*.

_____
_____
_____

Check your definitions against those in the dictionary.

How do the definitions of these two words support the concept of early-intervention natural environments?

_____
_____
_____
_____
_____
_____
_____

all the conditions, things, and circumstances that surround something living and help it grow. The two words used together in early intervention denote all the places and relationships that surround a child and help him or her grow and develop and that are expected and accepted by the family raising that child. The legal definition of *natural environment*—as first used in the Individuals with Disabilities Education Act (IDEA) of 1990 (PL 101-476)—that applies to early intervention is explained in more detail later in this section. The importance of this concept is that children thrive and develop best when surrounded by people, places, and community activities they would be involved in with their families and similarly aged children if they did not have disabilities. This is the concept of inclusion rather than exclusion or segregation.

Infants and toddlers live and interact in a range of settings: in homes with their immediate and extended family members, in communities and neighborhoods where they go to preschool or child care, in parks and neighborhoods where they play, at the library, and in places where their families shop and participate in other community activities. Supporting families of young children by visiting them in their homes and communities is not a new concept. In fact, providing help in families' homes is documented back to the 1880s, when organized efforts to assist the masses of poor immigrants flooding into major U.S. cities were put into practice. In 1899, Mary Richmond, a worker with the poor, published a text titled *Friendly Visiting Among the Poor*. In this publication, she outlined six principles for providing relief for families. In spite of the language difference and passage of time, her principles sound quite similar to many of the family-centered practices of today. (Complete Give It a Go! 2.4.)

GIVE IT A GO! 2.4.

Mary Richmond's six principles of relief are included in the following list (Wasik, Bryant, & Lyons, 1990, p. 47). In the space provided, convert the meaning of each principle into family-centered practices as they are or should be practiced today.

1. Relief should be given individually and privately in the home and the head of the family should be conferred with on all questions of relief.

   _____

   _____

2. We should seek the most natural and least official sources of relief, bearing in mind the ties of kinships, friendship, and neighborliness, and we should avoid the multiplication of sources.

   _____

   _____

3. Relief should look to not only alleviate present suffering but promote the future welfare of the recipient.

   _____

   _____

4. Instead of trying to give a little to very many, we should help adequately those that we help at all.

   _____

   _____

5. We should help the poor to understand the right relations of things stating clearly our reasons for giving or withholding relief, and by requiring their hearty cooperation in all efforts for their improvement.

   _____

   _____

6. We must find the form of relief that best fits the particular need.

   _____

   _____

By the 1930s and through the 1980s, social work and public health nursing were the major disciplines delivering services to families in their homes and community settings. Home visitation programs were added to Head Start in the 1960s, and other home visitation and parenting programs began to spread by the 1970s. Prior to the 1986 passage of Part H (now Part C) of IDEA, young children with disabilities received most services in clinics, special-purpose schools, or university demonstration programs. As mentioned in the first chapter of this book, many of these model demonstration projects first published the benefits of young children learning, playing, and being with typically developing peers. Families of young children with disabilities began to advocate for services to be different as well.

The idea of putting an 18-month-old in a car seat on a school bus to attend a special school for 6 hours while watching the neighborhood children play and learn in the context of family life is heartbreaking to some families. Taking a child who is medically fragile out in inclement weather to twice-a-week clinic-based therapy appointments and sitting in the waiting area while the child is treated also makes little sense to many families. Furthermore, anticipatory guidance and intervention activities that do not relate to real family life are less likely to get implemented. For example, a provider explaining the importance of playing with other children and suggesting that the family provide opportunities for their young daughter to play with same-age peers at a playgroup may not be realistic for a family in a rural area who has one car that the father uses every day to get to work. Another mismatched example is a provider who discourages a mother from breastfeeding her child at age 1 or encourages a mother to introduce table food and a cup when the mother values breastfeeding as special bonding. Families want and need help and support for their children but they also want their children to be a real part of their families and the community.

The term *natural environment*, first used in the 1986 legislation, means a setting that is "natural or typical for a same aged infant or toddler without a disability, and may include the home or community settings," and the term has remained in the statute and regulations ever since (§ 303.26). The regulations explain that, to the maximum extent appropriate, early intervention services are to be provided in the natural environment. In section 303.344 (B) (2), more guidance is provided, stating that if the child's outcome(s) identified on the IFSP cannot be achieved satisfactorily in a natural environment, then the IFSP must contain a statement as to why this is so. The nation has made great strides in implementing natural environments. In 2010, 94.5% of all children receiving early intervention in the United States primarily received services at home or in community settings, the natural environment as defined by federal law (Annual Performance Plan, 618 data tables). There are, however, a handful of states in which children with disabilities continue to primarily receive their services in clinics, special-purpose child care, or day treatment centers.

Moving services out of already established clinics or special-purpose programs into the family's home or other community settings has not occurred without resistance or challenges for programs, service providers, and families. Some common challenges described by providers and programs include the amount of time spent driving to family homes and the increased cost of gas, visits to homes and neighborhoods that do not feel safe, availability of team members for consultation, difficulty transporting large equipment, families not having the types of toys needed and therefore having to bring things into families' homes, and dealing with home activities that may not have the same perceived therapeutic benefits as those provided in a clinic (Campbell, Sawyer, & Muhlenhapt, 2009). Parents, however, more readily understand the benefits of services provided in their home and community. Parents report that home visits are more convenient, as they do not have to take children to multiple appointments in a variety of places. Children are likely to be more at ease and engaged when they are at home or in a familiar setting. Opportunities to play with same-age peers who do not have disabilities can offer more opportunities to promote learning than being sheltered in a group of children who all have similar disabilities. Parents understand that natural environments provide many more opportunities for learning, and most important to families, the home and community afford the child and family with full inclusion, places to meet friends, and opportunities to be active participants in daily community life (Campbell et al., 2009).

Providers sometimes indicate that their professional organizations do not support providing services in children's homes. However, professional organizations such as the

American Speech-Language-Hearing Association (ASHA), American Physical Therapy Association (APTA), American Occupational Therapy Association (AOTA), and the Division for Early Childhood (DEC) have developed clear position papers or statements that endorse the provision of early intervention services in family homes and community settings.

As the emphasis on natural environments continues, it is important to recognize that natural environments encompass more than the location where services are provided. Simulating clinic-based sessions in the family's home or community setting and using therapist-selected materials does not equate to services in natural environments (Hanft & Pilkington, 2000). Services in natural environments need to capitalize on using the materials, activities, routines, interactions, and locations in the family's repertoire. To help clarify natural environments as more than locations, Dunst and others talk about *natural learning environments.* Everyday community and family activities that are sources of child learning opportunities are the true natural environments for a child and family (Dunst et al., 2010). For example, bath time could be an opportunity for a child to develop and use language to request certain toys; learn concepts such as on, off, full, and empty; practice scooping and stirring with a spoon; experiment with pouring; practice taking turns with a favorite toy; figure out how to activate a water wheel; practice getting undressed and dressed; and the list goes on. A trip to the grocery store is likewise rich in opportunities for development of a myriad of skills important for successful functioning in that setting.

Natural settings are daily routines and activities that are unique to the child and family and that promote growth and development throughout the day. Providers and families work together to identify these natural learning opportunities and to apply agreed-on developmentally enhancing modifications that fit into existing family or child care routines and activities. Conceptualized this way, families, caregivers, and early intervention providers work side by side to discover and build upon children's interests that occur naturally throughout the day as well as to identify any adaptations needed so that the child can explore, engage, and master new skills or competencies. The concept of natural learning environments supports the parents' and other care providers' understanding of the importance of everyday activities as the sources of children's learning opportunities (Shelden & Rush, 2010). The family and caregivers have greater contact with the child and a greater capacity to enhance the child's development than do early interventionists who would have seen the child less frequently. Early interventionists must recognize and respect the family as the constant in the child's life. Families are the true change agents, and early interventionists are the support personnel helping the family make the desired changes for their child and family.

Early intervention services occurring within the context of family routines and activities exemplify services in natural environments. For example, a provider might help a family of a child with cerebral palsy who has difficulty riding in the grocery cart by brainstorming with the family and trying different adaptations to help the child sit upright and securely in order to see and point to items and more actively participate in the outing. Taking a child with autism to a fast-food restaurant may require the provider and family to work together to discover behavioral prompts to limit disruption. Including a child in a wheelchair when taking the dog for a walk may require some adaptations to secure the leash so a family member can push the chair. All these examples represent activities and routines that may occur naturally as part of a family's day-to-day life so that the child with a disability can truly participate and benefit from the many learning opportunities. To achieve this goal, the parent and the provider must work closely together. These examples reinforce the idea that natural environments go beyond physical location alone. Intervention that is part of family routines and activities becomes functional, relevant, useful, and meaningful for families.

3. CHILDREN'S LEARNING

Children are busy learning from the moment they are born and held in their parent's arms. As the relationships between the mother and child and other important caregivers develop, they support and form an essential foundation for future learning. It is vital for all early intervention providers to know about typical infant and toddler development, including important developmental milestones, the influence of temperament, and the influence of nature and nurture. It is equally important that interventionists understand how children learn through repetition of meaningful activities with familiar and trusting caregivers. Children need the opportunity to practice things repeatedly. Think about how many times and in how many different ways a child explores a new toy before mastering and then expanding on its playful use. Although it is possible to conduct drills with children to encourage their learning of specific information, such approaches do not promote children's real understandings of the information or facilitate their applications of the information in meaningful contexts. This is true for children with disabilities as well. Of course, some children may need adaptations and accommodations, or more time, practice, and repeated opportunities to learn many of the same things typically developing children do.

Common themes of children's learning include being motivated by what they are interested in and needing lots of opportunities to practice new skills through play and repetition at their own speed. Young children learn by participating and engaging with objects and people. They are hands on—playing, manipulating, vocalizing, moving, and experimenting. Children need the next challenge once they have mastered a new skill or competence. This new challenge, or next step, must build upon the previous skill. Children's interests and their temperament affect what they are willing to engage in and try for themselves (Keilty, 2010).

Natural learning opportunities consist of many locations for learning in the life of a family and child. Locations are the physical places and the social contexts a child and family find themselves in each day. Each location provides a variety of activity settings. It is within the activity settings that a variety of learning opportunities are available (Dunst & Bruder, 1999). One example of this concept is the neighborhood park as a location; the activity settings at this location may be swings, slides, sandboxes, and other children to play with. The learning opportunities may include pumping legs to make the swing go; climbing up the stairs on the slide; using language such as "push," "higher," and "1-2-3-go"; and taking turns with other children.

Family routines can also be regarded as learning opportunities. Routines are the activities the family or child care center engages in, perhaps not every day but with some regularity (McWilliam, 2010a). All families have routines. Routines may include such things as getting up and getting dressed, eating meals, riding in the car, taking a nap, going to bed, and playing with toys. A family routine such as getting up allows for practice with taking clothes off and putting new ones on, washing hands and face, brushing teeth, using language to name the clothing items, expressing desires, using words such as *on* and *off*, and so much more. Depending on the age and interests of the child and his or her previous skills, the family's routines allow for many skills and concepts to be practiced and mastered throughout the day. (Complete Give It a Go! 2.5.)

Children's interests, family everyday activity settings, increased learning opportunities, and parent-mediated child learning are the basis for Dunst's (2006) model of child learning titled *Contextually Mediated Practices* (CMP). Providers who use CMP first help parents and other primary caregivers identify children's interests and everyday community and family

GIVE IT A GO! 2.5.

Given the following information, identify three learning opportunities.

24-month-old boy

Location: bathroom

Activity: bath time

Learning opportunities:

1. Identifying his big and little boats

2. _____
_____
_____

3. _____
_____
_____

4. _____
_____
_____

18-month-old girl

Location: yard

Activity: playing in a sandbox

Learning opportunities:

1. Pouring sand from one container to another

2. _____
_____
_____

3. _____
_____
_____

4. _____
_____
_____

12-month-old girl

Location: kitchen—highchair

Activity: breakfast

Learning opportunities:

1. Picking up cereal and eating it

2. _____
_____
_____

3. _____
_____
_____

4. _____
_____
_____

24-month-old boy

Location: car—car seat

Activity: going to Grandma's house

Learning opportunities:

1. Repeating the names of the people he will see

2. _____
_____
_____

3. _____
_____
_____

4. _____
_____
_____

activities that are part of the child's life. For example, a child who loves to play with cars and trucks can use those toys as the basis for learning colors, one-to-one correspondence, sequencing play actions, taking turns, putting them away when finished, and so much more. The interesting activity and objects hold the child's attention far longer than an activity designed to reinforce similar skills but that uses objects or activities in which the child is not interested. Together the parent and provider identify the activities that will give the best opportunities for interest-based learning. Next, they figure out ways to increase the child's participation in these learning opportunities by offering support and encouragement to family and caregivers. Then together they evaluate how the activities are going and suggest any needed adaptations, supports, or other techniques to facilitate the child's learning (Dunst, 2010). A final important note about this model is that the focus is on supporting the family or other caregivers to help the child, hence the emphasis on *parent/caregiver*-mediated child learning.

Children do not learn as well in isolation during weekly home visits provided by even a highly skilled early interventionist or therapist focusing on therapy-driven goals to fix a problem. Assuming a child in early intervention received 6 hours of early intervention services per month over a 12-month period for a total of 72 hours, that is about a week and a half of therapeutic intervention spread out over the year. However, if that time was spent supporting the family and other caregivers to understand the importance of natural learning opportunities, identifying interests, discovering ways to increase the child's participation and enjoyment, and helping parents capitalize on contextually based learning, then the child is receiving optimal intervention every day in meaningful and contextually relevant places with familiar others. This is where and when real learning takes place for both the child and the family. In the end, helping parents and caregivers understand how children learn is an essential component of helping parents and caregivers capitalize on children's natural learning opportunities.

4. ADULT LEARNING

For adults, all life experiences—positive and negative—are opportunities for learning. Some of these experiences are planned, such as attending classes or workshops. Others are unplanned and can happen in all kinds of settings and experiences. Life events such as the birth of a child, a divorce, a new job, or having a child with disabilities can create circumstances that can motivate adults to learn new information, skills, or strategies in order to address the situation at hand.

Most early intervention providers receive training at the preservice level on working with infants and toddlers with the expectation that the focus of their work will be with young children. Although some training focuses on building partnerships and involving families, there has traditionally been little training on adult learning styles in the field of early intervention. However, a focus of the field is enhancing the family's capacity to help their child develop. This means that early intervention is not just about working with children; it is about helping families, and doing so requires understanding adult learning principles and using those principles to support the parent, caregivers, and team members.

Malcolm Knowles (1980) is often given credit for proposing a model of adult teaching that views adult learners as very different from children or even young adolescents. Some of these differences include that adults are usually self-directed, they have a lifetime rich in experiences that can be resources for new learning, and they often have a life task or problem-centered orientation to learning and want to use what they learn to immediately solve or resolve a situation. They are motivated by internal or intrinsic factors, such as a sense of accomplishment, a need to do something different, an increase in self-esteem at mastering something, or the fulfillment of a longtime personal goal—not outside rewards. He also spoke about adult learning as an interactive process encompassing the relationship between the learner and teacher, which ties some of the needed practices back to relationship-based practices discussed previously.

Brookfield (1986), another leader in the field of andragogy (adult learning), highlighted six principles that are important to keep in mind when facilitating adult learning. Accentuating these adult learning principles in early intervention reinforces family-centered and relationship-based practices. Adults play an active role in what they want to learn, and their openness to take on new information, concepts, or strategies is their choice. The learning they value most will be what links to their priorities (Knowles, Holton, & Swanson, 1998). This means we cannot coerce adults into learning something that is not meaningful, useful, or interesting to them. Learning must also happen in a climate of reciprocal respect, where parents, providers, and colleagues feel comfortable sharing their impressions, ideas, and viewpoints; together they flesh out the best ideas. According to Brookfield (1986), and parallel to family-centered philosophy, a collaborative spirit should exist that yields relevant learning based on the learners' identified needs versus predetermined plans. The experience of learning must also be coupled with application in real-life situations and opportunities for reflection. Real-life practice reinforces everyday learning and allows for consideration of situational circumstances, and motivating critical reflection promotes active rather than passive learning, as well as proactive input. Adult learning is not a separate field of study. It has direct application to early intervention and facilitating learning with families and colleagues.

Brookfield's (1986) Six Principles of Adult Learning

1. Voluntary participation
   - Learners decide for themselves what is important for them to learn.

2. Reciprocal respect
   - Learners need to know that their perspectives are valued, making them feel comfortable to share impressions, ideas, viewpoints, and more.

3. Collaborative exchange
   - Learners have a wealth of past experiences and accumulated knowledge, and new learning should be linked with their prior experiences.

4. Praxis
   - Learners need opportunities to practice what they are learning in meaningful contexts.

5. Critical reflection
   - Learners should be encouraged to question and discouraged from acquiescing simply because the *teacher* said something was so.

6. Self-direction
   - Learners ultimately gain the ability to establish and maintain personal learning goals.

There are three perceptual channels that assist learning: visual, auditory, and kinesthetic. Although some adults have a preference for one over the other, all three are necessary for learning and doing something new or different (Markova, 1996). Visual learners learn by watching, reading, and writing—making the written word very important to them. They like descriptions and may stop while reading and gaze away with intense concentration as they imagine the scene. They also often write things down, take notes, and organize thoughts by making lists. Auditory learners prefer hearing something first and then engaging in conversations and discussions about the material. They like verbal instructions. They also talk through problems—come up with verbal solutions through self-talk or by talking with someone else. Kinesthetic learners learn most comfortably by doing something and then having someone share either written or verbal information following their attempts. They tend not to be avid readers. They remember best by what they have done versus what was talked about or seen. Kinesthetic learners resolve problems actively and often choose the solution that includes the most activity. They seem to not focus well on visual or auditory presentations of information (Garmston & Wellman, 1998).

Interestingly, all three of these modalities work together for adults in learning and mastery, but one may be the first preferred method followed by the others. It is vital to acknowledge that your preferred learning style may not match the learning style of the families or team members with whom you work; therefore, having a variety of methods for sharing information and facilitating learning is essential as you work with the adult family members and team members. (Complete Give It a Go! 2.6.)

As an early intervention provider, you will be working with many different families and family members who all have likely had both positive and negative experience as learners. As you work toward building positive relationships with families, remember

GIVE IT A GO! 2.6.

After reading about different learning styles, take a moment to identify your optimal learning modalities (visual, auditory, or kinesthetic).

_____

_____

Identify which modality is first and which is second for you.

_____

_____

Now think of a family you work with. How would you describe their first and second learning modalities?

_____

_____

After jotting down your thoughts, check your assumptions by asking the person you wrote about. Did you identify their learning modality correctly?

_____

_____

adult learning principles and individual learning styles in your intervention interactions. You and the family will exchange information and learn new things together throughout the early intervention journey.

Early intervention programs and providers often rely on sharing written information with families by giving out brochures about early intervention, parent rights, parent booklets, and anticipatory guidance information sheets about what to expect. These publications may appeal to those who are visual learners but are not necessarily well matched to other learner modalities. When and how the information is shared may or may not result in "learning." When giving out handouts, it is wise to read them first and personalize the information you think is most pertinent to an individual family by highlighting and taking the time to review and discuss them. Simply giving brochures, handouts, and articles without some discussion is nearly pointless. Take the time to bring the material to life for the family.

Demonstration is another practice used to show a particular strategy that a parent or caregiver might be encouraged to try between visits. Yet, if the parent acts only as a passive observer, the learning value of demonstration is questionable. Rather, consider the adult learning principles and collaboratively discuss the strategy first, offer practice opportunities, and make time for feedback and reflection. Providers must consider how they present and exchange information with other adults in light of adult learning principles.

Approaches that apply foundations of adult learning include modeling, mentoring, consultation, and coaching. All these methods use a type of communication exchange that is built on trust, respect, and openness. It is a balanced conversation that uses active, reflective listening that allows time for thinking and responding. The interactions between adult learners should not be one-sided telling, arguments, or win-lose situations. They should focus on a balance of sharing information and inquiring about the other person's thinking to collaboratively blend the expertise of both parties to apply strategies toward accomplishing the desired goal (Garmston & Wellman, 1998).

Coaching, as an adult teaching and learning practice, was introduced into the early intervention field by Hanft, Rush, and Shelden (2004). They defined *coaching* as

> an adult learning strategy in which the coach promotes the learner's ability to reflect on his or her actions as a means to determine the effectiveness of an action or practice and develop a plan for refinement and use of the action in immediate and future situations. (p. 3)

Included in coaching is an interactive process of reflection, information sharing, and action on the parts of the learner (parent or team members) and the early intervention provider as the coach. It is used to help the learner develop new skills and then to help them continually assess, adapt, and practice what they have learned. Coaching fits well within the proactive help-giving model described previously in family-centered practices, as it builds upon the strengths and resources of the learner and assists them with building new competencies.

The coaching methodology proposed by Rush and Shelden (2011) included five key practices that the early intervention provider should use within each coaching conversation. These practices consist of joint planning, observations, action/practice, reflection, and feedback. Although not all early intervention providers engage in specific coaching practices, they are encouraged to use quality relationship-based conversation practices, apply effective help giving, and engage in adult learning and teaching methods to optimally achieve the outcomes each family prioritizes for their child and family.

5. QUALITY TEAM PRACTICES

The final pillar supporting early intervention practices is quality teaming. No early intervention provider works alone; rather, they work side by side with a team of others, which always includes the family. The team may also include other professionals and agencies coming together to help meet the diverse needs of the child and the family. All this requires collaborative teamwork, which is not always as easy as it sounds.

Senge (1990) noted that systems do not struggle because of lack of individual skill but "because they are unable to pull their diverse functions and talents into a productive whole" (p. 69). This is apparent in early intervention teams, as each member is generally skilled in their respective area of expertise. However, each team member may require continued learning to gain the experience and proficiency to provide optimal family-centered services on an early intervention team.

The federal law mandating the delivery of services to children with disabilities and their families, IDEA, mandates that a team of professionals representing more than one discipline, including the family, conduct the evaluation of children to determine initial and ongoing eligibility for early intervention services (Title 20, U.S.C. § 1433, 2004). The emphasis on teaming, working across disciplines and agencies, and involving all stakeholders (i.e., the parents and individuals they choose to involve) reinforces the team-based intent of early intervention. Although IDEA requires a coordinated, family-centered approach to early intervention services, it does not dictate specific methodologies to successfully provide team-based services. What is important is that early intervention must represent a system of services uniquely tailored to meet the diverse needs of individual families with infants or toddlers with disabilities. The different disciplines on an early intervention team represent different entities of the system that must integrate and function collaboratively to optimally support families of children with disabilities within the system framework of early intervention and within the natural environments of the family.

Over the past two decades, the most common team structures in use in early intervention are called multidisciplinary, interdisciplinary, and transdisciplinary. One can think of these on a continuum of how thoroughly the described pillars are applied and implemented. Multidisciplinary would be at the least thoroughly implemented end of this continuum, whereas transdisciplinary would be at the most thoroughly implemented end.

A multidisciplinary team comprises a number of professionals from different disciplines and/or different agencies who work independently of one another with the child and family. They each evaluate the child and family from their separate domain using measures particular to their discipline. They may write up separate evaluation reports and determine separate IFSP outcomes for each developmental area in which evaluation indicates a delay or need. Service delivery is then tied to each outcome, having a specific team member who works independently with the child and family. The child may be receiving speech therapy to help use words more clearly, physical therapy to help move around the environment more freely, occupational therapy to help with self-feeding, and service coordination to help the family address other family outcomes. All members of the team make separate visits or may do an occasional covisit in which part of the visit is spent with each provider focusing on their skill area. The team may come together during the initial IFSP meeting and again at the 6-month and annual IFSP reviews. They typically do not meet between these specified times. The professionals see themselves as specialists or experts and identify problems and activities designed to help the child in their particular area of expertise. Family input is for sharing information specific to the child, rather than for giving ideas, discussing daily activities they would like help with, or actively carrying out agreed-on strategies between visits.

The difference between the multidisciplinary and interdisciplinary teaming models is most evident in the interaction among team members (Garguilo & Kilgo, 2000; Woodruff & McGonigel, 1988). In the interdisciplinary team, the professionals conduct independent evaluations but come together to share results and to develop goals. Intervention strategies are collaboratively designed but separately implemented by domain-specific specialists. The team meets regularly for review and sometimes for consultation with one another. Child and family outcomes are assigned to separate disciplines, but there is communication among team members, and occasionally some joint goals are developed. For example, the physical therapist supports the child with crawling, the speech-language pathologist supports the child with requesting food by pointing, and the special educator works with the child and family to advance the child's play skills. Although families are more readily involved as a team member, their input remains secondary to the professionals and they are not regularly included in team meetings except for the 6-month and annual reviews of the IFSP.

The transdisciplinary team includes professionals from various disciplines and the family members; however, a major difference is that team members are committed to teaching, learning, and working across disciplinary boundaries to plan and provide integrated services by sharing roles and seeing the child as a whole within the context of the family (Garguilo & Kilgo, 2000; Mayhew et al., 1999; Woodruff & McGonigel, 1988). Within this type of teaming model, it is believed that sharing the expertise of all team members, including the family, provides a well-rounded approach without fragmenting services by professional specialty area or developmental domain (Dinnebeil et al., 1999). The family on the transdisciplinary team is valued as an active member with a recognized and respected decision-making role. The team members meet regularly with the family and work together to support one another.

Transdisciplinary team members accept and build upon each other's knowledge and skills. Often the terms *role release* or *sharing* are used to describe team members' actions. Members of a transdisciplinary team cross professional discipline boundaries to achieve service integration by consulting or coaching one another. They do not abandon their discipline but blend specific skills with other team members to focus on achieving integrated outcomes.

One member on a transdisciplinary team works the most frequently with the family. This person is frequently referred to as the primary service provider. This individual works collaboratively with the other team members to integrate information and to deliver efficient and comprehensive services to a child and family. The assignment of a primary service provider to a specific child and family should be based on the IFSP outcomes. They must have regular access to all needed team members to receive information, consultation, and coaching from them related to child and family outcomes and intervention strategies. The use of a primary service provider on a transdisciplinary team is not a watered down version of services. Rather, it is a service delivery method that is unified around functional family needs, uses specialists as effectively as possible, and allows for families to form a close and helpful relationship with one primary person (McWilliam, 2004).

Team structures are further complicated by how teams are formed. Team members may all work for and be housed in the same agency, and the agency may have adopted a particular teaming structure that allows opportunities for team members to meet and work together. Team members may work for agencies that are completely focused on providing

Quality Team Characteristics

- Working toward a common purpose
- Having agreed-on values and beliefs
- Having frequent opportunities to be together and share
- Keeping lines of communication open
- Sharing common tasks and understandings of each member's roles and functions
- Respecting one another
- Helping one another willingly
- Focusing on personal and team growth
- Supporting each other's learning and growth

only early intervention services or agencies that provide services to a greater population. Some teams are made up of private contractors who work independently and are housed in separate locations. Teams can also be composed of many combinations of the aforementioned and more. Essentially, there is a potpourri of system designs and team structures across early intervention programs, which can promote and complicate team functioning.

As an early intervention provider you may find yourself working in a team structure that may or may not be a comfortable fit because of your values, beliefs, training, or previous experiences with families. Some team members may be better than others at applying key principles of family-centered and relationship-based practices, adult learning techniques, natural environment learning approaches, or quality children learning strategies. Some team members may see families as equals, and others on the team may have a more traditional view whereby the professional is the key decision maker and the intervention focus is on the child's delays to be fixed by the professional. If this feels a bit confusing to you as a professional, then imagine how it might feel to a family who is involved with several professionals and is having to decipher and deal with the different expectations—not to mention all the different bits of information they are receiving. Hence a focus on quality teaming is essential. (Now complete Give It a Go! 2.7.)

There are some things all teams can do to improve not only how they work with each other but also how they work with families. All team members (private contractors, private and public agency employees) working in early intervention under IDEA are expected to follow the federal law and regulations governing Part C. All team members should participate in ongoing training to improve their practices in working with families and children. Ultimately, training should incorporate the early intervention foundations we discuss in this chapter, as they are truly essential to supporting families and helping them gain confidence and competence to help their young children develop and learn.

Effective teamwork across agencies, across disciplines, and with families demands time, mutual trust, respect, common goals, and open communication. The impact of a team that works together effectively is much greater than individuals working in isolation or a team that is having difficulty working together. Application of the key principles discussed

GIVE IT A GO! 2.7.

Name the type of team (multidisciplinary, interdisciplinary, or transdisciplinary) each of the following behaviors most likely represents (answers on page 36):

1. Generally, family members meet with team members separately, by discipline.   _____

2. Teams regularly meet to share information and to teach and learn across discipline.   _____

3. Members conduct assessment by disciplines and share results with one another.   _____

4. Families are always members of the team and determine their own level of team participation.   _____

5. Individualized Family Service Plan (IFSP) goals are developed by disciplines and shared with the rest of the team to form a single IFSP.   _____

6. Staff development happens independently and within individual disciplines.   _____

7. Members develop separate goals and plans for intervention activities.   _____

8. Team members and families participate in "arena"-type assessments, observing and recording across disciplines.   _____

9. Lines of communication among team members happen informally, and members perhaps do not think of themselves as a team.   _____

10. The IFSP implementation is done by specific team members, but covisits might occur when working on several goals or outcomes. _____

earlier in this chapter is paramount to effective teamwork, and teamwork is a hallmark of early intervention.

WRAP UP

The early intervention pillars we explore in this chapter drive your everyday practices in many ways, including how you meet and interact with children and families, conduct assessments and evaluations, discover family priorities for children and their parents, and work on a team to develop IFSPs. The pillars guide how team members work together to implement IFSPs, support and help children and adults learn, assist children and families with transition, and so much more. What you as a provider and as an individual believe, value, know, and put into practice will influence your desire or ability to put these foundational concepts into practice. In the next chapter, we look at the seven key principles for providing early intervention services in natural environments and explore what these look like and do not look like in relation to these vital key concepts. As a final activity for this chapter, complete Give It a Go! 2.8.

GIVE IT A GO! 2.8.

Drawing from the information presented on team structures earlier, consider the following questions and write your answers in the space provided.

- What type of team are you part of?
    - ❑ Multidisciplinary
    - ❑ Interdisciplinary
    - ❑ Transdisciplinary
- Is it a good fit for you? Why or why not?

_____

_____

_____

_____

_____

- Does the team structure and the way it presently works seem to be the best it can be with providing services and supports to children and families?

_____

- List three things you wish your team could do differently.
    1. _____
    2. _____
    3. _____
- Are there any barriers to making your three wishes possible? What can be done to resolve the barriers?

_____

_____

_____

_____

_____

_____

- What are three things you can do to improve the overall quality and function of your team?
    1. _____
    2. _____
    3. _____

GIVE IT A GO! 2.7. ANSWER KEY

1. Multidisciplinary
2. Transdisciplinary
3. Interdisciplinary
4. Transdisciplinary
5. Interdisciplinary

6. Multidisciplinary
7. Multidisciplinary
8. Transdisciplinary
9. Multidisciplinary
10. Interdisciplinary

CHAPTER THREE

Seven Key Principles
An Overview

This chapter reviews the seven key principles of providing early intervention in natural environments developed by the national workgroup discussed in this book's introduction. This workgroup included lead researchers, program developers, Part C coordinators, parents, representatives from professional discipline organizations, early interventionists, and technical assistance providers. The workgroup's diverse composition facilitated development of a mission statement and a set of evidenced-based principles and practices applicable to all disciplines and statewide early intervention systems. This chapter provides an overview of the key principles, and the following chapters delve into how the principles are implemented.

A *principle* is a value, belief, or mission statement that provides a rationale for a particular course of action. Many states have adopted the mission statement and principles developed by the workgroup or have developed their own similar mission or beliefs statements to guide their early intervention systems' work. Many examples of these statewide principles can be seen on the individual web sites for Part C programs. As you review these seven key principles, think about how the five pillars of early intervention discussed in the previous chapter influence these key principles and the associated practices. Table 3.1 provides a quick cross-reference of the early intervention pillars and the seven key principles.

This chapter defines each principle with an "At a Glance," which includes the major descriptors that providers, families, and communities should know and demonstrate in order to put each principle into practice. There is also a Give It a Go! to correspond with each principle. The activities list provider practices that may or may not support the key principle, and your job is to identify which provider practices you should or should not do as you work with children and families.

Table 3.1. Seven Key Principles and Foundational Pillars

	Early intervention pillars				
Mission	Family centered	Natural environment	How children learn	Adult learning	Teaming
Part C Early Intervention builds on and provides supports and resources to assist family members and caregivers with enhancing children's learning and development through everyday learning opportunities. **SEVEN KEY PRINCIPLES**					
1. Infants and toddlers learn best through everyday experiences and interactions with familiar people in familiar contexts.	x	x	x		
2. All families, with the necessary supports and resources, can enhance their children's learning and development.	x	x	x	x	x
3. The primary role of service providers in early intervention is to work with and support the family members and caregivers in children's lives.	x	x	x	x	x
4. The early intervention process, from initial contacts through transition, must be dynamic and individualized to reflect the child's and family members' preferences, learning styles, and cultural beliefs.	x			x	x
5. IFSP outcomes must be functional and based on children's and families' needs and family-identified priorities.	x	x	x	x	x
6. The family's priorities, needs, and interests are addressed most appropriately by a primary provider who represents and receives team and community support	x			x	x
7. Interventions with young children and family members must be based on explicit principles, validated practices, best available research, and relevant laws and regulations.	x	x	x	x	x

✳ Key Principle 1

Infants and toddlers learn best through everyday experiences and interaction with familiar people in familiar contexts.

At a Glance

Children

- Children are naturally curious and learn from everything they do throughout their day.

- Children learn best when they are engaged with familiar people and things they like and find interesting.

- Children are motivated to learn, and through play, they practice existing abilities and build competence.

- Children learn through engagement in daily routines. They use and master skills needed to successfully participate in family and community life.

Families

- Families are the crucial supporters of children's learning, growth, and development.

- Families are natural facilitators of their children's participation in daily routines and activities.

- Families have their own routines and rituals that can be used to expand children's learning, practice, and mastery.

Communities

- Communities provide many opportunities for enjoyable activities that can promote children's learning and mastery of important skills and abilities.

- Communities should offer children with disabilities the same opportunities for participation as other same-aged peers without disabilities.

- Community agencies and staff may need additional information, guidance, and hands-on help to assist children with disabilities to participate in community activities.

(Now complete Give It a Go! 3.1.)

GIVE IT A GO! 3.1. SHOULD OR SHOULD NOT

Based on Key Principle 1, review the following practices and identify those that early intervention providers should or should not do as they work with children and families.

Providers should or should not . . .	Should	Should not
1. . . . help families understand how their toys and everyday household items can be used or adapted		
2. . . . design activities to do during a home visit that focus on the skill delay or missed test items		
3. . . . understand that certain children, such as those with autism, do not benefit from family interactions and natural learning opportunities		
4. . . . observe the child in multiple settings, getting family input about the child's behavior in various family routines as part of the assessment and evaluation process		
5. . . . work with the child in sessions or activities apart from peers or other family members so the child can pay attention to the interventionist		
6. . . . help the family and other caregivers engage the child in enjoyable activities that allow for frequent practice of emerging skills		
7. . . . teach specific skills in a specific order through structured, adult-directed activities		
8. . . . bring a well-equipped toy bag into the home for each visit		
9. . . . consult with community providers as a regular part of their job to assist them with their work with children		
10. . . . assist families with understanding how their daily routines and activities naturally provide children valuable learning opportunities		

Answer key: 1) should, 2) should not, 3) should not, 4) should, 5) should not, 6) should, 7) should not, 8) should not, 9) should, 10) should

✳ Key Principle 2

All families, with the necessary supports and resources, can enhance their children's learning and development.

At a Glance

Children

- Children live in different types of families.

- Children's learning and development is influenced by familiar people and positive learning opportunities.

- Children's learning occurs within the context of the relationships with the primary caregiver(s).

Families

- All families have hopes, dreams, and wishes for their children.

- Families can focus on the learning needs of their child when the daily living needs for themselves and their family are in place.

- All families have strengths and capabilities to help their child grow, learn, and be happy.

- All families are resourceful, but not all have equal access to the assets that ease family life or make their dreams happen.

- Families have networks of formal and informal support that can be used as resources.

Community

- Communities offer resources that families can use, but not all communities have equal resources.

- Community activities should be available and welcoming to all families of children with disabilities.

- Communities should have a mechanism to identify and ultimately fill gaps in services and supports for young children with disabilities and their families.

(Now complete Give It a Go! 3.2.)

GIVE IT A GO! 3.2. SHOULD OR SHOULD NOT

Based on Key Principle 2, review the following practices and identify those that early intervention providers should or should not do as they work with children and families.

Providers should or should not . . .	Should	Should not
1. . . . base expectations for families on characteristics such as race, ethnicity, income, or education		
2. . . . match assistance to the family desires		
3. . . . suspend personal judgments and build rapport and trust to truly understand information gathered from the family		
4. . . . view families as not caring about their child or apathetic if they miss appointments or do not carry through with prescribed interventions		
5. . . . assume certain types of families need more help based on family circumstances or a child's type of disability		
6. . . . drive families to appointments or other services in order to make sure they keep appointments		
7. . . . understand that certain kinds of families have no routines that are useful or helpful to the child		
8. . . . explain to families that professionals can help them meet their needs in a better way than people in their informal support network can		
9. . . . help families feel comfortable with taking their children with disabilities to community activities and advocate for their children's participation		
10. . . . help families meet their needs by first using resources available in the family's own network		

Answer key: 1) should not, 2) should, 3) should, 4) should not, 5) should not, 6) should not, 7) should not, 8) should not, 9) should, 10) should

✳ Key Principle 3

The primary role of service providers in early intervention is to work with and support the family members and caregivers in children's lives.

At a Glance

Children

- Children's interests and engagement sparked by everyday opportunities are catalysts for their learning and mastery of important life skills.

- Children's functional learning does not happen in individualized sessions with an early intervention provider directing the activity.

- Children with disabilities may require adaptations to fully engage in daily learning opportunities.

Family

- Families are equal partners in the relationship with service providers.

- Families naturally offer children many opportunities to learn and practice skills.

- Family confidence and competence increase when a family has information to support their child's everyday learning.

- Families are the constant in a child's life, whereas early intervention providers come in and out.

Community

- Community agencies should support, not supplant, families' natural life activities.

- Community support should be readily available, easy to access, and respectful of individual families.

- Community providers should build relationships with families based on open and honest communication.

(Now complete Give It a Go! 3.3.)

GIVE IT A GO! 3.3. SHOULD OR SHOULD NOT

Based on Key Principle 3, review the following practices and identify those that early intervention providers should or should not do as they work with children and families.

Providers should or should not . . .	Should	Should not
1. . . . be nice to families with a primary focus on becoming a best friend to the family		
2. . . . show activities they have planned and then ask families to fit them into their day		
3. . . . evaluate progress or success by including how the family feels the learning opportunities and activities are going		
4. . . . offer information, materials, and emotional support to enhance the family's natural role in supporting their child's learning		
5. . . . involve the family in discussions and decisions about what it is they want their child to be able to do and what the child enjoys and can do		
6. . . . use professional behaviors that build trust and rapport to establish a working relationship or partnership		
7. . . . point out children's learning opportunities as they are seen and work with families to make any adaptations to enhance the learning opportunity and the children's active participation		
8. . . . give all families activity sheets or worksheets and ask parents to chart their child's participation in assigned activities during the week		
9. . . . provide feedback and encouragement as they see the naturally occurring incidental teaching moments the family uses		
10. . . . focus on the child during home visits but ask the parent to sit nearby and watch		

Answer key: 1) should not, 2) should not, 3) should, 4) should, 5) should, 6) should, 7) should, 8) should not, 9) should, 10) should not

 # Key Principle 4

The early intervention process, from initial contacts through transition, must be dynamic and individualized to reflect the child's and family members' preferences, learning styles, and cultural beliefs.

At a Glance

Children

- Children develop rapidly in their first 3 years of life.

- Children's interests and the skills needed to participate in activities change frequently.

- Children's means for adapting and adjusting to various situations change.

Family

- Family needs and priorities change according to life circumstances.

- Families have individual cultural values and beliefs that influence their priorities.

- Families are critical decision makers in all aspects of their children's learning.

- Families have their own learning styles and preferences for giving and receiving information.

Communities

- Community activities and support should be culturally sensitive.

- Community activities and support should be relevant to the needs and interests of families.

- Community agencies should be staffed with culturally competent personnel.

(Now complete Give It a Go! 3.4.)

GIVE IT A GO! 3.4. SHOULD OR SHOULD NOT

Based on Key Principle 4, review the following practices and identify those that early intervention providers should or should not do as they work with children and families.

Providers should or should not . . .	Should	Should not
1. . . . write broad Individualized Family Service Plan (IFSP) outcomes that can easily last for 6 months or a year		
2. . . . work with the team that includes the family to collaboratively decide and adjust the frequency and intensity of services		
3. . . . only change the IFSP at 6-month or annual review times		
4. . . . treat each family member as a unique adult learner with valuable insights		
5. . . . use the family's cultural beliefs and traditional activities as sources of learning for the child		
6. . . . suspend judgment and assumptions about how a family should do things based on the provider's own cultural expectations related to child rearing and family life		
7. . . . determine IFSP services by either asking the family what they want or providing what a referring medical provider prescribes		
8. . . . understand that families from certain cultural backgrounds are the same as other families of that same background		
9. . . . ensure that all families receive the same number of visits and information as part of the early intervention process so that all is equal and fair		
10. . . . help families understand that their children's participation in early intervention sessions and their follow-through with prescribed intervention strategies are what will help their children		

Answer key: 1) should not, 2) should, 3) should not, 4) should, 5) should, 6) should, 7) should not, 8) should not, 9) should not, 10) should not

✳ Key Principle 5

IFSP outcomes must be functional and based on children's and families' needs and family-identified priorities.

At a Glance

Children

- Children learn holistically, not in isolated, discipline-specific domains.

- Children's learning needs are best identified through authentic assessments of children's abilities in natural contexts.

- Children's participation in meaningful activities is maintained as a focus when the IFSP outcomes are necessary and useful.

Family

- Family participation in the assessment process is critical in order to identify what is and is not working and to identify the focus for early intervention.

- Family priorities and concerns are the basis for IFSP outcomes.

- Family desires as stated in functional outcomes keep the intervention focus on what is meaningful and helpful.

- Family routines and activities provide a context for addressing IFSP outcomes through strategies and activities developed with the family.

Community

- Services and supports from early intervention and the community are determined *after* the family's priorities are identified and IFSP outcomes are determined.

- Communities provide locations and social contexts that promote children's learning and are reflected in IFSP intervention strategies as applicable to individualized IFSP outcomes.

- Community agencies and providers, in addition to early intervention providers, can be part of the team with family members to address functional IFSP outcomes.

(Now complete Give It a Go! 3.5.)

GIVE IT A GO! 3.5. SHOULD OR SHOULD NOT

Based on Key Principle 5, review the following practices and identify those that early intervention providers should or should not do as they work with children and families.

Providers should or should not . . .	Should	Should not
1. . . . write Individualized Family Service Plan (IFSP) outcomes such as, "Johnny will get physical therapy to help him walk"		
2. . . . listen to and believe the family's needs and concerns about their child		
3. . . . write outcomes such as "Penny will gain six new skills in talking over the next 6 months"		
4. . . . help the family express their priorities and concerns in written outcome statements that are clearly stated		
5. . . . write outcome statements such as "Markus will participate in backyard playtime by walking using his walker in order to play more with his brother"		
6. . . . write IFSP outcomes only for the child, as that is the focus of the early intervention		
7. . . . list on the IFSP only the team members and providers that work for the early intervention program		
8. . . . write IFSP outcomes such as, "Mark and Ellen (parents) will get enough information about autism to comfortably explain Jeremiah's condition to family and friends"		
9. . . . include on the IFSP how families will know an outcome has been achieved by writing a measurable criteria that is easily understandable for anyone to review progress		
10. . . . write IFSP outcomes that are discipline specific		

Answer key: 1) should not, 2) should, 3) should not, 4) should, 5) should, 6) should not, 7) should not, 8) should, 9) should, 10) should not

✳ Key Principle 6

The family's priorities, needs, and interests are addressed most appropriately by a primary provider who represents and receives team and community support.

At a Glance

Children

- Children are at ease with familiar caregivers who receive support from a primary provider.
- Children's complex needs can be met by a primary provider when there is effective consultation and support from other professionals.

Family

- Families are better able to develop meaningful relationships with a consistent primary provider who keeps abreast of the ever-changing needs and priorities of the family.
- Families can receive consistent and coordinated information from a primary provider who works in partnership with other team members.
- Families in partnership with the primary provider have access to other supports and services as needed.

Community

- Community agencies beyond early intervention can be part of an IFSP team.
- Community agencies supporting families require time to collaborate with the IFSP team on shared IFSP outcomes.
- Community agencies understand the scope and purpose of early intervention and the value of a primary service provider approach.

(Now complete Give It a Go! 3.6.)

GIVE IT A GO! 3.6. SHOULD OR SHOULD NOT

Based on Key Principle 6, review the following practices and identify those that early intervention providers should or should not do as they work with children and families.

Providers should or should not . . .	Should	Should not
1. . . . share the message that, the more providers that are involved with the child, the more gains the child will make		
2. . . . plan and make consultative visits with other providers per Individualized Family Service Plan (IFSP) agreements		
3. . . . work independently with each family		
4. . . . regard a primary service provider as the family's gatekeeper to other disciplines and providers		
5. . . . determine the primary provider based solely on the child's delay or diagnosis		
6. . . . make covisits when they are beneficial to the primary provider and family		
7. . . . recognize that a primary service provider approach means that everyone on the team should be able to provide any service (e.g., an educator, OT, or PT can provide speech therapy)		
8. . . . recognize that functional IFSP outcomes are a shared responsibility		
9. . . . understand that cost savings is the main reason for using a primary service provider approach		
10. . . . visit other agencies and referral sources to assist them in knowing what early intervention approach the program is using and what that means		

Answer key: 1) should not, 2) should, 3) should not, 4) should not, 5) should not, 6) should, 7) should not, 8) should, 9) should not, 10) should

✳ Key Principle 7

Interventions with young children and family members must be based on explicit principles, validated practices, best available research, and relevant laws and regulations.

At a Glance

Children

- Children's activities and strategies toward IFSP outcome achievement must be individualized and based on quality practices.

- A child's progress is regularly reviewed and modifications are based on reliable information.

Families

- Families receive support and services from professionals with required competencies and credentials.

- Families are informed of regulations and laws that govern early intervention.

- Families, in partnership with professionals, have an understanding of the rationale for intervention strategies being used or suggested.

- Families are customers and stakeholders and have access to information about early intervention recommended practices and results as they desire.

Community

- Community agencies supporting young children and families stay abreast of and promote quality early intervention practices.

- Community agencies provide training opportunities to help staff support families of young children with disabilities.

- Community agencies engage in ongoing activities to maintain and improve the supports and services offered.

(Now complete Give It a Go! 3.7.)

GIVE IT A GO! 3.7. SHOULD OR SHOULD NOT

Based on Key Principle 7, review the following practices and identify those that early intervention providers should or should not do as they work with children and families.

Providers should or should not . . .	Should	Should not
1. . . . explain clearly the rationale for suggesting a particular intervention strategy to meet an IFSP outcome		
2. . . . understand that the law and regulations for IDEA are for monitoring purposes only and do not apply to the day-to-day application of early intervention		
3. . . . believe that having a professional degree or certification means that they do not need further training		
4. . . . refine their practices based on principles and values of the early intervention system they work for		
5. . . . hone their discipline-specific skills by only participating in discipline-specific training.		
6. . . . keep abreast of the recommended practices in the field of early intervention through reading, attending trainings, referring to professional organizations, collaborating with peers and others, and taking advantage of other learning opportunities		
7. . . . research intervention strategies and practices they are uncertain about before suggesting or trying them		
8. . . . base practice decisions for each child and family on family input and ongoing assessment		
9. . . . suggest learning or professional development topics to their agency or program		
10 . . . always implement all intervention strategies suggested by a medical doctor without question		

Answer key: 1) should, 2) should not, 3) should not, 4) should, 5) should not, 6) should, 7) should, 8) should, 9) should, 10) should not

PART TWO

Agreed-Upon Practices in the Early Intervention Process

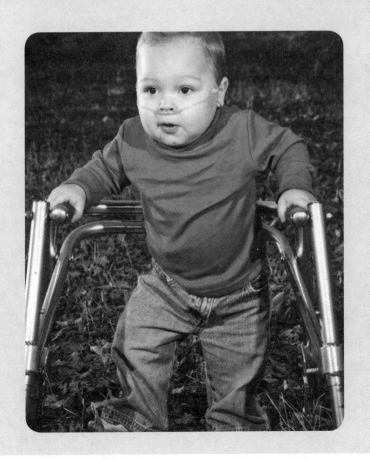

WRAP UP

Some of the principles and practices in this chapter may be familiar to you, and others may be new. In the activities, as you decided if the provider practice should or should not be done, some of your choices may have been easy and others more difficult. In the following chapters, you learn more about the details of these principles and how the associated practices apply to the everyday work of early intervention providers. After you complete this book, please revisit this chapter and see if your responses are affirmed or have changed based on what you have learned.

CHAPTER FOUR

Beginning the Journey
The Referral and Initial Visits

A Parent's Perspective

I was worried about what the doctor had said about Caleb not developing right. I had noticed he didn't do things as quickly as his sister, but the sitter said that it was just the difference of the two kids. The doctor gave me the number of this program to call, and I did. I was so nervous after the person from that program called back and asked to visit me and said they could evaluate Caleb and then help me help him if there was a problem. They were nice on the phone, but honestly, I didn't hear much of what they said after they asked about my concerns. They told me the name of someone who would come to my house and talk to me and see the things Caleb could do. They said the person would "evaluate" him to see if he was "eligible for their services." I picked a time next week that would work for me. I don't remember the name of the person who is coming. Now I think I should clean the house and have all the toys out that Caleb likes. Maybe I should have the sitter come and take his sister to the park. I wonder what else I should do. I'm not sure what they will do when they are here, but "evaluate" sounds like they are testing him somehow, and maybe they want to see if I'm a good parent and if we live in a clean house. I wish I didn't have to wait a whole week now, as I know I will just worry and worry. Should I have done something sooner? What will they think of me as a father? What might they be able to do?

> To achieve the essential collaborative relationship between practitioner and family, the family must be included, from the beginning, in all aspects of shaping the services to be delivered.
>
> —Pawl & Milburn, 2006

In this chapter, we explore the practices, vital behaviors, and specific steps and activities providers and families such as Caleb's engage in during the first two steps in a family's early intervention journey: 1) the initial contact following receipt of a referral and 2) the first visit(s) with the family. The agreed-upon practices for first contacts with families, from the Workgroup on Services in Natural Environments, are listed here. As you read this chapter, explore the resources presented, reflect on your practices, and compare them to the foundational themes discussed in the previous chapters; these agreed-upon practices will become more real to you. Early intervention providers' first contacts with families set the stage for all later work.

Community of Practice
Agreed-Upon Practices: First Contacts

- Become acquainted and establish rapport with families.

- Engage in conversations to find out why the family is contacting early intervention, and identify the next appropriate steps in the referral process.

- Describe early intervention as a system of supports and services for families to assist them in helping their child develop and learn.

- As applicable, conduct a developmental screening.

- For children proceeding to evaluation/assessment, explain the purpose and process, including the importance of gathering information about family concerns, priorities, and resources.

- Begin gathering information about the family's everyday routines and activities and the child's behavior and interaction with others in those contexts.

- Discuss with the family formal and informal supports they use or would like to use.

- Explore and identify the roles the family may want to play in their child's evaluation and assessment process.

- Provide written prior notice along with procedural safeguards, and ask the family to sign consent for evaluation and assessment and release of medical and other records.

(Workgroup on Principles and Practices in Natural Environments, 2008)

MEETING PARENTS AT THE STARTING
POINT OF THEIR EARLY INTERVENTION JOURNEY

Meeting parents at the starting point of their journey means taking time to understand what they know about and what they expect from early intervention and sharing how the program works. Caleb's father was worried, confused, and did not know what to expect. Other families may have completely different starting perspectives. It is vitally important to discover what the family understands and expects in order to start this journey with each family and to avoid conflicting or differing agendas. This means you are working on behalf of the family rather than working simply to accomplish the professional or program plan (Harrower, Fox, Dunlap, & Kincaid, 2001). Although challenges can exist and not all providers and families see eye to eye, it is imperative that providers follow the families' leads to facilitate development of collaborative relationships. Beverly and Thomas (1999) highlighted that collaborative relationships evolve and adjust to the situation at hand. It is important for providers to not let their own behaviors suggest that they are being judgmental about a family's lifestyle such as their living situation, parenting styles, beliefs and values, or cultural practices. For example, Caleb and his sister are being raised by a single father. He is divorced from the children's mother, who is incarcerated because of drug charges. No family will do things exactly as you do, and it is often very difficult not to impose your opinions and judgments on what they do. Likewise, you will bring assumptions into your work. Giving your opinion about something is helpful when it is asked for, but unsolicited advice is not always beneficial.

The way in which initial information is gathered influences the relationship between providers and caregivers. For example, if the provider's questions seem pushy or intrusive, the family may question the provider's intent and grow skeptical of the provider's ability to help. It is important to acknowledge that the information gathered by the provider is dependent on what the family elects to share. This further reinforces the importance of being responsive to the interests of the family rather than driven solely by a professional agenda and the paperwork demands of the program.

INFORMATION EXCHANGE

During first contacts, you are responsible for ensuring that information is gathered from and shared with the family in a respectful and understandable manner. During any contact with families, it is important to engage in an exchange of information rather than a one-sided giving or gathering of information. Remember that, although there is a wealth of information to give and gather during early contacts with the family, it is important to find a balance between the obligatory paperwork and listening to the family to discover what brought them to early intervention. Taking the time to listen to the family's story and helping them learn about early intervention are important roles of every early intervention provider. Family members have different preferences for how they like to receive information. Providers should have multiple ways of sharing important information, such as describing, providing written materials, or even sharing short video clips. Remember, telling someone something only one time or simply giving out a brochure does not mean he or she will understand.

TIP

Consider the following five questions when gathering information:

- How might we use this information?
- Is it pertinent to understanding the child's and family's strengths and needs?
- Is it pertinent to future intervention?
- Is it any of my business?
- Will this information help us meet the family's needs?

With these key points in mind, let us look at what should happen during early contacts with families.

FIRST CONTACTS

Children can be referred to early intervention in a variety of ways, including by parents, other family members, physicians, child care providers, and other types of professionals who are familiar with the child. They are referred because the child has a condition with a high probability of resulting in a developmental delay or someone has a concern about how the child is developing. For example, a doctor may have concerns following a routine check-up, a child care provider may believe a child is not achieving expected developmental milestones, or a parent is concerned that her child is not doing the things another other child did at the same age.

Referrals received by the early intervention program are given to a service coordinator, who facilitates the beginning of the family's early intervention journey by initiating a first conversation with the family, often via telephone. This first conversation is usually followed by a face-to-face visit or a series of visits by staff representing the early intervention program.

A family's early intervention journey begins when someone contacts them regarding the referral made to the early intervention program about their child. This first contact with the family is of utmost importance. It sets the stage for how the family views the early intervention program and their role and relationship with the providers. There are several tasks and functions that must be accomplished, and it is how these activities are completed that makes all the difference for families. Form 4.1 includes basic yet essential steps for making your initial phone calls positive and effective.

The following conversation starter provides a glimpse at an initial referral phone contact.

 CONVERSATION STARTER

Hi, my name is Neal Batton. I am calling from early intervention. Is this Mrs. Novo? [Yes.] Oh, good. I am calling about a referral we received from Dr. Wellborn regarding your son Luke. Are you familiar with this? [Yes, he said that he was concerned about Luke's speech.] Yes, that is the information we received in the referral. Did the doctor tell you anything about our program? [Well, not really; just that you help children who are behind.] Yes, that is a big part of our program. I would like to understand what questions or concerns you have about Luke? [I really was not concerned until the doctor explained to me that Luke is not talking like other 2-year-olds.] He is not talking like other 2-year-olds? [No, he mostly just points or takes us to what he wants. He can say a few words and jabbers, but it is hard to make out what he is saying.] Thank you for sharing that. I understand that Luke has a few words but uses more pointing or gestures. [Yes, that is correct.]

As part of the early intervention program, we work with families to help determine if children are behind in their development, and if so, we work together to help children make progress. One of the first things we do is meet with you and Luke and get a better understanding of the things he can do and if he has any needs. We do this by asking you questions and watching Luke play with the things he likes. The visit usual takes about an hour. Is this something you are interested in? [Yes, I guess so.] Great, we typically meet with families at their home or a place in your community that you and Luke like. We find that children do best meeting us in places that are comfortable and familiar to them. [You can come to my home?] Yes. Would that work for you? [That is better because our second car is in the shop.] Okay. Let's find a time that is good for you and Luke. Do you have any time later this week? [Would Wednesday morning work?] Yes, that would be great. How about 10:00?

The overall purpose of first contacts is for the family to learn what early intervention is all about, including what it can do for their child and family, and to understand their critical role in the early intervention process. Equally important is establishing the partnership relationship that will continue to grow over time. Notice that first contacts is plural not singular. This is because it may not be feasible to cover all the information you need and want to share with the family and to truly hear their story, discover their strengths and concerns, and begin to build the family-centered relationship in only one visit. During the first contacts, fundamental information is shared and materials are given to the family, information is gathered from the family, forms are signed, and paperwork is

FORM 4.1.

PROCESS CHECKLIST: INITIAL PHONE CALL

What to do as part of the initial phone call to a family following receipt of a referral

BEFORE THE CALL

❑ Review available information.

❑ Jot down any specific questions you need to ask.

DURING THE CALL

❑ Introduce yourself and the program you work for.

❑ Confirm that you are talking to the parents/guardian.

❑ Inquire if the family is aware that a referral was made on behalf of the child.

❑ Ask the family if they have questions or concerns about their child's development.

❑ Explain that you are calling to see if they are interested in following up with the referral and, if so, to set up an initial visit.

❑ Share some brief information about what early intervention is and check if the family is interested in early intervention.

❑ If the family is interested, share the purpose of the initial visit. Include a description of what the family can expect and how long it will take. Let the family know that they can choose what they would like to share and who they would like to be there.

❑ If the family is not interested, thank them for their time and invite them to contact early intervention in the future if they have any concerns or questions.

❑ If appropriate, inquire about the need for interpreters.

❑ Set up a time with the family that is convenient for both you and them. Consider the child's sleeping, waking, and feeding schedules and if both parents and other family members may want to participate.

❑ Give the name of the person(s) who will be making the initial visit.

❑ Provide contact information if the family should need to reschedule.

❑ Get directions to their home or an agreed-upon location for the initial visit as needed.

❑ Thank the family for their time and let them know that you are looking forward to meeting them in person. Encourage them to jot down any questions they think of to address during the first visit.

AFTER THE CALL

❑ Mail (or e-mail) a reminder including the program name, contact information, the name of the person making the initial visit, and the date, time, and duration of the scheduled visit. Include a program brochure or other information about early intervention.

❑ Compile information received from the referral so that the family does not have to repeat information already shared. Keep in mind that some of the information you have may need to be confirmed with the family; don't assume the reason for a referral from a doctor matches the precise concerns or questions of the family.

GIVE IT A GO! 4.1.

The following are some conversation topics you may discuss with the family early in the process that can help pave the way for better understanding of the services and supports the family will receive. Compare the information in the topics to information your program shares with families. Use a highlighter to mark words you already use and another color to indicate words you might consider using with families.

❖ "As the process gets started, early intervention providers help families address their concerns about their child's development. Addressing potential concerns may involve an evaluation to determine if the child has a delay and if he or she may be eligible for early intervention. Together, families and providers determine the amount and type of supports and services needed. These decisions are based on family concerns, priorities, and resources."

❖ "Early intervention providers know how young children grow and learn as well as conditions that may affect development—but families know their children best. We value the expertise that families have about their children and want you to be a key decision maker throughout the process."

❖ "Children learn during families' day-to-day routines and activities. Early intervention support and services are provided in locations where children and families spend time."

❖ "Although early intervention draws on the expertise of various disciplines, services are most frequently delivered through a primary service provider. The primary service provider works in partnership with the family to address their concerns and identify and enhance children's natural learning opportunities."

❖ "Early intervention providers work collaboratively with families to address identified child and family needs. Early intervention support and services can include informational support such as providing information about child development, material support such as making connections with community resources, and emotional support such as validating and empowering family efforts."

(From Department of the Army, Educational and Developmental Intervention Services and Comprehensive System of Personnel Development. [2013]. *Individualized family service plan process document: Linking early intervention processes*. Retrieved from http://projects.fpg.unc.edu/~eco/assets/pdfs/IFSPPDHandbook5May2013finaldraft.pdf)

completed. There is much to be communicated and done, and ample time must be allotted to covey the purpose, listen to the family, gather information, and complete all the necessary tasks. (Now complete Give It a Go! 4.1.)

The federal timeline to have the meeting to develop the IFSP is within 45 calendar days from the referral (§ 303.310 and § 303.342[a]). This may seem like a short time for providers, who sometimes try to condense volumes of information into one phone call and a single visit. If you think about it, 45 days is nearly 6 weeks. This should ultimately allow for several calls to be made, materials to be sent to families, and several visits to occur to ensure the optimal foundation for the important work that is occurring and that will lie ahead. Starting the process early within the 45-day timeline is important so that families are not left waiting to begin the journey with early intervention.

INITIAL FACE-TO-FACE VISIT WITH A FAMILY

Following the referral and the initial phone call, the first face-to-face visit with the family and child is optimally in the family's home or at another community location convenient for and familiar to the family. In some early intervention programs, this first face-to-face visit is called an *intake visit*.

As you visit families in their homes, think of yourself as a guest. Confirm that it is a good time for the visit when you arrive. For the first few visits, make sure you introduce yourself by giving your name and the program's name. Ask where they would like you to sit. Greet and include other family members that may be present. Ask if it is okay to pick up or hold the child before attempting to do so. Always treat the family with respect and kindness and regard them as you would want to be treated as a guest in someone's home. Also remember that you are a professional building a relationship using positive and effective helping practices. You are not a best friend, yet you should act in a friendly way while acknowledging the boundaries of your duties and responsibilities as an early interventionist.

As part of the initial visit, be sure to allow sufficient time in your schedule so that you do not have to rush off, but also honor the time arranged with the family. If the meeting was set for 60 minutes, it is not okay to stay for 3 hours. Rather than going way over, set up a subsequent visit if needed or ask if it is okay to continue.

During the initial visit or visits, there is much to cover, including the following:

• Discovering the family's concerns

• Describing early intervention as a system of supports and services to assist families to help their children develop and learn

• Sharing information about family rights

• Determining if a developmental screening is needed

• Deciding if evaluation for determining eligibility is necessary

• Planning for evaluation, if needed

These activities are not necessarily straightforward. Although there are consistent steps and practices that should be in place, the actual conversations and decisions that will be made are as unique as the individual child and family. Foundational to the visit should be the key practices and common behaviors that exemplify the core pillars discussed in Chapter 2: family-centered and relationship-based practices, natural environments, respect for how children learn, knowledge of principles of adult learning, and quality team practices. These pillars of early intervention should optimally guide your interactions with families during early contacts and throughout the family's early intervention journey. Let us now look more closely at the different decision points that happen as part of first contacts.

DISCOVERING THE FAMILYS CONCERNS

Do not assume that the concerns presented in the referral match the concerns or questions the family has. Let the family tell you what their concerns are, if they have any. Do this by asking questions, taking the time to hear their responses, clarifying responses, and allowing the family to ask questions. When asking questions, start with open-ended ones that invite the family to share what they would like, rather than closed-ended or multiple choice ones that might imply there is a *correct* answer. For example, consider the difference between asking, "What questions or concerns do you have about Caleb's development?" versus "Are you concerned about Caleb's communication?" Of course, sometimes you will need to ask yes/no or multiple choice questions, such as when more specific information or clarification is needed. But remember that it is best to start with open-ended questions, as they invite families to share details of their child's everyday activities.

Also listen for *red flags* indicating an appropriate referral or a diagnosis that would make a child automatically eligible. If the child has a diagnosis, ask questions such as "What has your doctor told you about Keyshawn's diagnosis?"; "What questions do you have about the diagnosis?"; or "What questions or concerns do you have about how it might affect your child and family?"

As you engage in a conversation with the family about their concerns regarding their child's development, listen with intensity by concentrating on the message being conveyed, not simply the words being spoken. Make an effort to listen more than talk. Families know their child better than anyone else, and you will want to capitalize on their expertise to truly understand their child's functioning. This requires gaining family insight by listening and asking good questions.

These questions facilitate a richer description of the parents' concerns; they go beyond simply identifying a developmental domain (e.g., I am concerned about Suzy's speech). These types of questions also reinforce the collaborative nature of early intervention and the important role the family plays. Gathering more specific information about the family's concerns improves everyone's understanding and is essential for guiding the early intervention process in a family-centered manner.

TIP

The following sample questions may help facilitate discovery of a family's concerns. It is not intended that each question be asked. Rather, these are suggestions to initiate dialogue about what brought the family to early intervention and what they would like to gain through their involvement with early intervention. Use the questions you think might best match the family and the information being sought.

- What can you tell me about your child that will help me get to know her or him better?

- What questions or concerns (if any) do you have about your child and family?

- What do you wish your child could do that he or she is not doing at this time?

- Is there anything you would like your child to do, do better, or be more independent at?

- Are there times during your day when things could go better than they do?

- What would you like to happen through your involvement with early intervention?

- What are your most frequent topics of conversations you have with others about your child?

- What does he or she like and want to do? Who does he or she enjoy being with?

- How does he or she prefer to participate in the things that happen day to day?

- What kind of information would be most useful to you regarding your child?

- What kinds of things would best assist you with helping your child?

In addition to asking questions, you will also have to respond in ways that are respectful and move the conversation along. Throughout the conversation, remember that taking the time to genuinely understand the family's questions or concerns is time well spent in building the relationship and ensuring that the next steps are congruent with the family's concerns. The following tip box highlights effective interviewing techniques.

EARLY INTERVENTION AS A SYSTEM OF SUPPORTS AND SERVICES

As you describe early intervention, explain the general purpose of the program and how children and families are eligible. Share public awareness materials and use them as a guide as you describe the program to the family. Never just give a brochure to a family or simply mail it ahead of your visit. Always open it up and explicitly point out the pertinent information you are referring to and then invite them to review the brochure and ask questions. Include in your explanation of early intervention an abbreviated discussion about how children learn best through everyday experiences and interactions with familiar people in familiar places throughout their day. (Now complete Give It a Go! 4.2.)

SHARING INFORMATION ABOUT FAMILY RIGHTS

As you describe early intervention, you will want to explain that the program has rules and procedures that providers must follow as well as safeguards for families. This topic must be covered early in the process and periodically repeated thereafter. These family rights "convey the law's central principles of respect for families' privacy, diversity, and role as informed members of the early intervention team" (Hurth & Goff, 2002, p. 2).

This important role and obligation of early intervention helps families understand

---

TIP

- "Use open-ended questions" (e.g., How does he let you know when he wants something? Tell me more about that. Think about the last time he did that and please describe it for me).

- "Use restating by repeating the exact words." Repeating the parent's exact words without paraphrasing or interpreting invites further conversation and clarification (e.g., The parent says at play time that the child watches television. You respond, "She watches television." The parent says, "Yes, she likes . . .").

- "Summarize and invite opportunities to correct." Summarize the parents' statements and give them the opportunity to correct you if you have misinterpreted something they have said (e.g., So he mostly plays by himself when you go to the park, and that is worrisome for you).

- "Avoid back-to-back and compound questions" (e.g., Does she use a sippy cup or regular cup? Has she had the opportunity to drink from a regular cup? Or does she spill a lot?).

- "Avoid leading questions," which tend to orient the person to a particular response (e.g., "Does he eat lunch at the table?" versus "Where does he eat lunch?" or "Where do you eat lunch?").

- "Cautiously use why questions." Be aware that these questions can sound judgmental. It is okay to ask for a parent's thinking (e.g., Why do you think he does that?). But avoid asking questions about why they do not do something (e.g., Why don't you get rid of the pacifier?).

- Make an effort to "listen more than talk."

(*Source:* Westby, Burda, & Mehta, 2003)

CONVERSATION STARTER

I would like to spend a few minutes talking about a very important part of early interven-tion that builds on what we know about how children learn: *natural environments*. These are the natural learning opportunities that occur in all the places, activities, and things you do as part of day-to-day life that help your child grow and learn. We know that children learn best and remember things much better when they engage in meaningful activities they enjoy that occur frequently and with familiar people.

Also explain how services work to support caregivers in making the most out of the myriad of learning opportunities that are already a part of their everyday lives. Also reinforce that families are team members and experts in knowing and understanding their child and family interests and that it will be essential to gather information from them along the way.

CONVERSATION STARTER

Because young children learn so much from their families and the things you do together every day, you and your family are at the crux of the work we do. It is important for you to feel a part of the team and a part of the entire process, so please let us know if you have any questions or suggestions along the way. To help us understand Jon and what is important for your family, we will ask you to share information with us about Jon, such as what he enjoys, things he does well, things that may be challenging for him, as well as his medical and developmental history. If it is okay with you, we will also want to learn a little more about your family. We will be looking for things you are interested in, day-to-day activities, and supports you have in the community. As we begin this process, please share what you would like.

their rights and safeguards as they apply to the early intervention system and process. As the rights are reviewed with families, it is important that the review is done in a family-friendly way by minimizing the legalese embedded in the safeguards without minimizing the rights themselves. Simply providing families with a copy of their rights is not satisfactory. The rights are more than just paperwork that parents have to sign as an acknowledgement of receipt. Every effort must be taken to ensure that providers do not inadvertently imply the message that these are not really important or simply something to file away without looking at them. Although sharing rights so early in the journey seems a bit overwhelming, it sets up a foun-dational element that families are primary decision makers in the process. Families should understand their rights in the contexts they apply. For example, as the family is getting started in early intervention, it is important to explain in more detail how the rights of *confidentiality* and *consent to release information and their consent to move forward with screening or evaluation* apply to this part of the process and the decisions the family will need to make to proceed. This helps the family see how the rights apply within the context of the early intervention process.

Another important conversation to have with families early on in the process is about getting their consent to share information about the child's and family's participation in early intervention with others outside of the program. For example, referral sources often want to know if their referral has been acted upon; this requires parent permission for early inter-vention to respond to the referral source. Children's doctors and child care providers are other important partners that may need information from early intervention; this can only be shared with parent consent. Families must grant consent for early intervention to share

GIVE IT A GO! 4.2.

Think about ways to enhance conversations you have had or heard with families about the purpose of early intervention and the family's role. Write two ways you would start a conversation with a family about the purpose of early intervention.

1. _____
   _____
   _____

2. _____
   _____
   _____

CONVERSATION STARTER
Sharing Family Rights

As a part of this program, you have rights that I will review with you now. Please feel free to ask any questions. I will give you a copy of the rights and will offer you additional copies each time we have a formal meeting.

As we get started with the early intervention process, it is important for you to know that you have rights and responsibilities. For example, you have a right to confidentiality. This means I will not release the information you share with me to others outside our program without your written consent. I want to be sure you know what you can expect from our program in terms of the rules and laws that govern us. These rights have been established to protect families and to help maintain quality services.

CONVERSATION STARTER

As we get started with the early intervention process, it is important for you to know that we do not share any of this information with anyone without your signed permission. With your permission, we would like to send a letter to Dr. Heffner, who referred you to early intervention, telling him we have followed up and have spoken with you. It would also be helpful to get from him health records or information that could help us to determine eligibility or contribute to the evaluation. May I have your permission? Please look over and sign this form. Let me know if you have any questions.

---

information with others, such as a letter acknowledging the family is enrolled in early intervention, screening or evaluation results, the IFSP, and so forth. In addition, families must grant their consent for early intervention to receive information from others. Professionals who work with the child and family may have valuable information that could help with an eligibility determination, assist with the development of an IFSP, support the provision of services, and so forth. The bottom line is that early intervention cannot share or gather any information from other agencies without first securing the family's written consent.

DETERMINING IF A DEVELOPMENTAL SCREENING IS NEEDED

Children who are referred to early intervention may already have a medical diagnosis or condition that makes them eligible for early intervention services, so there is no need for the early intervention program to do screening in those cases. These children will need a multidisciplinary assessment to identify the family's priorities and to determine which services and support will be provided. Other children may have been given a developmental screening in the doctor's office or in their child care setting, and that information is shared with early intervention. These children also do not require a developmental screening if one has already been completed. Therefore, depending on the information available from the screening, they could go on to a multidisciplinary evaluation to determine eligibility and, if eligible, assessment to identify family priorities and determine what services and supports are needed. Finally, there are children referred by parents or other primary referral sources that suspect there may be an issue with a child's development. It is this group of children for which the first step may be to conduct a developmental screening. This screening will help guide the team's decision of whether or not to go on to evaluation to determine eligibility.

Using the aforementioned guidelines, review information from the referral source and listen to the family describe their child to help you and the family decide if a developmental screening is needed. If no prior screening was conducted and if initial information is inconclusive (i.e., delays in development or presence of a biological risk are not indicated), then a developmental screening would be wise. To make this decision with the family, explain that there is an age range when children learn certain skills and abilities and that screening is a quick way to determine if there are any possible areas of delay. Discuss what is known about the child and determine with the family if screening is necessary.

 CONVERSATION STARTER

The screening takes a quick look at all areas of Jenna's development. Together we will use a checklist called the [insert name of developmental screener]. This is to see if she is doing what is expected at her age and to help us decide together if there is a need to look more deeply at her development. If the screening indicates she is not doing what is expected in one or more areas of her development, then the next step is to do an evaluation, which takes a bit more time and involves two or more professionals taking a closer look at Jenna's development. Because you know Jenna best, much of the screening will involve me asking you questions about what Jenna does. There may be some items on the checklist that I will ask Jenna to do or that I will ask you to do with Jenna. Do you have any questions about what a screening is or what we will be doing?

Form 4.2 includes key steps that should be evident in the developmental screening process.

FORM 4.2.

PROCESS CHECKLIST: DEVELOPMENTAL SCREENING

What to do as part of the developmental screening

BEFORE THE SCREENING

❑ Clearly describe the process with the family. Include what will be done and what information will be gathered. Reinforce that screening is a snapshot in time of the child's current skills.

❑ Obtain parental permission for the screening and follow program procedures for prior written notice and providing rights and procedural safeguards.

DURING ADMINISTRATION OF THE SCREENING

❑ As questions are asked and the child is asked to perform certain tasks, explain what you are doing and what you are seeing. Provide a commentary of what you are doing, what you are looking for, and what you are seeing.

❑ Invite the family to facilitate screening items and/or check if what you are seeing is typical for the child.

❑ Talk with the family about what the screening is showing and ask for their observations of their child's behavior or other information they want to share.

AFTER ADMINISTRATION OF THE SCREENING

❑ Discuss the results of the screening with the family and decide together what the next steps should be; for example, "pass screen," "no further action," "rescreen at a later time," or "go on to evaluation."

❑ If the screening shows no concerns and the family does not want their child to be evaluated, describe other available community resources, as appropriate.

❑ Explain that the family can contact the early intervention program any time up until the child turns 3 years old.

❑ Leave the family with necessary information, such as how to contact the early intervention program, resources on developmental milestones, and information about other community resources.

❑ If the team decides that further evaluation is warranted, or if the family desires an evaluation, begin discussing the evaluation process.

❑ Follow state and local protocols about notifying the referral source about action taken on referral.

❑ Conduct agreed-upon next steps.

Before moving on, let us quickly review a few important points about gathering information on a child's health. As you know, early intervention provides support and services to families of children with disabilities. In doing so, providers see children whose health ranges from well to severely compromised and at risk. The amount of medical information gathered should reflect this range. When gathering information for any child, keep in mind the educational nature of early intervention. The information sought should be necessary to appropriately evaluate and extend support to the child and family. Beyond pertinent developmental milestones and health information related to the referral, providers should focus on the child's current health facts and the information that is of use now and in the future rather than trying to take the child's and family's full medical histories. Make certain that the information being gathered is information needed to facilitate the early intervention process.

DETERMINING IF AN ELIGIBILITY EVALUATION IS NEEDED

Based on the information gathered and shared, the team must determine if an evaluation for eligibility is needed. It is important to review all the available information with the family and involve them in the decision-making process.

CONVERSATION STARTER

When you called early intervention, you were concerned about Gordy's speech. His child care center did a screening of Gordy's spoken language and what he seems to understand when others talk to him. The screening indicated that there are some concerns in how he talks and understands language. Now that we have talked about the early intervention program and your concerns, we need to decide about the next step. Based on the great information you have provided, we have a better understanding of Gordy's strengths and the concerns you have. Gathering additional information through an evaluation will help us determine whether or not he is eligible for early intervention. How would you like to proceed?

PLANNING FOR EVALUATION IF NEEDED

For children going on to evaluation, it is essential that the purpose and process is explained to the family. Part of evaluation planning should involve exploring and identifying the roles the family may want to play in their child's evaluation and assessment process. Ask the family who they would like to include. When deciding on the evaluation procedures, be sure to use information gathered earlier to help guide the process and ensure that the tools and procedures fit the needs, interests, and culture of the child and family. Drawing upon earlier information also reduces the need for the family to repeat information they have already shared. In helping families decide how they want to participate, provide them with some examples and offer concrete descriptions rather than vague statements about their participation. Ask if they would like to observe or assist by engaging the child in play and other types of activities.

CONVERSATION STARTER

The primary reasons for this initial evaluation are to determine if Irma is demonstrating delays in development and whether or not she is eligible for early intervention. The evaluation will tell us a lot more about her development. We will actually look at how Irma plays and interacts with you and others. We will talk with you about what she is able to do and what is challenging for her. This will help us understand Irma's skills and how she approaches learning. Completing an evaluation is just one more way of getting to know Irma. Because you know your daughter best, you will be an important part of the evaluation team. You have already provided us with a lot of information about Irma, which is a great start. During the evaluation, Irma may need your reassurance. If she is not interested in things she is asked to do, we may ask you to present them to her. As we go through the evaluation, we will talk about what we are looking for and how she is doing. You are a partner in this process, so please let us know your thoughts.

Explain that gathering information about the family's everyday routines and activities and about the child's behaviors and interactions may also be part of the assessment. Knowing how the child functions within the context of day-to-day life provides an authentic glimpse into the child's skills and abilities beyond what structured evaluations can provide. Assessment will also include a discussion with the family about the formal and informal supports they use or would like to use. This information is important for understanding the family's concerns, priorities, and resources.

Similar to the first contacts, the evaluation should be scheduled at times convenient to the family and respectful of the child's sleeping, waking, and eating times. To ensure a collaboratively planned evaluation, discuss the following arrangements with the family:

- Who should be involved in the evaluation process?

- Who will do what (roles/responsibilities)?

- What will the evaluation look like? What can the family expect?

- Where should the evaluation take place?

- When can the evaluation occur?

- How much time is needed?

- How will results be shared?

WRAP UP

The initial contacts with families form the foundation for future interactions. Therefore providers must take the time to listen and understand families' concerns as well as share information about the program, adhere to regulatory requirements, and invite family participation. Consider the following dos and don'ts for initial contacts with families.

TIP

Initial contacts dos and don'ts:

Do

- Listen to the family's story
- Focus on understanding the family's concerns and the child's strengths and needs
- Acknowledge the child in the context of the entire family
- Tailor questions to the individual needs of the family
- Find out what the family wants to know

Don't

- Tell the family what they need to do next based on the referral
- Focus only on completing the paperwork
- Focus exclusively on the child
- Use the same approach with all families
- Just give the family what you think they need

The initial phone call from early intervention sets the stage for future interactions. During the call take time to listen to the family concerns, explain the program, and ask and answer questions. At the initial visit build upon the relationship by reviewing what was talked about over the phone verifying the information received. As the visit goes on listen to the family as they talk about their concerns and describe early intervention as a system of supports and services, share information about family rights, and together discus screening and evaluation and decide upon the next steps. As the visit wraps up schedule any required next visits, answer any remaining questions, provide contact information, and encourage parents to contact if they have questions. Providers should also take time to reflect on how the visit went.

Thinking how the initial contact had gone for Caleb's Dad, the service coordinator who contacted him could have done a better job listening, explaining the program, and planning the first visit with the Father rather than telling him what would be done.

CHAPTER FIVE

The Importance of Evaluation and Assessment

A Family's Perspective

We have had two children in early intervention separated by 6 years and a move to a different state. What happened during the evaluation and assessment process was so very different for each of our children.

Our first child, Damien, was diagnosed at birth with Down syndrome. Although we were heartbroken about the diagnosis, Damien was darling, peaceful, and fortunately healthy. When he was 6 weeks old the early intervention program contacted us. They had received a referral from Damien's doctor and wanted to evaluate Damien so he could be in the program. When I expressed some hesitation, they told me we really needed get started *now*, as each day was a day lost in helping him. I gave in reluctantly, and they told me a date for Damien's evaluation.

On the appointment day, four people showed up at my home. They had bags of things and lots of papers. After quickly introducing themselves by their titles, one lady, the service coordinator, started asking me questions about my prenatal care and if I had smoked during my pregnancy. While she was doing this, someone else began undressing Damien, saying they needed to checkout his muscle tone. He was fussy, and when I said he was not usually like this, they seemed not to believe me. As Damien started to cry harder, I picked him up, put his PJs back on, and cuddled him. Another person started asking me questions about breastfeeding and said that she would work with us on that, as children with Down syndrome are hypotonic, whatever that meant, and needed help with feeding. As I gave Damien his pacifier, she piped in again saying that pacifiers were not a good idea. The four of them talked together while I held and rocked Damien to sleep. They looked over their papers and then told me he was eligible and proceeded to give me lots of papers. Some I had to fill in, others I was to read and sign. Even though I was apprehensive, they kept saying that my doctor made the referral and that Damien needed their services if he was to progress. As they were leaving, they said they would call me to set up the next appointment to make a plan of what to work on and what services to provide. I spent the next week reading all the papers and wondering what would happen next. What delays did they think he already had? My whole family thought he seemed very much like other babies his age even though he had Down syndrome. I worried a lot about what they thought was wrong with Damien and what I had missed.

My experience with Rachel was entirely different! She arrived 8 weeks early, weighed 3 lbs., 2 oz., and had health problems. At discharge, the hospital staff told us about early intervention and asked if they could make a referral. Early intervention contacted us and the person calling introduced herself, saying they had received the referral and asked if we were aware of it. Her name was Marilyn, and she explained her role as an early intervention service coordinator. She congratulated us on Rachel's birth and asked how things were going now that we were at home. She said I could decide if I wanted to set up an appointment to talk about how the program might be able to help. We set up an appointment that worked around my schedule, and I was invited to visit the program's web site.

The appointment was much different from the one with Damien. When she arrived, Marilyn introduced herself and told me she was the person I talked to on the phone. She asked if this was still a good time for the visit and where I would like her to sit. As we reviewed the information she already had, she asked a few questions and then let me talk about Rachel's surprise birth and her ongoing health issues. Marilyn said Rachel was eligible for their program due to her early birth and health issues. She talked about how their program worked with families to help their children. I mentioned that we had been in early intervention in another state, but I could already tell that this would be different in a good way! After I expressed interest in the program, we talked about the assessment process and set up an appointment that worked around Rachel's nap time and my husband's work schedule. Toward the end of the visit, Marilyn asked if she could hold Rachel. She had been talking to her and watching her on my lap and then seemed so pleased to hold her.

During the second visit, Marilyn was accompanied by two team members, a nurse and a special educator. We watched Rachel together, and they explained what they saw her doing and what children her age typically do. They also asked my husband and me to try a few things with her. Throughout the evaluation assessment, they explained the purpose of different activities. We also talked about Rachel's health issues and spent time talking about a typical day for our family, including the easy and difficult times, not only for Rachel, but for our whole family. As we talked, they really listened. By the end of the visit, we had identified many things they might help with and set up a next appointment to develop her IFSP. As they left, my husband and I talked about how much we had learned and about how they were so interested in learning from us. It was very different from the experience with Damien and felt so much better.

EVALUATION AND ASSESSMENT PROCESS

The next step of the early intervention journey for children, families, and providers is the evaluation and assessment process. It is important to note the emphasis on process, as this should not be thought of as a single event or the administration of a single evaluation tool. One purpose of this process is to determine if the child meets the state's eligibility criteria, but equally important purposes are to gather information about the child's functional abilities, collaboratively determine family needs, and if eligible, identify family priorities for intervention. An underlying focus throughout this process is to involve the family as a full team member and respect them as the experts on their child and family.

Once a referral is made to the early intervention agency, a 45-day timeline is imposed by federal regulations. Any screening by the early intervention program—evaluation, assessment, eligibility determination, and if eligible, the meeting to develop the IFSP—must happen within this period. From a program perspective, this seems like a lot to accomplish in about 6 weeks. Yet from Rachel's family's perspective, 6 weeks can be a long time to wait to determine their child's eligibility and, if eligible, to develop a plan before any services actually begin.

A screening may be done prior to a referral by other professionals who then make a referral. Screening can also be done by the early intervention program following the referral. This is often done to see if the referral is appropriate and/or to help guide the evaluation and assessment process. It is important to note that screenings cannot be used to confirm a delay or disability or determine a child's eligibility for early intervention. Screenings do, however, provide information about the possibility of delay and the need for further evaluation. If screening is conducted by the early intervention program, it cannot delay the 45-day timeline, and all Part C procedural safeguards apply. A family can request to move directly to an evaluation and assessment even when the screening indicates there may not be a possible delay. (Now complete Give It a Go! 5.1.)

Commonly Used Screening Instruments for Infants and Toddlers That Look at Multiple Areas of Development

Ages & Stages Questionnaires® (ASQ)

Bailey Infant Neurodevelopment Screening

Battelle Developmental Inventory Screening

Brigance Early Childhood Screening

Denver II Developmental Screening

GIVE IT A GO! 5.1.

List the screening tools you are familiar with and then star those that you have administered in the past 12 months.

1. _____
   _____
   _____

2. _____
   _____
   _____

3. _____
   _____
   _____

FEDERAL DEFINITIONS OF EVALUATION AND ASSESSMENT

Children under the age of 3 referred to early intervention are entitled to a timely, multidisciplinary evaluation by qualified personnel. If a child's eligibility has been established based on having a diagnosed condition that has a high probability of resulting in a delay, then it is not necessary to do an evaluation for eligibility. Rather, the multidisciplinary assessment is conducted to identify the child's functional abilities and family priorities. This was the case for Rachel. She was born extremely premature and had health complications, which automatically made her eligible for early intervention, and the multidisciplinary assessment was done to identify family priorities for intervention. (Now complete Give It a Go! 5.2.)

Evaluation and Assessment Defined by Federal Regulations

Evaluation: "the procedures used by qualified personnel to determine a child's initial and continuing eligibility. An initial evaluation refers to the evaluation to determine his or her initial eligibility." (§ 303.321[a][2] [i])

Assessment: "the on-going procedures used by qualified personnel to identify the child's unique strengths and needs and the early intervention service appropriate to meet those needs throughout the period of the child's eligibility. Initial assessment refers to the assessment of the child and family prior to the IFSP meeting." (§ 303.321 [a][2][ii])

Other regulations regarding evaluation and assessment are found in IDEA Part C in the following sections:

45-day time line: 303.310(a)

Optional screening procedures for use by an EI (early intervention) program: 303.320

The evaluation and assessment of the child and family (all details): 303.321

What if the child is *not* eligible?: 303.322

TYPES OF TESTS AND INSTRUMENTS

Evaluation and assessment tools include standardized tests, rating scales, developmental profiles, checklists, questionnaires, observation records, and more. The type of test used should be based on the information available and the information needed. Traditional evaluation serves to distinguish typical from atypical development and to help determine eligibility based on state-established criteria. Although a child's test performance provides useful information, it is important to reinforce that the results of a test alone should not be the sole information source used to determine a child's eligibility or ineligibility. Regardless of the test used, it is always important to augment that information with observation, parent reports, and review of other available information.

Some early intervention programs require a particular instrument or type of test for eligibility determination. The following box includes a list of the most common instruments used by early intervention programs to assist with eligibility determination.

GIVE IT A GO! 5.2.

What do you already know about the regulations regarding evaluation and assessment (answers on page 90)?

1. What is the cost to the family?

_____

_____

_____

2. When is *permission needed*?

_____

_____

_____

3. How many people are needed to conduct the evaluation for eligibility?

_____

_____

_____

4. Who can be part of the team?

_____

_____

_____

5. What role do families play?

_____

_____

_____

6. Who can families invite?

_____

_____

_____

7. If the family does not speak English, what should happen?

_____

_____

_____

8. What are some of the important legal documents parents must receive prior to the evaluation and assessment?

_____

_____

_____

Standardized, Norm-Referenced, and Criterion-Referenced Tests: What Is the Difference?

Standardization refers to the manner in which a test is administered. Standardized tests are those that must be administered in a structured, prescribed manner.

Norm-referenced tests are designed to examine a child's performance and compare that to a representative group. Norm-referenced test are largely standardized.

Criterion-referenced tests determine a child's performance in relation to a set of skills. Criterion reference instruments are not usually standardized.

Commonly Used Instruments for Determining Eligibility

- Assessment, Evaluation, and Programming System for Infants and Children (AEPS®)
- Battelle Developmental Inventory, 2nd Edition (BDI-2)
- Bayley Scales of Infant and Toddler Development, 3rd Edition (Bayley III)
- Carolina Curriculum for Infants and Toddlers with Special Needs
- Developmental Assessment of Young Children (DAYC)
- Early Learning Accomplishment Profile for Young Children (E-LAP)
- Hawaii Early Learning Profile (HELP)

EXPLAINING THE EVALUATION AND ASSESSMENT TO FAMILIES

Prior to the evaluation, early intervention staff must spend time with the family to understand their concerns, gather information about the child, explain family rights, secure permission to conduct evaluation, and clarify the logistics—including who will be involved and how, where, and when the evaluation will take place. These conversations can take place as part of the intake process once the team decides to conduct further evaluation.

The evaluation process is often new to a family. This is important to keep in mind, as the terms used in your everyday work may seem foreign to someone just getting started in early intervention. Be careful not to use jargon and to explain the terms or acronyms used. Also be careful not to rush through the information; rather, encourage questions and check for understanding. It may also be necessary to review information covered during prior contacts to ensure the family's full understanding of the information shared and the upcoming process. Use Form 5.1 to guide your process.

METHODS AND PROCEDURES FOR FORMAL EVALUATION

Beyond test administration requirements, it is important for providers to encourage a child's optimal performance. This is done by taking time to get acquainted with the child

FORM 5.1.

PROCESS CHECKLIST: EVALUATION AND ASSESSMENT

Things that must happen as part of the evaluation and assessment process

BEFORE

- ❑ Explain the purpose and process.

- ❑ Discuss eligibility for the program and what happens if the child is or is not eligible.

- ❑ Review available information and determine whether or not the child is automatically eligible, assessment is needed, and/or evaluation for assisting with eligibility determination is needed.

- ❑ Secure parent permission for release of any needed medical or other records. Ensure that they understand their rights before evaluation/assessment.

- ❑ Explain what will happen during evaluation and assessment sessions.

- ❑ Determine who will be involved and who will do what, and identify any special accommodations that may be needed.

- ❑ Emphasize that parents know their child best and that their input is essential.

- ❑ Explain the importance of gathering information about family concerns, priorities, and resources.

- ❑ Provide *written prior notice.*

- ❑ Share family procedural safeguards.

DURING

- ❑ Evaluate and assess the functional needs and strengths of the child.

- ❑ Throughout the process, observe and document what you see the child doing.

- ❑ Openly share your observations with the family and encourage their input.

- ❑ Begin gathering information about the family's everyday routines and activities and the child's behavior and interactions with others in those contexts.

AFTER

- ❑ Establish eligibility and collaboratively determine next steps.

- ❑ Complete any program reports and share them with the family.

The Family's Role

Now that we have had a chance to meet and talk again, I have a better understanding of your concerns about Jared. Do you have any new questions? So let us talk about the next step in the process. This step is to do an evaluation to help us determine if Jared has a delay in his development and if he and your family would be eligible for our services. To do this, we will look at Jared's overall development, which includes the five domains we talked about earlier. We use a tool called the [insert tool name here]. Would you like to look at it with me? When we do the evaluation, it will look a lot like the play activities we did during the screening. You can ask questions and comment on what we all see Jared doing at any time. We will share our observations as well. We may also ask you to help Jared do some things. It is important for us to work together during the evaluation, because Jared is most comfortable with you and you know him the very best. We will talk about the results right after we are done. Do you have any questions so far?

---

before beginning test administration. After all, a child is not likely to initially demonstrate his or her typical behavior to a stranger. Optimally, testing should take place in a location comfortable and familiar to the child, include the child's parents or caregiver, and occur at a time when the child is awake and alert. It would be of little benefit to anyone to attempt to evaluate a stressed infant or child.

There may be some flexibility in the administration and order in which items are conducted depending on the test. If such flexibility is allowed, it is often helpful to follow the child's interest and allow him or her to demonstrate his or her most typical skills and abilities and then match these to the test items. It can also be helpful to involve the parents or caregivers in presenting a test item or getting the child to demonstrate a particular skill because the child is most familiar with them. It is of utmost importance that the providers administering the test are well versed in its administration, scoring, and interpretation of results as well as stay true to the test administration requirements. During evaluation, ask the parent if the behavior you are seeing and scoring is typical. Not only should parent reports be included, but they are a vital part of the evaluation and assessment process and help providers gain a complete picture of the child.

Following the formal evaluation, the parent/caregiver and early intervention staff should take some time to share general impressions. Remember that parents may be anxious about knowing what you learned about their child and what that information means; therefore, this should not be postponed until a final report is written. When possible, the general impression about a child's eligibility to early intervention should be discussed when an evaluation is completed, and team members should discuss what the next steps will be. Sharing information openly helps all team members make informed and collaborative decisions.

FUNCTIONAL ASSESSMENT

Formal evaluation methods are useful in helping to determine eligibility for many children referred to early intervention. They do not, however, provide rich information about the child's functional abilities in the context of day-to-day routines, do not determine what the child likes to do or needs to do, and do not provide the information needed to develop functional IFSPs that can be implemented in natural environments (Bagnato, Neisworth, & Munson, 1997). To understand the child's abilities in meaningful contexts and to identify the outcomes and priorities a family has for intervention, assessment beyond formal evaluation is necessary. That is why the regulations require that each eligible child receives an evaluation *and* assessment. Functional assessment yields relevant information about what the child and family do during daily activities and routines. It is culturally sensitive and individually focused. Functional assessment involves using methods and activities to learn about the child and family in contexts meaningful to them. This yields rich information about what the child can do, likes to do, is interested in, and how well he or she does it throughout the day. It helps providers and families understand what in the family's day is challenging, what is going well, what learning environments are available, and in what situations the parents want help. Ultimately, functional assessment helps providers and families focus on the child's participation, interactions, and independence in family and community activities that are meaningful and important to the family. Rachel's family stated that they too learned a lot from the assessment. It was easy to talk about their day-to-day routines, and they were impressed with how Marilyn and other team members genuinely listened and even learned from them.

Community of Practice Agreed-Upon Practices: Functional Assessment of the Child

- Use prompts and observations to encourage the family to describe their child's engagement, participation, independence, and social interaction in various routines and activities.

- Ask open-ended questions to explore what goes well or may be challenging throughout the day for the child and family.

- Use assessment procedures that ensure collaboration among the family and the providers, including encouraging the family to participate in the way they choose.

- Identify the child's skills that seem to be emerging.

- Observe the child's authentic behaviors in typical routines and activities.

- Use assessments that capture information about the child's interests, engagement, social relationships, and independence.

- Give equal weight to the family's observations and reports about their child's behaviors, learning, and development.

- Throughout the assessment process, reflect with the family about observations of the child's behaviors, summarize results, clarify and confirm that the family understands the process and results, and record the findings.

- Observe and discuss with the family how they help their child learn.

- Offer compliments about how the family uses specific strategies that support the child's learning.

- Use concrete examples of how the family supported the child's skills during assessments.

(Workgroup on Principles and Practices in Natural Environments, 2008)

FUNCTIONAL ASSESSMENT METHODS

Observation, Observation, Observation

Observation is an essential part of the assessment process. In this early stage of relationship building with the family and getting to know the child, much can be learned and understood through naturalistic observation. By observing the child doing things he or she typically does, you can learn about his or her interests, abilities, temperament, responses to others and surroundings, relationships, and challenges. By observing parent and child interaction, you can begin to understand parent interests and interaction styles as well.

Observation is an important component of all steps in the early intervention journey. Initially, observations provide insight about the whole child in the context of the family. You may observe the child playing with toys, being outside, getting upstairs to his or her bedroom, or even eating a snack or meal. Later on, observations may be focused on a particular challenge, such as a child's ability to sit in the grocery cart during shopping outings or to participate in meal time with the family. Observations are also helpful for identifying intervention strategies and progress monitoring.

There are three important ingredients of observation. First, it is important to know what you hope to learn from your observation—why are you observing and for what purpose? Knowing the answer to this critical question will help you focus your observation and yield desired information. Second, abandon your biases by being nonjudgmental. This means not getting hung up on your values. For example, observations such as an unclean house, a cluttered yard, an overattentive parent, a beautiful house, or expensive toys are examples of judgmental statements and are not needed in your evaluation and assessment. Third, concentrate on the actions and behaviors versus your thoughts about someone's feelings or why things are happening—be objective, not subjective. For example, rather that stating, "Johnny enjoys playing with trucks," document the behavior that Johnny demonstrates: "Of all the toys available, Johnny went straight to the trucks. He pushed them and rolled them down the ramp and smiled as he did it." As is with all information gathered, it is important to review it with the family and collectively reflect on what it means and what, if any, action is needed. Sharing your written observations with family members and asking for their input is an important practice in building collaborative relationships. It can also keep you from straying into value or judgment statements. (Now complete Give It a Go! 5.3.)

Gathering Information from Families

Information gathered from parents about themselves, their child, and other family members is so important for understanding family priorities and, in turn, determining meaningful outcomes and the supports and services needed to assist with achievement of those outcomes. By understanding what is going well and what is challenging, early intervention providers and parents can partner to identify or enhance natural learning opportunities based on child and family interests, strengths, and resources.

Gathering family assessment information should not be thought of as a one-time activity or as a box completed on initial and annual IFSP forms. It should be part of the ongoing dialogue and ongoing monitoring of progress toward IFSP outcomes. When gathering family assessment information, be respectful of the family's prerogative to share the information they choose to share. Remember, as you build trust and rapport

GIVE IT A GO! 5.3.

For the three example pairs, circle which example in each pair is the objective observation (answers on page 90).

1a. Jessica built a tower of five blocks. She laughed as she knocked them over.

1b. Jessica built with her blocks and seemed to get frustrated when the sixth one fell off. I think that is too much for her.

2a. Benjamin held one cup in each hand and banged them together. He smiled each time they hit and looked over to his mom. His mom smiles back and Benjamin repeated his game. He did this five times, each time looking over at his mom. Mom and Benjamin laughed.

2b. Benjamin tried to get his mother involved in a game by banging his cups together. Mother did not seem very interested, but she did smile and then Benjamin continued for a while.

3a. Tamika appeared depressed and not very interested in what we were doing. She seemed tired.

3b. Tamika told me she was tired. Matthew had been awake off and on during the night. He fussed for about 3 minutes while on his tummy. He quieted down when Tamika picked him up and held him.

with families, as in any relationship, there will likely be changes in the depth of the information shared.

Interviewing

Gathering information from families often happens through interviewing families and caregivers. Like observation, interviews should have a clear purpose, be unbiased and non-judgmental, and be conducted in a manner that yields authentic information. Some interviews have more formal methods and protocols, others are less formal, and some involve questionnaires and/or checklists for families to complete with you as part of a conversation. One strategy for interviewing is using open-ended rather than closed-ended or multiple choice–type questions. Open-ended questions allow the family or caregiver to elaborate or describe the important details. A closed-ended or multiple choice question—"Does Anthony drink from a regular cup or a sippy cup?"—may lead to a yes-or-no response or may imply that those two choices are the only acceptable cups he should use. Asking, "Can you tell me about how Andy drinks?" allows the parent to tell you many more details:

> He still uses his bottle for milk, and I have been trying to get him to drink some things from lots of different types of cups, but he does not seem to like them. Here, let me show what cups I have tried.

You can see this yields much more quality information. Open-ended questions allow the parent or caregiver to tell you what he or she has seen and how things are as well as reduce the risk of applying bias or judgment. Think of the difference between asking, "Does Katy sleep in her own bed?" versus "Please tell me about Katy's sleeping?" The first seems to imply that all children, including Katy, should sleep in their own bed/crib. The second allows the family to describe Katy's sleeping.

Conversation Starters to Use with the Assessment Process

- What activities do you and your child do on a typical day?

- Tell me how your child participates in _____.

- Tell me how he or she interacts with others during _____.

- What are some things you like to do as a family?

- What are your child's favorite things to do in a day?

- What are things your child does not seem to like or has trouble with?

- Tell me about any times or activities that are difficult for you to do as a family.

- What is the best time of day for your child and family? What is the most challenging? Why?

- Who helps you out with child care?

- If something really good happens, who do you tell about it? If something really bad happens, who might you talk to?

- Who do you see and do things with regularly?

- What community activities and places do you participate in for yourself? As a family?

- What kinds of activities in the community would you like your family (or child) to participate in?

Some IFSP forms include these types of questions and record the responses as a means to document the regulatory requirement of family assessment—with family consent, of course. Recommended practice, however, would indicate that family assessment is more than a list of questions on a form. Yet a beginning list of questions can be helpful, provided the questions are used to facilitate conversation rather than asked in a perfunctory manner. The information gathered should be used as the IFSP is developed and not simply be filed away.

USING EVALUATION AND ASSESSMENT INFORMATION

Eligibility Determination

Eligibility determination is a required step in the early intervention journey. Some children are referred to early intervention with a diagnosed condition that makes them automatically eligible and should move directly to assessment. In other instances, multidisciplinary

Examples of
Interviewing Tools and Resources

Ecomap: A diagram of connecting circles that depicts a specific family's support systems. It documents people, agencies, and community programs that a family names or describes and their relationships with those people. It is useful in discovering the strengths and resources families have and the degree of helpful support that is provided. It is best developed collaboratively with the provider and the family.

Routines-Based Interview (RBI): A semistructured interview developed by Robin McWilliam. It is one part of his Routines-Based Early Intervention Approach. The RBI facilitates relationship building and leads directly to developing functional outcomes for the IFSP and, therefore, to routine-based early intervention. McWilliam uses the ecomap as one strategy of gathering important family information. The specific questions and interviewing techniques are described in McWilliam's (2010) text *Routines-Based Early Intervention: Supporting Young Children and Their Families*. Certification courses in the RBI are offered through the Siskin Institute in order for the methods and material to be used with fidelity. You can find more information at http://www.siskin.org/www/docs/112.190.

Juliann Woods: A professor, researcher, and model developer who has a number of family interview techniques and forms available for use at http://fgrbi.fsu.edu. Especially useful resources from her include "Meeting the Family," "Getting to Know Your Child," and "Family-Guided Routines-Based Intervention (Family Routine Categories)."

Community of Practice
Agreed-Upon Practices: Eligibility Determination

- In order to make the eligibility decision, review and summarize findings and share perspectives among the team, which includes the family.

- If the team determines that the child is eligible, provide written prior notice for both the eligibility decision and the IFSP meeting.

- If the child is not eligible, discuss the team decision, provide written notice for the eligibility decision, including procedural safeguards, and explain the process for filing a complaint if the parent disagrees with the decision.

- If the child is not eligible, discuss and give information about available community resources, developmental milestones, and ways of contacting the early intervention program in the future.

(Workgroup on Principles and Practices in Natural Environments, 2008)

evaluation is needed to determine if the child meets the state's eligibility criteria. It is important to remember that all team members, including parents, are part of the eligibility decision.

Eligibility determination should not be made from a single source of information but from all the information gathered throughout the evaluation and assessment process. Qualified personnel must use informed clinical opinions when conducting evaluation and assessment to determine eligibility. Informed clinical opinions may be used to determine eligibility even when a test does not indicate the required percentage of state-identified delay or if the state-approved instrument is not appropriate for the particular child. Informed clinical opinion uses all assessment information. It is not merely a *feeling* by professionals that this child could benefit from early intervention. Although it may be used as an independent basis to establish eligibility, it cannot be used to negate the results of evaluation instruments.

Measuring Family and Child Outcomes

In 2007, the U.S. Department of Education's Office of Special Education Programs (OSEP) began requiring programs to establish a system for measuring the outcomes or results of early intervention for families and children served. This is different from parent satisfaction surveys that many programs gathered in the past. These measuring requirements capture data about the benefits experienced as a result of participation in early intervention versus how pleased someone was with services. Three family outcomes and three child outcomes were chosen to capture the benefits a family and child might experience as a result of early intervention. All states now participate in gathering these data and reporting to OSEP yearly. The following are the nationally approved child and family outcomes for all early intervention programs:

Family Outcomes

1. Knowing their rights

2. Effectively communicating their children's needs

3. Helping their child develop and learn

Child Outcomes

1. Positive social-emotional skills (including social relationships)

2. Acquisition and use of knowledge and skills (including early language/communication [and early literacy])

3. Use of appropriate behaviors to meet needs

These child outcomes represent the integrated nature of how children develop and learn and cut across the five developmental domains that must be included in multidisciplinary evaluations. The shift away from measuring test scores in domain-specific areas toward looking at how skills and behaviors are functional and meaningful in a child's early day-to-day life coincides with the body of evidence-based practices shared in previous chapters. Each of the three outcomes encompasses actions that children need in order to function successfully across a variety of settings and to ultimately be successful in school.

Although not directly linked to evaluation, assessment, or eligibility determination, measuring the three child outcomes can be integrated into evaluation, assessment, and IFSP development. The Early Childhood Outcomes (ECO) Center cross-walked several evaluation and assessment tools by aligning the three child outcomes with the different test items. The ECO Center has also developed and shared numerous resources and training materials around assessment, evaluation, outcomes measurement, and integration of outcomes into the IFSP process. Recognizing that another book could be written on this topic alone, you are encouraged to go to the ECO web site at www.fpg.unc.edu/~eco. (Complete Give It a Go! 5.4.)

Writing Functional Individualized Family Service Plan Outcomes and Measuring Progress

In the following chapter, we explore the details of how the evaluation and assessment information is applied in the development of the IFSP. Functional assessment information lets the provider know how things are going, what new things may need to be addressed, and which outcomes have been achieved or are no longer needed. Without quality functional assessment and the wealth of information it should yield, it would be impossible to develop a quality IFSP that then guides quality intervention. The early intervention journey is an intricately linked process guided by the foundational pillars addressed in Chapter 2 and builds on the information you gather during the first contacts with families and throughout their stay in early intervention.

GIVE IT A GO! 5.4.

Example 1: Which of these two descriptions provides an authentic assessment of Molly's abilities? Which description provides information useful for identifying functional IFSP outcomes and intervention strategies?

A. Molly demonstrated the ability to stack six blocks, put rings on a dowel, and turn pages in a book. She used her pincer grasp to pick up small objects but did not put the small bead in the pill-shaped bottle. She walked and ran without falling. She could climb up steps but did not demonstrate reciprocal foot motion in stepping. She could not balance on one foot or skip and was not successful on the balance beam. She pointed to the pictures when asked to find a specific item in the picture and was correct 80% of the time. She named 5 out of 10 objects when asked, "What is this?" She took nearly 20 minutes to warm up to the evaluators. She demonstrated inconsistent attention to the various tasks presented to her and did not say any true words.

B. Molly's family is concerned that she is very shy and does not play alongside other children unless her mom, dad, or sisters are right there. When playing at the park, Molly will cry when her sister leaves her side. Molly is able to use most of the playground equipment, but has difficulty going up the five steps on the slide, which is something she wants to do each trip to the park. Molly lets us know what she wants by pointing and using "Molly words," which sound like jibber-jabber. Molly plays in the sandbox and often scoops sand into the dump truck and uses the small lever to dump it out. Molly has several toy animals that she plays with and will carry around. If her sister takes one of her animals, she gets upset and has even bitten to get the animals back. Molly can identify the different animals by giving you the one you ask for. She also pretends to have them eat and will tuck them in to go to bed before she goes to bed.

(continued)

GIVE IT A GO! 5.4. *(continued)*

Example 2: Which of these two observations would provide team members with the most useful information for developing outcomes and intervention strategies? Highlight the particular descriptions you would find the most useful.

A. Annabelle is a darling little girl who shows interest in learning. She is aware of new situations, enjoys exploring her surroundings, and likes playing with toys. She explores new toys in a variety of ways, and her parents report that she can occupy herself for longer periods of time. During a shape-matching activity, she is able to match shapes in a form board but is not successful with other shape-matching activities. She does, however, demonstrate the understanding of one-to-one correspondence. She also shows an early understanding of colors. Annabelle enjoys looking at books and likes to play with her baby dolls. During her play, she demonstrates an understanding of functional relationships and demonstrates object permanence by searching for items that are removed. She will also solve problems by figuring things out. She understands pointing and will imitate some actions. At this time, she is not identifying many items or following simple directions. She makes sounds but is not saying true words.

B. Annabelle most often chooses dolls and books as her play items. In play, she generally jabbers or is quiet rather than using words. Annabelle points, gestures, smiles, vocalizes, fusses, and cries to communicate. She typically pairs sounds with her gestures. She imitates others' talking by using similar inflections, making it sound like she is saying something. However, she does not say many consonants in her imitation attempts, so it is hard to understand her unless you already know what she is saying. For example, she imitates her parents saying, "Where's the cat?," and what she says sounds somewhat like that, but you cannot make out the words. Annabelle typically plays with a chosen toy for 3 to 5 minutes. During play time, she pretends to feed her baby dolls and gives hugs to her kitty, typically linking one or two actions with the toys (e.g., picking up a baby doll and feeding it). When her mom plays "hide kitty," Annabelle will search for it until she finds it if she saw the direction of where her mom put it (e.g., behind her back, under the couch). During play with shapes, Annabelle matched the shapes when putting them in a form board but does not match them without the structure of the form board. She also shows one-to-one correspondence by putting one shape on each shape picture, even if they are not the same shape. During the day, Annabelle imitates her mother's actions like putting clothes in the dryer or trying to wipe off the table after meal time. When her parents dance with her, she tries to imitate them as well. At bedtime book reading, Annabelle looks at the book, turns pages, and points to pictures while looking up at her parent as if to say, "What's this?" She is not yet consistently pointing to the exact picture asked for or named (e.g., Where's the cat?). As her parents ask her questions or give her directions during the day, Annabelle follows some simple familiar directions like "Give me that." However, she is not following directions without having several gestures or hand-over-hand help.

NEXT STEPS

Following the evaluation, eligibility determination, and assessment process, the team should have information about the child, the family, and the community of support that surrounds the family. This information will be useful in the next step of the process, the IFSP meeting. The rich information gathered through intake, evaluation, and assessment helps the family identify their priorities for intervention, helps the team develop functional IFSP outcomes that address the family-identified priorities, and assists the team with identifying and enhancing natural learning opportunities that complement family routines, activities, resources, and interests. (Now complete Give It a Go! 5.5.)

In the following chapter, we begin to explore how the information gathered up to this point in the process is drawn upon to develop an IFSP, including recommended practice strategies for writing functional child and family IFSP outcomes.

GIVE IT A GO! 5.5.

Think of a child and a family for whom you have recently completed the evaluation and assessment process. In the following spaces, list all the information you have that you think is important as you developed the IFSP.

Child: List *all* the information you have and know about the child.

_____
_____
_____

Family: List all you know about the family.

_____
_____
_____

Community: List all you know about the family's community of support: the people and the places.

_____
_____
_____

Finally, what did the family identify as their top three to four priorities?

1. _____
   _____

2. _____
   _____

3. _____
   _____

4. _____
   _____

GIVE IT A GO! 5.2. ANSWER KEY

1. There is no direct cost to the family.

2. Parent permission is needed before conducting a screening and before beginning any evaluation or assessment activity.

3. Two or more professionals of different disciplines, one of which can be the service coordinator

4. Team members can include special instructors, speech language pathologists, occupational therapists, physical therapists, social workers, psychologists, or other specialists as needed.

5. Families play an active role throughout the process.

6. Anyone else they wish to include, often other caregivers or other family members

7. The evaluation must be conducted in the native language of the child and family whenever possible. An interpreter can be included at the family's request.

8. Permission, prior written notice, provision of due process, and procedural safe guards

GIVE IT A GO! 5.3. ANSWER KEY

You should have circled the following examples:

1a.

2a.

3b.

CHAPTER SIX

Developing an Individualized Family Service Plan

A Family's Perspective

After we determined that Abby was eligible for early intervention, our service coordinator, Marilyn, said the next step would be to have a meeting to develop the plan, an IFSP. She explained that our IFSP would include outcomes that were statements about what we wanted Abby and our family to be able to do. Based on our outcomes, we would then identify the early intervention services we needed. Marilyn reinforced that, although she would facilitate the meeting, I was an equal team member and should share my thoughts about what to include on our plan. She also explained who would be at the meeting and that I could invite whomever I would like.

On the day of the meeting, my mother was with me when the three people from early intervention arrived at my home. I knew Marilyn and had met the speech therapist and teacher during the evaluation.

Marilyn introduced everyone, and I introduced my mother, explaining that she cared for Abby when I worked. Marilyn reviewed the evaluation and assessment information, and we had a chance to ask questions. As Marilyn started putting that information into the IFSP form on her computer, she turned the screen so that I could see what she was writing. As she typed, she encouraged input from everyone; I liked that. In one section of the plan, we put things about Abby's abilities, including how she is talking, moving around, and thinking. Marilyn filled in the information I shared about Abby's health, and then we started talking about the things I wanted to work on; I remembered these were called outcomes. Because we had talked about this some at our earlier visits, it was easier than just coming up with things out of the blue. Marilyn had asked me about our day-to-day routines, and I had identified five things that stood out for me. Marilyn had brought the list and shared it with everyone. I agreed that those were still things I wanted to work on, and I added a new one that my mother had mentioned. My mom explained a bit more and that led to further discussion. As we talked about the things I wanted to work on—my outcomes—Marilyn wrote them into simple statements and everyone talked about a few things to do over the next few months to help meet the outcomes and how we would know when each was achieved. After this, Marilyn read them back, and I made some suggestions of words I liked better for two of them. I did not feel shy anymore!

What I liked best was talking and thinking about ideas (called strategies). Everybody, including Mom and myself, started sharing ideas. They kept looking back at information they had about Abby and our family, such as what she liked to do and what we did during the day. As we came up with ideas, they kept asking if those might work for us. I had a pretty good idea of what their visits might be like when we finished that as well as what things Mom and I could do between their visits.

After finishing the outcomes and strategies, we talked about services. Marilyn filled in a page that showed who on the team would help, what they would each do, and how often they would each come. Cyndi would be the main person who would visit. She was the teacher, But the speech therapist would work with her and sometimes visit too. The hour and a half seemed to fly by. I signed the papers, including the IFSP, and Cyndi and I set up a time for her first visit with us.

After they left, Mom and I had a cup of coffee and looked over the plan again. They had printed us a copy on a printer they had brought. We both felt pretty good that we now had the right support to help us help our Abby. We were glad that we could get started the next week and that we did not have to wait any longer; it had been almost 5 weeks since I had gotten brave enough to call the program.

THE INDIVIDUALIZED FAMILY SERVICE PLAN MEETING AND DOCUMENT

Once the team has determined eligibility and the family chooses to participate, the next step in the early intervention journey is developing the IFSP. Even though the IFSP process actually begins at the time of referral, the IFSP development meeting occurs following the evaluation, assessment, and determination of eligibility. All the information gathered from the point of referral up to the actual IFSP meeting should be drawn on for the meeting and subsequent intervention. The IFSP is more than a document to be completed and then filed away. It is not a static plan or a plan that requires professionals to do whatever the family wants. Rather, it is a plan written with families for families. It is the dynamic plan that ultimately guides ongoing delivery of early intervention support and services, and it shifts and adjusts as changes occur in the family. As early intervention providers partner with families during this step in the early intervention journey, it is critical that the pillars discussed in Chapter 2 remain in the forefront, as they are vital to quality IFSP development and implementation.

Beyond being a dynamic agreement with the family and the early intervention program, the IFSP is used to record important dates and information for program monitoring to ensure adherence with federal requirements. It should, however, always be thought of as the family's and the team's document, not a program monitoring tool. The purpose of the IFSP is to support the child and family by documenting the agreement of what will be the focus of intervention, who will be involved, and when, where, and how long supports will take place.

Although IFSPs must be developed in a timely manner, the effort to develop each IFSP should not be hurried. A focus must be on functionality and what the family identifies as needed in the context of their day-to-day lives. For example, Abby's mother wants her to be able to ride in the car without unbuckling the car seat. This becomes one of the IFSP outcomes the team will help her achieve. Abby's family identified that meal times are difficult because it is a guessing game trying to figure out what she wants or does not want. This too became an IFSP outcome: to help Abby use words to request desired food or drink. As changes occur, the IFSP must be revised to reflect those changes. The IFSP is essentially the individualized curriculum for a child and family that can be changed and revised as needed, based on individual child and family circumstances.

It is important that families have a good understanding that the IFSP process and document guides intervention. Remember, developing an IFSP is most often a new experience for the family, so take the time needed to ensure they are in fact full team members in IFSP development and decision making. Foundational to the IFSP must be the recognition that the family is a child's greatest resource and that the child's needs are closely tied to the family's needs. Abby's family, for example, will be the ones who ultimately do the things the team collaboratively identifies to help achieve the IFSP outcomes. The services listed on the IFSP build upon the family's abilities to help Abby learn how to keep her seatbelt buckled and to use words at meal times to tell others what she wants. Therefore, addressing family priorities and building upon family strengths is the best way to support children and families. Respecting this, the IFSP is a plan for the whole family, not just the child with a delay or disability.

CONVERSATION STARTER

What Is an Individualized Family Service Plan?

The IFSP is the personalized document that is the driving force of our work together. It describes what Jacob is doing now, and what you would like to see him doing over the next few months. It outlines a plan of action by highlighting your priorities. It details what support and services will look like for Jacob and your family. You are central to the development of this plan and will be asked to participate in each step of its development and implementation. The IFSP is a fluid document, meaning that, if and when changes need to be made, they will be; it will change and grow with Jacob and your family. At a minimum, it will be reviewed every 6 months. The IFSP is essentially the roadmap for our work together.

INDIVIDUALIZED FAMILY SERVICE PLAN LEGAL REQUIREMENTS

The IDEA defines the required components of the IFSP, the general steps for developing the plan, and who must be present. The IFSP must include the eight IDEA-required components. These are spelled out in section 636(d) (1) of the IDEA statute. In Give It a Go! 6.1, see if you can fill in the required components.

The meeting to develop the IFSP must be held within 45 days of receiving the referral. Thereafter, IFSP services the family agrees upon must begin "as soon as possible" after the parents consent to the services (§ 303.344 [f] [1]).

Each state is allowed to determine what *as soon as possible* means. In the Annual Performance Plan (2011), 41 states defined this as within 30 days from parent consent of the IFSP.

Each family participating in early intervention has at least three IFSP meetings in a year—the initial meeting to develop the IFSP, a periodic review 6 months into the plan, and an annual meeting to evaluate the IFSP. More frequent meetings can occur at any time the family and/or providers feel there is a need to make changes to the IFSP.

The IFSP itself is an agreement with the best thoughts of the team and the family about how to address the agreed-upon outcomes. If things are not working as anticipated, the team should change the IFSP so that it accurately represents what is being provided. If the child is not making progress toward the outcomes, then with family input, the services or strategies may need to be modified.

Although the federal requirements define what must be included in the IFSP, there is great variation in what the IFSP form looks like across states and local programs. You can find examples of IFSP forms on state early intervention web sites.

GIVE IT A GO! 6.1.

Fill in the blanks. These are the IDEA-identified required components of the IFSP (IDEA 2004, Title I, Part C, Section §636 [d]). To help you get started, the first three blanks have been filled in.

1. The infant's or toddler's present levels of development include __cognitive__, __communication__, __social-emotional__, _____, and _____ development

2. A statement of the family's _____, _____, and _____

3. A statement of the measurable _____ or _____ expected to be achieved for the infant or toddler and the family, and the _____, _____, and _____ used to determine the degree to which progress toward achieving the results or outcomes is being made

4. A statement of the specific early intervention _____ necessary to meet the needs of the infant or toddler and the family, and the _____, _____, and _____ of delivering services

5. A statement of the _____ in which early intervention services will appropriately be provided, including a _____ of the extent, if any, to which the services will not be provided in a natural environment

6. The _____ for initiation of services and the anticipated length, _____, and _____ of the services

7. The identification of the _____ from the profession most immediately relevant to the infant's, toddler's, or family's needs

8. The steps to be taken to support the _____ of the toddler with a disability to preschool or other appropriate services

Federal Regulations

Section 303.342: Procedures of IFSP development, review, and evaluation

Section 303.343: IFSP team meeting and periodic review

Section 303.344: Content of the IFSP

Section 303.345: Interim IFSP

THE INDIVIDUALIZED FAMILY SERVICE PLAN MEETING

**Community of Practice Agreed-Upon
Practices: Individualized Family Service Plan Development**

- Establish a welcoming and respectful climate for family members and caregivers as equal members of the IFSP team.

- Review the purpose and process (agenda) of the IFSP meeting. Describe the IFSP document as a dynamic plan that will guide the provision of supports and services.

- Collaboratively review information regarding the family's concerns, priorities, and resources collected since first meeting the family.

- Collaboratively review information gathered previously about the child's health, development, and learning.

- As needed, build upon information about the family's everyday routines and activities and the child's behavior and interactions with others in those contexts to collaboratively identify family priorities and write functional outcomes based on those priorities.

- Discuss with the family the formal and informal supports they use or would like to use.

- Collaboratively plan and write strategies and activities that can be implemented to work toward outcomes.

- Select the needed services and supports to address the agreed-upon IFSP outcomes.

- Identify the criteria, procedures, and timelines to help determine progress and achievement of each outcome.

- Identify the team member who will provide ongoing service coordination.

- Ensure that the family understands relevant procedural safeguards and next steps.

(Workgroup on Principles and Practices in Natural Environments, 2008)

WHAT HAPPENS BEFORE INDIVIDUALIZED FAMILY SERVICE PLAN MEETINGS?

All IFSP meetings—whether they are the initial, periodic review/change, or annual—should be coordinated with the family and include the service coordinator. The service coordinator and other early intervention program participants should prepare for the meeting by reviewing available information and ensuring that the required documents and materials are ready. Meetings should be held at a time and in a place that is convenient for the family and other participants. The early intervention program must also give the family an invitation or notice that states the purpose of the meeting. This notice must be given with sufficient time for the family to arrange and invite the people they wish to attend. Although some early intervention programs convene an initial IFSP meeting immediately following the evaluation and assessment, recommended practice supports holding these on separate dates to allow the family time to review the information provided and, if desired, to talk with others in their support network and invite others to attend. Before IFSP meetings, the early intervention program must also ensure that the family has been provided their rights and procedural safeguards. The purpose of each IFSP meeting should be fully explained to the family. Their important role as full team members and the contributions they make cannot be stressed enough. (Complete Form 6.1.)

WHO ATTENDS INDIVIDUALIZED FAMILY SERVICE PLAN MEETINGS?

The family can invite whomever they wish to attend the meetings. It is often helpful to include other family members and people who are directly involved in the care of the child. Each initial and annual IFSP meeting must include the parents, the service coordinator, and other people who were directly involved in the evaluation and assessments. If appropriate, the people who will most likely provide early intervention services should also attend. If the people who participated in the evaluation and assessments cannot attend, there are provisions allowed for reports to be sent, or they may participate through a conference call or video teleconference. A periodic IFSP review can occur with only the family and the service coordinator. It is important to note that an IFSP meeting can never be held without the family. No changes regarding eligibility, placement, or services can be made to the IFSP before providing the family prior written notification and securing their permission for any agreed-upon change.

WHAT HAPPENS DURING INDIVIDUALIZED FAMILY SERVICE PLAN MEETINGS?

The service coordinator is often the person who facilitates and sets the tone for the IFSP meeting. Family members can, however, be invited to facilitate the meeting if they wish to do so, and other team members can take on this role as well. All parties should be welcomed and introduced equally. For example, if the early intervention team members are introduced as Mrs., Miss, or Mr., then introduce the family and guests by similar titles. Ask parents how they would like to be referred to (e.g., full name or first name). Referring to parents as Mom and Dad is never encouraged. Their name to you is not *Mom* or *Dad*: Those are the names the child uses for his or her parents. When speaking directly to the parents at any time, use their names, Mr. and Mrs., or their first name if they prefer. Using their name demonstrates you have taken the time to see them each as an individual and equal member of the team and that the meetings together are about their particular child and family. The

FORM 6.1.

CHECKLIST

Information to share with the family prior to the meeting

- ❏ The purpose of the meeting
- ❏ Who will attend, including anyone the family wants to invite
- ❏ Family concerns and priorities are what drive the development of IFSP outcome statements.
- ❏ The outcomes inform the services the child and family receive.
- ❏ As applicable, the fees or how public and private insurance may be used to help pay for services, which will vary depending on the state and early intervention program
- ❏ What happens next after the meeting
- ❏ When services will start
- ❏ The service coordinator's ongoing role with the family and the team members

meeting facilitator should keep the purpose and agreed-upon start and end times in mind and move the meeting along by encouraging conversation, taking time for questions and answers, and providing clarification as needed, especially to define any jargon or acronyms that might get used. (Complete Form 6.2.)

To reinforce the importance of team collaboration, everyone should be involved in developing and determining what is documented in the IFSP. Most importantly, the meeting facilitator makes sure the family's concerns and priorities shape the agreed-upon outcomes and that the child's and family's strengths, interests, networks of support, and resources are drawn on to form strategies for addressing the outcomes. In Abby's story, Marilyn, the service coordinator, actively involved Abby's mother and grandmother in developing the IFSP along with the teacher, speech therapist, and physical therapist. It is important to reinforce that decisions about which services the child and family will receive are made only *after* the outcomes are determined. Services are not based merely on areas of delay; rather, they are based on the agreed IFSP outcomes, which can be for the child and/or the family. All strategies for both the child and family outcomes include the family's active participation in working toward meeting those outcomes. The entire process is about supporting the family and promoting their confidence, competence, and even enjoyment as they work with early intervention to meet the needs of their child and family. If you do not have the information you need going into the IFSP meeting, writing outcomes that are genuinely useful and meaningful and that address the concerns and priorities of the family becomes extremely difficult, if not impossible. The IFSP should *never* be written by the team before the meeting and simply presented to the family for their signature. (Complete Give It a Go! 6.2.)

GIVE IT A GO! 6.2.

What information should you have going into an initial IFSP meeting?

What should you know about the child?

_____
_____
_____
_____

What should you know about the family?

_____
_____
_____
_____

What knowledge or skills do team members bring into the meeting?

_____
_____
_____
_____

So how did you do? See if what you wrote matches the following presented information.

FORM 6.2.

CHECKLIST

Tasks to accomplish during the IFSP meeting

- ❑ Begin with introductions.
- ❑ Discuss the purpose and process for the IFSP meeting.
- ❑ Together review information from the evaluation and assessments.
- ❑ Clarify, correct, or add any additional information, as needed.
- ❑ Based on family priorities, determine functional outcomes and measurable criteria.
- ❑ Begin to problem solve activities and strategies to address agreed-upon outcomes.
- ❑ Decide upon the needed services to reach the outcomes.
- ❑ Address transition, including transition at 3 years of age.
- ❑ Provide and ensure family understanding of their rights.
- ❑ Secure required signatures.
- ❑ Make plans to implement the IFSP.
- ❑ Ensure the family understands what is included in the IFSP before they sign it.

Child information gathered before the IFSP meeting should include specifics about the child, including such things as age, developmental skills, strengths and needs, formal evaluation results, a pertinent health history (including any known conditions), things the family would like their child to be doing or not doing, opportunities the child has to play and interact with others, things the child does on a typical day (including what is going well and what is difficult), other services the child may receive, and other caregiving settings the child is in and how those are working for the child.

With the family's permission and their input, family information gathered before the IFSP meetings should include such things as who lives in the household; extended family members, friends, or neighbors that provide support; cultural beliefs or practices that are important to know about as part of intervention; groups or activities the family participates in; and/or formal services they receive from other agencies. Other important information includes things the family enjoys doing, things the family wishes they could do, times of the day that go well, times of the day that are difficult, how the child participates in daily routines, and worries and wishes the family has concerning the child and their family as a whole.

In addition to specific information about the child and family, providers bring their knowledge and understanding of child development, specific information about a variety of disabilities and risk factors, expertise in their particular field, evidence-based practices from a general early childhood perspective and from their particular discipline, adult learning methods, and teaming practices. It is the blending of all this information that contributes to a useful and meaningful IFSP for each child and family.

CHILD OUTCOMES

- Related to functional skills or abilities of the child (e.g., learning to interact and play with peers, entertaining self by playing with toys, sleeping through the night, etc.)

- Addressed within the context of meaningful routines and activities with a focus on function, not domains or isolated skills

- Focused primarily on the child with the caregivers as one resource to help it happen and the team supporting the caregivers using a variety of strategies and roles

- Skill-based only if the skill is tied to a useful behavior the child can use to engage in an activity or to become more independent

- Participation-based, showing what activities the child will participate in using those skills

FAMILY OUTCOMES

- Related to the needs of the family with *help* focused on the parent/caregiver

- Sometimes are indirectly child-related (e.g., getting information about a diagnosis, learning ways to do something for the child)

- Sometimes related to one family member in particular or for the whole family (e.g., finding a place to live that feels "safe," finishing a GED)

- Parent participation based—the parent or parents are the doers or learners

WRITING INDIVIDUALIZED FAMILY SERVICE PLAN OUTCOMES

Writing IFSP outcomes based on family priorities is undoubtedly the recommended practice. However, if you start a discussion about family concerns and priorities by asking broad questions such as, *What do you want for your child?, What would you like to see your child doing in X months?*, and *What would you like to work on with early intervention?*, you will likely get broad responses. For example, *I want him to talk more; I wish he were doing things that other children his age are doing; I want him to walk; I want him to behave better.* These broad statements are too general to simply reword into functional, measurable, and meaningful IFSP outcomes. Without first understanding the details of what is currently happening in meaningful contexts, details about the child's skills and behaviors in those settings, and precisely what the family would like, it is impossible to sincerely develop family-driven, functional IFSP outcomes.

Functional refers to things that are useful and meaningful in the context of everyday living and represent an integrated series of behaviors or skills that allow a child to achieve important everyday goals and participate in day-to-day routines. Think about how a child uses skills in action across settings and situations to accomplish something meaningful. Do not only think about the child's ability to show a specific or isolated skill. For example, extending an index finger in a pointing position is an isolated skill, but pointing to request a cookie from the cookie jar on top of the fridge is functional because it is meaningful in a contextually relevant circumstance. Outcomes that are written to improve only an isolated skill such as *stack five blocks* or *use five words* are not functional outcomes. Rather, functional outcomes are those that define skills or behaviors needed for participation in developmentally appropriate activities or daily routines and are specific enough to be clearly observable and understood by anyone reading the IFSP.

To identify functional and contextually relevant outcomes, interviews such as Robin McWilliam's (2010) "Routines-Based Interview" (RBI) and conversations with families about their day-to-day routines, activities, and challenges are essential. These conversations not only help the team identify the real concerns that a family wants to address, but they are also helpful for identifying natural learning opportunities to help meet a family's desired outcomes. For example, you might learn that car rides are a lot of fun for Rena and her family; they sing songs and listen to music. This, in turn, might become a great learning opportunity to reinforce Rena's ability to use words to request desired items, such as a favorite song. With another family, you could learn that a part of their daily routine is scooping dog food out of a big bin and putting it in the dog's dish. This might be a great motivator to encourage the child to walk over and help out, because you also learned that the child loves the family's Great Dane, Tiny.

It is important to clarify the distinction between concern and outcome. A family concern alone is *not* the outcome, but it is a starting place to explore what needs to happen to resolve the concern or make it better. For example, a family may be concerned that their child is not talking, but the child does point and cries to let others know what he or she wants. Through further discussion, you learn that this presents a real challenge during meal times and at the grocery store. By understanding the context and desired behavior, a functional outcome can be crafted. For example, *Ryan will use words to let others know what he wants during meal time and when grocery shopping, so that he can be understood.* By understanding the concern, knowing it is a family priority, drawing upon information about the child's skills, and determining the context in which the new ability is needed, the team can delineate an outcome to work on in the next few months.

Functional outcomes define what the family would like to see happen; include where, when, or with whom an outcome should occur; and describe why it is important by stating what will be better. They also focus on active participation in family routines, not passive types of activities or drills. After all, learning opportunities capitalized on—in the context of family and community life—have a greater impact on a child's progress than periodic sessions (Jung, 2003; Dunst, 2004; Hanft et al., 2004), and interventions that fit the daily routines and are compatible with family priorities are more likely to be sustainable (Bernheimer & Keogh, 1995).

IS THERE ONLY ONE WAY TO WRITE A FUNCTIONAL, QUALITY OUTCOME?

Even though each of the national experts suggests wording outcome statements in a specific way, there is not only one way an outcome *must* be written. There is, however, common content that must be there in order to write functional outcomes.

At the most basic level, an outcome is a simple statement that consists of the following elements:

1. Name of the person the outcome is for

2. An action verb

3. Where the outcome will be practiced or demonstrated

4. The reason the person is doing this, which ties back to the priority

Example: Carson **(1)** will sit and look **(2)** at books or play with small toys while getting his haircut **(3)** in order for the haircut to be a positive experience for all involved **(4)**.

ROBIN MCWILLIAM'S SUGGESTION
The child will participate in _____ by _____ + criteria.
   Example: "Lance will participate in breakfast, lunch, and dinner by feeding himself independently."
   Example's criteria: "We will know he does this when he uses his hands, with or without a spoon, to put 10 bites into his mouth at breakfast, lunch, and dinner in 1 week" (McWilliam, 2010b, p. 97).

DATHAN RUSH AND M'LISA SHELDEN'S SUGGESTION
Example: "Sanjay will play with his toys and be happy during bath time while sitting up in the tub." (Shelden & Rush, 2009)

BONNIE KEILTY'S SUGGESTION
Example: "Dianne will explore objects by touching, banging, and shaking them to learn and to have fun." (Keilty, 2010, p. 74)

The following list gives a few tools to judge if the outcome you have written is quality and functional:

SMART OUTCOMES (Jung, 2007)

Specific: Is the outcome clear and unambiguous?

Measurable: Will the outcome be obvious when it is met? What is the criteria and under what conditions?

Attainable: Can the outcome be expected to happen in the next few months?

Routines-based: Is the routine within which the outcome is embedded clear?

TIP

Another way to judge the outcome statements—using the SMART measure (Lucas, Gillaspy, Peters, & Hurth, 2012)`

- The outcome statement is necessary and functional for the child's and family's lives.
- The statement reflects real-life contextual settings (not test items).
- The outcome is discipline-free.
- The wording is jargon-free, clear, and simple.
- The wording emphasizes the positive.
- The statement avoids passive words (e.g., tolerate, receive, improve, maintain).

Tied to a priority: Is the rationale evident? Is it tied to a family priority and not discipline or instrument driven?

(Now complete Give It a Go! 6.3 and 6.4.)

CHILD AND FAMILY OUTCOMES AND CRITERIA

The rubric in Form 6.3, developed by author Naomi Younggren, offers a common lens for examining the quality of child and family IFSP outcomes and measurable criteria. It can be used as a training or monitoring tool. A 5-point scale with descriptors at 0, 2, and 4 represent degrees of quality (0 = *unacceptable*, 2 = *getting there*, and 4 = *recommended practice*). Ratings are determined based on the presence or absence of rubric criteria only. To complete the rubric, check all applicable boxes for each child and family outcomes and criteria you are reviewing. Then determine the overall rating for outcomes and criteria using the scale. For example, if all items under response option 2 are checked and none of the items in response option 0 or 4 is checked, the overall rating for that section is 2. If some responses under 0 are also marked, then the overall rating is 1. When some items in response option 2 are checked and some in option 4 are checked, the overall section rating is 3. The reviewer must look at the items checked under each of the anchored response categories (0, 2, and 4) before determining the total rating for the outcome or criterion. Response options 1 and 3 are included to rate subtle differences, such as when items in two anchored response categories are checked.

CRITERIA AND MEASUREMENT PROCEDURES: CHECKING THE STATUS OF THE OUTCOME

Criterion is the standard used to determine achievement of the outcome. The measurement procedures define *how* the team gauges if progress is being made and when the outcome is achieved. Knowing how to identify achievement and measure progress of the outcome are other important parts of the IFSP. Some IFSP forms and state training encourage including the criteria and measurement in the outcome statement. Other IFSP forms have a separate place for criteria and measurement procedures. Remember that this is the family's document. The criteria and measurement procedures included need to have family input, make sense to all, be doable from the family perspective, and have family endorsement. In addition, criteria and measurement procedures must be linked to the family priority and the associated IFSP outcome.

FORM 6.3.

INDIVIDUALIZED FAMILY SERVICE PLAN
RUBRIC FOR CHECKING OUTCOME QUALITY

Child outcome: Outcome is understandable, observable, functional, and linked to family concern. Child outcomes are developmentally appropriate.

0 *Unacceptable*	1	2 *Getting there*	3	4 *Recommended practice*
❑ Too vague, too broadly stated, or includes jargon ❑ Not linked to family concern ❑ Not developmentally appropriate or realistically achievable ❑ Outcome is to tolerate or only extinguish a behavior		❑ Written in family-friendly language ❑ Linked to family concern ❑ Answers 2 of the 3 following questions: • What would the family like to see happen? • Where, when, and/or with whom should it occur • What will change for the better?		❑ All items from Response Option 2 are checked ❑ Specific and functional; necessary for successful functioning in routines or to meet the family's desires ❑ Answers all 3 of the following questions: • What would the family like to see happen? • Where, when, and/or with whom should it occur (i.e., routines-based)? • What will change for the better?

Child criteria: Each criterion represents a functional measure of progress toward the outcome. Criteria address function, context, and measurement.

0 *Unacceptable*	1	2 *Getting there*	3	4 *Recommended practice*
❑ Vague or not understandable ❑ Appears to be a direct repeat of the outcome ❑ Not functional ❑ Not measurable		❑ Functional ❑ A measure of achievement of the outcome ❑ Answers 2 of the following questions: • Can it (i.e., behavior, skill, event) be observed (seen or heard)? • Where or with whom will it occur? • When or how often will *it* occur (conditions, frequency, duration, distance, measure)?		❑ All items from Response Option 2 are checked ❑ Obviously linked to the outcome but not a direct repeat of the outcome ❑ Answers all the following questions: • Can *it* (i.e., behavior, skill, event) be observed (seen or heard)? • Where or with whom will it occur? • When or how often will *it* occur (conditions, frequency, duration, distance, measure)?

(continued)

Adapted from Department of the Army, Educational and Developmental Intervention Services and Comprehensive System of Personnel Development. (2013). *Individualized family service plan process document: Linking early intervention processes.*

In *The Early Intervention Workbook: Essential Practices for Quality Services* by Lynda Cook Pletcher & Naomi O. Younggren (2013, Paul H. Brookes Publishing Co., Inc.)

Family outcome: Outcome is understandable, observable, functional, and linked to family concern.

0 *Unacceptable*	1	2 *Getting there*	3	4 *Recommended practice*
❑ Vague or too broadly stated ❑ Includes jargon. ❑ Not linked to family concern		❑ Written in family-friendly language ❑ Linked to family concern ❑ Answers the following question: • What would the family like to see happen?		❑ All items from Response Option 2 are checked ❑ Specific ❑ Not compound

Family criteria: Each criterion represents a functional measure of progress toward the outcome. A criterion includes a measurement.

0 *Unacceptable*	1	2 *Getting there*	3	4 *Recommended practice*
❑ Vague or not understandable ❑ Appears to be a direct repeat of the outcome ❑ Not realistic		❑ Functional ❑ A measure of achievement of the outcome ❑ Answers 1 of the following questions: • Is the time frame, date, or family satisfaction measurement included? • Can it (i.e., event, receipt of information) be observed and reported?		❑ All items from Response Option 2 are checked ❑ Obviously linked to the outcome but not a direct repeat of the outcome ❑ Answers both the following questions: • Is the time frame, date, or family satisfaction measurement included? • Can *it* (i.e., event, receipt of information) be observed and reported?

Adapted from Department of the Army, Educational and Developmental Intervention Services and Comprehensive System of Personnel Development. (2013). *Individualized family service plan process document: Linking early intervention processes.*

In *The Early Intervention Workbook: Essential Practices for Quality Services* by Lynda Cook Pletcher & Naomi O. Younggren (2013, Paul H. Brookes Publishing Co., Inc.)

GIVE IT A GO! 6.3.

Here are some examples of outcome statements. Use one or more of the aforementioned tools to determine which of these statements is a functional and high-quality outcome (check *yes* or *no*). Answers can be found on page 114.

		yes	no
1.	Lucy will participate in breakfast, lunch, and dinner by drinking from her cup independently without spilling.		
2.	Jamie will increase his vocabulary to 10 words.		
3.	Suzie will engage with playmates at child care by using words to request toys during free play time. She will use 5 names of toys over a 2-week period.		
4.	Jazzie will successfully sit up without help 5 out of 6 times.		
5.	Rachel and her children will spend 1 hour together in a fun activity they enjoy one time a week for a month.		
6.	Family would like Lynda to continue to move forward in her development by doing the next step of activities to continue to encourage independence, problem solving, and play skills.		
7.	Darla will sit in her high chair during dinner so that her parents do not have to hold her and so she can be more independent.		
8.	Jacob will have PT visits two times a week in order to help him walk.		
9.	Abby will eat two different types of food at lunch and dinner in order to increase the amount of both fruits and vegetables in her daily diet.		
10.	Donnie will move around the house with a walker in order to get things and go places by himself.		
11.	Sarah will locate a child care center she feels is good quality so that Ben can be cared for in a place Sarah feels comfortable with when she returns to work.		
12.	Michael will sleep all night in his own bed 5 out of 7 nights in order for Ed and Sue to get some uninterrupted sleep.		
13.	Matthew will use a spoon at lunch and dinner in order to feed himself so that Jen can focus on feeding the baby.		
14.	Erica will participate in her family's bike outings by riding in the supported seat on the back of Naomi's bike.		
15.	Izzie will tolerate sitting in her adaptive bath seat.		

How did you do? Check the answer key at the end of the chapter.

GIVE IT A GO! 6.4.

Use your information from *Give It a Go!* 5.5.

1. Write down the concerns the family shared that they would like to address with early intervention.

_____
_____
_____
_____
_____
_____

2. Consider the child and family evaluation and assessment information you have gathered.

_____
_____
_____
_____
_____
_____

3. Turn the family's expressed concerns into functional outcomes.

Concern: _____
_____

Functional Outcome: _____
_____

Concern: _____
_____

Functional Outcome: _____
_____

Concern: _____
_____

Functional Outcome: _____
_____

4. How do you feel your functional outcomes measure up? Check your outcomes against one of the outcome tools. Are there elements you could improve? If so, try rewriting them.

_____
_____
_____
_____
_____
_____

Some teams use a number as the criterion such as *4 out of 5 times*, a behavior such as *without spilling*, or sometimes a combination of both. When thinking about criteria, first consider the number of opportunities available. For example, if something such as going to the grocery store only happens two times a week, then having a criterion of every day would be unrealistic.

Appropriate measurement procedures are often parent report, observation, or in some instances, a chart of data collected over a period of time. If you ask a family to measure something during the week, be sure you are not imposing homework on them. Charting something, such as how many times a behavior or skill was demonstrated, may be appropriate for a classroom to measure progress, but busy families may see this as an additional burden. On the other hand, some families may enjoy keeping a simple chart for a week or so to document the successful attempts. The bottom line is to make certain that the measurement procedures fit the family. In addition, they must be linked to the outcome and criteria. For example, you probably would not use provider observation as a measure for an outcome about the child sleeping in his bed through the night. The measurement method written into the plan must be carefully thought of just as all other elements of the IFSP.

Just as the outcomes must be carefully documented to accurately reflect the desired result, so too must criteria and measurement procedures. Criteria must provide sufficient information to define what outcome achievement will look like and be developed with family involvement. Following are a few examples of outcomes and criteria to measure outcome achievement. Notice that the first two examples are child outcomes and the third example is a family outcome.

Outcome: Toby will participate in car outings by playing with the toys provided so he does not mess with and unbuckle his car seat.

Criteria: When Toby plays with toys rather than opening his car seat buckle for 3 car outings a week for 3 weeks

Outcome: Leona will sleep through the night in her own bed.

Criteria: When Leona sleeps in her bed the entire night, every night, for 2 weeks straight

Outcome: Jordan's parents, Kasha and Anthony, will have enough information about Cornelia de Lange syndrome to comfortably explain his condition to family and friends.

Criteria: When Kasha and Anthony have information to explain Jordan's condition to their satisfaction

STRATEGIES, ACTIVITIES, AND/OR STEPS: WHAT WILL WE DO TOGETHER?

The intervention strategies and activities, in part, begin to establish the home visiting plan and the plan for the caregivers between home visits. This does not mean the family members become the teacher or therapist while you are not there or that what is written in the IFSP is the family's "assignment." Remember, *together* you are coming up with ideas for activities within the family's natural routines, not adding things for families to do in one-to-one sessions during their day. Strategies and activities can be thought of as steps or actions that, when done, are anticipated to help achieve the outcome. They need to be written in enough detail so that if the provider or providers were no longer involved with that family, someone else on the team or on a subsequent team could step in and know what was being done by whom and where. The strategies and activities clarify who is doing what, what is being done (method, role, or tasks), and when and where these things are happening. The following examples provide a few strategies that could be used to help achieve the outcomes. Remember, though, that just as outcomes are unique and individual to the child and family, so too are the strategies.

Outcome: Toby will participate in car outings by playing with the toys provided so he does not mess with and unbuckle his car seat.

Criteria: When Toby plays with toys rather than opening his car seat buckle for 3 car outings a week for 3 weeks

Strategies: Parents will continue to provide Toby a mix of toys for car outings.

Family and EI providers will work together to complete an interest inventory for Toby.

Family and EI providers will explore alternate ways to safely secure the belt buckle.

Outcome: Leona will sleep through the night in her own bed.

Criteria: When Leona sleeps in her bed the entire night, every night, for 2 weeks straight

Strategies: Parents will continue to make sure Leona has the things that comfort her when she goes to bed (her dolly and her tulip blanket).

Parents and EI providers will brainstorm ways to respond to Leona when she gets up in the night.

The team will explore ways to darken the room and create a soothing routine before bedtime.

Outcome: Jordan's parents, Kasha and Anthony, will have enough information about Cornelia de Lange syndrome to comfortably explain his condition to family and friends.

Criteria: When Kasha and Anthony have information to explain Jordan's condition to their satisfaction

Strategies: EI staff will link the family with other families who have children with Cornelia de Lange syndrome and to reliable web sites.

Parents will schedule a follow-up appointment with the geneticist to get updated information.

Parents will practice explaining Jordon's condition with their EI provider.

Developing strategies and activities involves the family, the early intervention providers, and other community providers working together toward outcome achievement. Strategies and activities blend the family routines, activities, resources, and ideas with what providers know about children's learning, the particular disability, and evidence-based recommended practices. Just as other parts of the IFSP change, so too can activities and strategies. After all, it would be impossible to think of or list all the possible strategies that may be attempted to achieve an outcome. Keep in mind, though, that all must be linked back to the family priority and functional outcome. If the outcome is too broad, too vague, or not a quality functional outcome, it is impossible to develop specific quality strategies that will work and that you can know have led to success. For example, an outcome such as *Iyana will do what other children her age are doing* is much too broad. With an outcome this broad, it is difficult to identify strategies to work toward it. Yet, if you knew the details and the family's desire was to have Iyana climb on the playground like the other children at her child care center, then you and the family and the child care providers can identify strategies to help Iyana. An outcome such as *Zoe will improve her communication skills* is too vague. It does not specify what the team wants to see happen. An improvement to this, depending on the individual child, might be *Zoe will use words to tell others what she wants at meal and play times.* By knowing what the family wants to see happen, it is much easier for the team to collaboratively identify strategies. Sometimes an outcome might be specific but not functional; for example, *Armani will bring hands to midline* or *Nadi will tolerate being on her tummy.* With outcomes like these, the focus is on an isolated skill rather than a functional ability that has a focus on increasing the child's successful participation in regular routines or activities. In essence, the activities and strategies families use between visits *are* the intervention, and for the intervention to be meaningful, you have to start with high-quality, functional, contextually based outcomes derived from family-expressed desires. When developing the strategies and activities, remember to include enough detail about what is being done as well as with whom and by whom, so that if the provider were no longer working with the family, someone else could step in and keep going.

TIP

CONSIDERATIONS FOR DEVELOPING INDIVIDUALIZED FAMILY SERVICE PLAN STRATEGIES

What is already being done?

- Brainstorm options and ideas with the family.
- Consider the child's interests and the family's strengths.
- Think about evidence-based strategies.
- Consider opportunities (people, places, interactions, activities, and routines).

When can we use these strategies?

- Collaboratively explore and identify the routines and activities within which the strategies could be used.
- Determine how often the strategies can be used.

How will we use these strategies within the identified routines?

- Collaboratively explore and identify how the strategies can be used.

Who can help?

- Consider support needed and how often.
- Strategies should include the family and others in the family's networks.
- Team members can participate.
- Other sources of support and help may be available to assist.

Included here is another example from Dr. LeeAnn Jung from the University of Kentucky. In her training materials, she provides the following guidelines for writing routine intervention strategies (Jung, 2007):

Routines-based: Embed intervention into the family routines.

Outcome-related: Strategies must fit the outcome.

Understandable: Others must be able to understand what is being done (jargon-free).

Transdisciplinary: Strategies integrate disciplines and domains (not just speech strategies or OT strategies).

GIVE IT A GO! 6.5.

In this activity, there are a series of 10 strategy statements (A–J) for each outcome. Read the entire list of strategies for each outcome and identify the 5 statements you feel are well written and reflective of the information presented earlier. For this activity, *EI* is used as a placeholder for the name(s) of the staff involved that you would include if this were a real IFSP and not simply an exercise (answers on page 114).

1. **IFSP outcome:** Dylan will participate in teeth brushing by letting his parents brush his teeth without fussing. We will know he can do this when he lets his parents brush around in his mouth once a day (morning or night) for 3 consecutive weeks.

    STRATEGIES:

    A. The family will continue to include teeth brushing as part of the morning and evening clean-up times.

    B. EI and the family will explore different types of toothbrushes.

    C. EI will select the best toothbrush for Dylan and teach the family how to use it with Dylan.

    D. Family will follow through with the ideas discussed.

    E. EI and the family will discuss ways to model teeth brushing on Dylan's favorite toy dinosaurs or some other toys.

    F. EI will support the family.

    G. EI will share information to ensure that the family understands the importance of starting teeth brushing at a young age.

    H. EI will explore with the family a teeth-brushing song that could be sung while Dylan brushes his teeth.

    I. EI and the family will brainstorm ways to positively reinforce Dylan for his efforts.

    J. EI will provide a teeth-brushing home program for the family.

2. **IFSP outcome:** Dylan will participate in meal time by independently using his spoon. We will know this is met when he uses his spoon with minimal spilling at one meal a day for 3 consecutive weeks.

    STRATEGIES:

    A. An occupational therapist will provide occupational therapy.

    B. EI staff and the family will examine how Dylan is using his spoon and brainstorm ways to make it less messy.

    C. EI and the family will explore how repetition and sameness can help Dylan practice eating using his spoon.

    D. EI will help Dylan move beyond using his current transverse palmar radial grip.

(continued)

GIVE IT A GO! 6.5. *(continued)*

E. EI and the family will find ways to give Dylan more time to practice with a spoon during play times.

F. EI will give family an adaptive spoon and home program for using it.

G. EI and the family will consider Dylan's favorite foods and think about ways to include spoon foods at more meal times.

H. EI and the family will discuss foods that are going to be easiest for Dylan to eat with a spoon.

I. EI will model ways to help Dylan use the spoon and parents will implement strategies.

J. EI will instruct the family on appropriate postural stability, jaw and oral motor skills, and coordination of sensory systems.

3. **IFSP outcome:** Jules will find an acceptable child care program that Dylan can attend to up to twice a week. We will know this is met when Jules is satisfied with her selection.

STRATEGIES:

A. EI will provide the family with information about community child care options.

B. EI will locate the best child care program for Dylan.

C. Jules will select a child care program for Dylan by October 1.

D. EI and the family will review markers of quality child care and make a list of what Jules wants.

E. EI will help Jules make a list of questions to ask child care facilities in which she is interested.

F. EI will help Jules think through the pros and cons of possible options she is considering.

G. Jules will select a child care program and stay with it at least 6 months before changing.

H. EI can accompany Jules and Dylan to child care facilities to help determine if any are a good fit for everyone.

I. EI will provide services to help the family.

J. A family service coordinator will take Dylan to various programs and report back to Jules about the one he seems to like best.

Implemented by others: In the context of the day-to-day routines and activities

Nonjudgmental: Not professionally directed; considerate of the family's culture, preferences, and interests

Evidence-based: Empirically based strategies that stay abreast of new developments in child development and professional fields (complete Give It a Go! 6.5)

DETERMINING SERVICES AND SUPPORTS

The services portion of the IFSP summarizes the early intervention services to be provided. These should only be decided *after* the outcomes and the strategies have been determined. The early intervention services defined in the federal regulations include 17 specified services (§ 303.13). More important than the list of services is the associated description of what each service provides. Many of the descriptions overlap and could be provided by a number of different providers on the team. Team discussion centered on a variety of questions should determine which services will be used and who the provider will be. The following box highlights these key questions.

Questions to Assist with Service Decisions: Following Individualized Family Service Plan Outcome Development

- Which provider can best address the identified outcomes, and what support does that provider need from other disciplines on the team?

- Are there specific strategies that rely on the specific knowledge and skills of a certain discipline?

- Which disciplines need to have face-to-face opportunities with the child and family?

- What frequency of face-to-face visits is needed?

- Which services can be provided via covisits with the primary provider or periodic consultation?

In addition to deciding upon the mix of services needed, the team must also determine frequency, intensity, roles, and methods of each service. If using a primary service provider approach, which is regarded as recommended practice, the family would have one main provider that may come from any discipline on the early intervention team. Ultimately, the primary provider is the person who can assist the family best with addressing the outcomes they have set for the child and family with, of course, the support of other team members as needed. The other team members are also listed on the services page, but their frequency, intensity, and methods would be documented differently than the primary service provider's. Support and services provided by other agencies can be listed on the IFSP as well. These services are not early intervention services provided under Part C but may also be working with the family and the child. Examples may include such things as support from a school for the blind, a parent-to-parent support group, a library program for children, a local playgroup, or a specialty doctor. The need for supports and services outside Part C depends on the individual child, the family, and the IFSP outcomes. Listing all the supports and services helps both families and providers get a complete picture of who is helping and providing what to the family.

The expected norm for services in natural environments is the home or other community settings in which children of the same age and without disabilities participate. If there is a determination that a particular outcome cannot be achieved for the child in a natural environment, then the team must write a justification statement on the IFSP explaining why the child's outcome cannot be achieved in a natural environment and include the steps that will be taken to move the services to a natural environment as soon as possible. Because justification for services in a setting other than a natural environment must be based on the individual child's needs, it is difficult to provide an example of an outcome that would always need to be addressed in an unnatural setting. Given that, a possible example might be trying different assistive technology devices that are difficult to transport before selecting one that will be used in a natural environment. The date that each service will begin is also documented in the services section of the IFSP so that everyone is clear when the service will begin.

Another component of the IFSP includes the payment arrangements for the services. The payment arrangements vary from state to state and are determined by each state's system of payments. Some states use sliding family fees and/or public and private insurance. In other states, there are no direct costs to families for the ongoing services. Early on in the IFSP process the costs of services must be explained so they are not a surprise as the IFSP meeting comes to a close. It is very important for providers to understand their state's policies and procedures around billing.

The IFSP development process and the meeting itself cannot be rushed, as there is too much to do and do correctly. A well-developed IFSP that the family has been instrumental in developing lays the ground work for all future relationships and sets up the expectations of the home or community visits for the next few months. At the conclusion of the meeting, the family can sign the IFSP there or take a few days to review it on their own and sign at a later date. It is the date of the family signature that starts the legal requirement that services begin in a timely manner as specified on the IFSP. By this point in the early intervention journey, providers have met with family's several times, answered many questions, provided support, and collaboratively developed a plan that is ready for implementation.

GIVE IT A GO! 6.3. ANSWER KEY

1. Yes	6. No	11. Yes
2. No	7. Yes	12. Yes
3. Yes	8. No	13. Yes
4. No	9. Yes	14. Yes
5. Yes	10. Yes	15. No

GIVE IT A GO! 6.5. ANSWER KEY

1. A, B, E, H, I
2. B, C, E, G, H
3. A, D, E, F, H

CHAPTER SEVEN

Moving Forward

Individualized Family Service Plan Implementation and Ongoing Intervention

A Family's Perspective

Willie and I (Tasha), and I guess you could say my ma and nana, have been work-ing with the Babies First program since Willie was 9 months old; he is almost 2 years old now. He just didn't seem to be developing right. I am a teenage mom, and it seemed everyone thought I was just not a good parent and that nothing was really wrong with Willie. After the evaluation and assessment, the early inter-vention team discovered that Willie was deaf. I was shocked because he had always made noises. I felt like saying to everyone, "See, I told you so! Something was wrong. It is not my fault!" Our teacher—that is what I call Ms. Cyndi—and some other people from the program visit Willie and me in our home. We live with my mom and nana in an apartment in the projects. So I was really surprised when they said they would come to our house and other places in our community to work with us. For the first few visits, I was not comfortable around Ms. Cyndi. It seemed like I did not have much in common with her because she was as old as my nana. I thought she was just going to tell me what and how to do things like my ma and nana do. I don't think I was very nice to her in the beginning. I didn't talk much to her and just said "yes" or "no" to lots of her questions. Ma and nana were at the visits too, and they seemed to do most of the talking, mostly about me. But Ms. Cyndi always asked me what I thought, even when my ma butted in. After a while, I started to realize that she was treating me like I counted for some-thing and that I was Willie's mother. She always greeted me first and looked at me when she talked.

Ms. Cyndi has been coming for about a year now. Our visits have even been fun. She, Willie, and I play together and talk about what we are doing, and she listens to me and my ideas. We have taken Willie to the park and to the store because I was having trouble controlling him there. That was great because we tried our ideas out right there. Ms. Cyndi even came to my church. She helped me teach the nursery care attendants some of the signs we were teaching him. I felt really proud that it was me showing them what signs he knew and how to do them. That is a lot of what we do on the visits, learning to talk with our hands and fingers (sign language) and helping Willie do other things little kids should do even if he cannot hear me. I worried that I wouldn't do so well learning those signs because I quit school after eighth grade; I didn't think I was very smart. But it seemed sort of easy the way Ms. Cyndi did it. I would tell her words that I thought Willie should say, and then we would try them out. At some meals, Willie would get so mad because I didn't know if he wanted his cup or his food or more of something. So we started with word signs to help with that. Now we have lots of signs he uses.

Other things we have done are get him to a special hearing doctor who did a lot of tests. Now Willie has two hearing aids that he got 4 months ago. I have learned how to help him keep them in, and I can check them to see if they are working right. He didn't like them at first, but now he wears them almost all the time. I can now take the bus with Willie by myself to the doctor for check-ups. Ms. Cyndi helped me think of good questions to ask the doctors and how to keep a notebook of information about Willie.

One time, another man came to the house with Ms. Cyndi and helped us try some real words with his signs. That was after we got the hearing aids. Then Ms. Cyndi and I did things the man showed us like make sure Willie was looking at us when we said the words and repeating a word again, making sure to speak clearly. Now Willie says some words out loud, along with his signs. They don't always sound just right, but I know what he means. I think he is so smart! Now Ms. Cyndi is helping me with an idea I had about me getting my GED. I told her I wanted to go to school and help little kids like Willie who have problems.

I like our visits. Ms. Cyndi doesn't tell me what to do. She shows me things, I show her things, we figure things out together, and she really listens to me. Sometimes she gives me an idea and then helps me do it. I can tell her if something doesn't seem like a good idea for me or my family, and she and I work on it a different way. She isn't bossy, and I don't feel like she thinks I'm a bad parent because she always tells me things I do that are good and tells me that she is learning from what I am doing too. We always start each visit by looking at Willie's plan about what we agreed to do. Sometimes we change things on the plan or mark off the things he is doing now or that I don't want to do anymore. Ma and nana don't come to all the visits much anymore. It's like they get it that I am his mama. Don't get me wrong; they still help me out a lot. I really like how the visits go and how Ms. Cyndi treats me like Willie's mama, not just a teenager. I may not have money, a fancy house, a man, or my schooling done, but I am Willie's mama, and I really love him, I want good things for him, and I know I can help him.

THE DYNAMICS OF ONGOING INTERVENTION

Once the initial IFSP is developed, the ongoing work of intervention begins. This does not mean that the plan is filed away; it means that the IFSP is actively used to guide visits with the family and child in their home or in other community locations. It also guides interactions such as phone calls, meetings, and written communication from the program. A great deal happens on and between visits.

As a provider, you work with a variety of families. Your roles and responsibilities may include being a service coordinator, a primary service provider, a supporting provider, another team member role, or a combination of these. During ongoing intervention, you work with the family to discover intervention strategies that work toward achieving the IFSP outcomes. You evaluate progress and add or change intervention outcomes. You partner with other team members and community providers to assist the family, strengthen their capacity to meet future needs, and celebrate their accomplishments. You also coordinate IFSP reviews, evaluations, and assessment activities as well as complete necessary paperwork. An important role—that affects everyone involved—is using your relationship-building skills to help each family develop a working partnership with you. Within this relationship, you will encourage participation and engagement as families discover new skills and competencies that help them and their child achieve progress. Some providers are good at building relationships but may be less skilled at ensuring opportunities for families to be actively engaged in learning new skills in a way that truly increases their competence and confidence. For example, a provider may be great at small talk and gathering information about how things are going, but less skilled at helping the family discover intervention strategies that make sense in their daily routine. It is vital that the balance of these roles be present throughout each visit. Considering the short amount of time you have to work with families, some less than a year, every effort should be made to make each visit the best it can be.

You will work in a variety of homes and community locations. You will make home visits as well as visits to child care, libraries, play groups, parks, and other community settings. Home visits will look a bit different for each family, yet the guiding principles described previously in this book should

TIP

Ten Visit Reminders That Should Be Part of Each Visit

1. Conduct yourself as a guest.

2. Greet all members present.

3. Check in and see how everyone is doing.

4. Use IFSP outcomes to guide the visit.

5. Use active, reflective listening (use open-ended questions before closed-ended questions).

6. Decide together what activities to do and explicitly discuss strategies.

7. Encourage parent input, ideas, and problem solving.

8. Balance time between listening and doing.

9. Make a plan for the next visit.

10. Thank everyone for their time and say good bye.

remain core to each visit, no matter who the family is. As you make home visits, there may be some that are easier than others. This is demanding work that requires you to represent the program and make visits both independently and with other team members or community agency representatives. You will work with families from cultures different from yours, families with values and beliefs different from yours, families of all ages and different compositions, and children with a different conditions and needs. Home visiting is never dull and never the same from visit to visit, as families' lives are dynamic and ever changing. It is, however, rewarding work.

GETTING STARTED AFTER THE FIRST INDIVIDUALIZED FAMILY SERVICE PLAN MEETING

As the family begins their early intervention journey from referral to eligibility to the IFSP meetings, they participate in a variety of different activities and meet a variety of people doing various tasks with their child and with the family. Considering the mix of activities that happens before ongoing intervention begins, it is no wonder that it can be difficult for families to truly know what to expect when it is time to implement the IFSP and get started with ongoing intervention. Parents may think that intervention is just about their child because many prior activities involved some direct work with the child and because eligibility for the program is based on their child's disability or delay. A parent might also draw upon past experiences with other types of providers or from an understanding of special education and child-centered services for children. With that said, parents can be uncertain about what IFSP implementation and the ongoing home visits will actually look like. For this reason, early interventionists must help families know what to expect. The visits should be designed to facilitate family engagement and participation (Keilty, 2010).

On the first visit after the initial IFSP meeting, the provider should share again (and again) the purpose and intent of early intervention and the roles of the provider and the family. The words you use and the materials you share set the stage for reinforcing intervention as family-centered support versus direct services provided to the child. If the purpose of early intervention has been explained well, parents can understand from the beginning that they do not simply leave the room as you show up to "work with Willie" or sit back and passively participate. To get intervention visits on the recommended practices path, the provider must help families understand what early intervention visits are, what they are not, and how early intervention can assist them with addressing their concerns and priorities. Even if you previously gave out program brochures or shared a program video about how early intervention works, this may be a good time to watch the video together again or look back over the brochures so that you can emphasize the key points that now will happen and invite family comments and questions. You should also discuss the practical aspects of the visits, such as who the family can invite, the general length, where visits can happen, how to get in touch with the provider, and program cancelation policies. On this first visit, the IFSP should be reviewed as needed with the family to answer any new questions or concerns that may have come up since it was developed. If not previously done, the family needs to sign the IFSP and any other necessary documentation.

Before the day of the visit, the provider should always call and make sure it is still a good day and time for the visit. If the family needs to cancel, accept their reason and set

---

 CONVERSATION STARTER

The Call to Confirm the First Visit After the Individualized Family Service Plan Meeting

Hi, Tasha. This is Cyndi Pillsbury from early intervention. How are you? (response)

I am just checking to make sure tomorrow is still a good time to visit you and Willie at your home. You said at the meeting last week that tomorrow (Tuesday) morning at 10:30 would be a good time. Will this still work? (response *yes*)

Oh, good. It's building 4, apartment 803; is that right? (response)

Our first visit will be about an hour. I will bring the IFSP, which is the plan we developed together last week. We will first talk about any questions you have about everything we have done so far. That has been a lot of information to take in. (response and question)

Sure, it is fine if your mom and grandmother want to be there—and Willie too! We will also talk more about what future visits will look like and who else on the team will be coming from time to time. Tomorrow it will just be me coming out. (response)

Great! I will see you tomorrow at 10:30.

another date. Before arriving at the visit, spend time thinking about the specific family and review information from any prior visits that have been made during the evaluation and assessment or the notes of others who did those activities. Be prepared, but also be flexible.

In some early intervention programs, the ongoing provider may have started with the family during the initial referral or worked with the child and family during the assessment and evaluation. In other programs, the provider may have met the family for the first time during the IFSP meeting. Still in other programs, the provider may be meeting the family for the first time during the initial intervention visit following IFSP development, meaning that they need to begin the process of getting to know the family and child and building the family-centered relationship that is so critical to continuing success.

The first few visits can feel the most awkward to you and the family as you are both getting to know one another and as the family is figuring out what participating in early intervention is all about and what kinds of things happen when you and other teams members are there. It is very important to keep the first few visits balanced with you helping the family know about ongoing early intervention visits and spending time doing things together. Remember, you will both be observing each other and making first impressions. Some may be true and others might be early assumptions that will change over time. Remember also not to lose sight of the purpose of early intervention and the family's priorities as stated in the IFSP. Get started together on the stated outcomes and keep a focus on building the relationship as you work together.

Community of Practice
Agreed-Upon Practices: Ongoing Intervention

- Use the IFSP as a guide to decide which outcomes and activities to focus on during the visit.

- Jointly revise, expand, or create strategies to continue progress toward achieving outcomes.

- Listen, observe, model, teach, coach, consult, and/or join the ongoing interactions of the family and child as the means to address the outcomes with the family.

- Together, plan next steps including what will happen between this visit and the next.

- Modify services and supports to reflect the changing family priorities and outcomes.

- After the visit, reflect on how you think it went and discuss with other team members as needed.

- Document the visit and progress toward the outcomes.

- Initiate any activities agreed upon with the family.

- Begin to prepare for the next visit.

(Workgroup on Principles and Practices in Natural Environments, 2008)

CRUCIAL ASPECTS OF ONGOING INTERVENTION

To help define the complexity of visits, we must consider three crucial aspects that shape each visit or interaction. These important components are using the functional outcome to guide the interventions, explicitly focusing on the intervention strategies, and promoting family engagement that leads to capacity building. This is what your ongoing work with the family in their home or other community settings is all about. It is what you do on each visit. This ongoing work is always supported by the foundational pillars discussed in detail in Chapters 2 and 3.

This dynamic work is illustrated later as a series of interlocking cogwheels. The center of each wheel is one of the crucial aspects: 1) functional outcomes to guide intervention, 2) explicit focus on intervention strategies, or 3) promotion of family engagement that leads to family capacity building. The cogs are the foundational pillars: 1) family-centered and relationship-based practices, 2) children's learning, 3) natural environments and routine-based learning, 4) adult learning practices, and 5) quality teaming.

FUNCTIONAL INDIVIDUALIZED FAMILY SERVICE PLAN OUTCOMES TO GUIDE INTERVENTION

The IFSP functional outcomes are at the core of every home visit and should be used to guide the discussions and activities that happen during the course of the visit. By explicitly using the outcomes to focus the home visit, you ensure that the family's priorities are being addressed and that changes are made as needed. There will be times when outcomes need revision or new ones need to be added. By addressing IFSP outcomes regularly as part of each visit, the team is able to stay focused and address any needed changes. This practice yields a dynamic IFSP that reflects changes that naturally occur in families' everyday lives.

It is likely that there is not enough time in a home visit to address each outcome at every visit. Sometimes an entire visit might be spent on just one outcome, and at other visits more outcomes may be addressed, or on other occasions the family may need to address something else that has come up. Using the IFSP outcomes to guide the visits helps providers and families keep track of the progress being made.

By having a shared focus and plan for intervention visits, families are better equipped to be informed, empowered, and engaged in ongoing visits. Of course, successful implementation of home visits is only possible if the IFSP is truly based on family priorities and if the outcomes are meaningful and useful to the family. The strategies and activities designed to meet those outcomes must work within the daily activities and routines that the family wanted to address. If the IFSP outcomes are based on missed assessment items or are broadly stated, the home visit becomes less effective because the outcomes are not about the functional skills the child needs to be successfully engaged in the family's day-to-day life or about the specific desires of the family.

EXPLICITLY FOCUS ON INTERVENTION STRATEGIES AND ACTIVITIES

In early intervention, we can think of intervention as the strategies and activities that are applied toward achieving the outcomes described in the IFSP. Considering the two broad types of IFSP outcomes (child and family), the focus of a visit may shift between outcomes and strategies that are specifically for the child and those that are for the family.

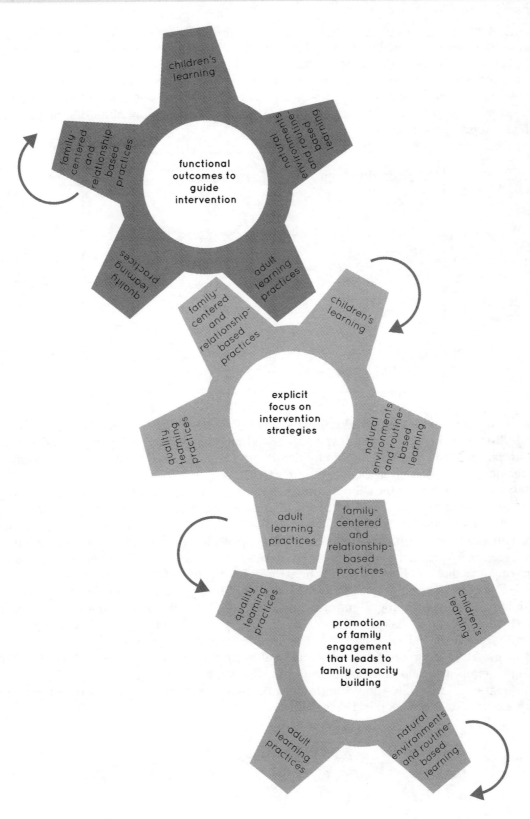

Figure 7.1. Crucial Aspects of Ongoing Intervention

When thinking of intervention, it is important to think about the use of actual strategies that may be applied to a particular outcome. Recognizing that all children are individuals and part of unique families, there are infinite types of intervention strategies and activities. The box below includes a small sampling of evidence-based intervention strategies you may have learned in your professional training. Each one has an array of ways it could be applied depending on the actual outcome, the individual child, the family, and their resources and routines.

General Intervention Strategies

Wait time

Following the child's lead

Offering choices

Environmental arrangement

Hand-over-hand prompting

Praise

Redirection

Adaptive equipment

Providers are not expected to be encyclopedias of all possible techniques. However, based on your knowledge and experiences and augmented with team input and crafted with family ideas, you will be able to identify and collaborate with families to implement specific intervention strategies. It is important to be able to specifically and effectively communicate with families about strategies rather than simply model them. It is equally important to collaboratively identify and define intervention strategies if families are going to understand, contribute to, and ultimately use them in meaningful routines. Remember, you are not trying to make parents be minitherapists, teachers, or students responsible for carrying out your intervention strategies. Rather, the strategies can be used to craft meaningful ideas that will help the family help the child accomplish family priorities.

Consider Figure 7.2 as a framework for identifying outcome-specific strategies and applying them to meaningful routines and activities. When thinking about strategies, start with what the family has already tried or thought of; consider the child's interests and the family resources and supports. This framework helps ensure that teams understand the strategies, including when and how they will be applied as well as who will apply them. These details also help guide regular intervention visits.

Figure 7.3 illustrates how the framework may be applied to address functional outcomes. It is the outcome, the child's skills and abilities, and the family routines that guide

Figure 7.2. Framework for Identifying and Applying Strategies

the types of routines-based strategies that are implemented. It is important that the strategies be collaboratively identified and explicitly defined if they are to be understood by all and ultimately integrated into routines that are meaningful and doable for the family.
Example:

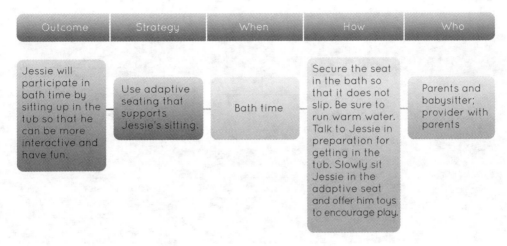

Figure 7.3. Example of Framework for Identifying and Applying Strategies

(Complete Give It a Go! 7.1.)

FAMILY ENGAGEMENT AND CAPACITY BUILDING

Conversation with families is an integral part of the home visiting and early intervention process. Conversation alone, however, is not enough. Effective communication requires active and impartial listening, continuous clarification, and a desire to truly understand all parties in the conversation. Such dialogue assumes that each member of the conversation can contribute ideas toward a workable solution. It is a collaborative style that is responsive to the family's needs and does not involve telling others what to do. A focus on family engagement and building their capacity promotes their involvement as well as their confidence and competence in identifying, applying and refining strategies to achieve to achieve their outcomes. Caregiver engagement is not a measure of the parent's follow-through with provider suggestions.

Intervention Interactions

Intervention visits are guided by the IFSP outcomes and the strategies to achieve those outcomes. Keeping in mind recommended practices of adult learning theory, your interactions with families should include listening, engaging in coaching or consulting conversations, problem solving, exchanging information, indirect and direct teaching, modeling, inviting the family to try out an idea, and providing feedback, encouragement, and support. The family is engaged and participating as you work with them as they help their child. The visits and the conversations are the blending of the wealth of knowledge and experience of the parents and of the interventionists. It is not enough to have a good relationship with the family if that relationship is not used to build the family's capacity to gain new skills, demonstrate their competency, solve a problem, or accomplish a goal that they feel is important in

GIVE IT A GO! 7.1.

Think about a family and one of their outcomes and write an intervention plan that includes the *what*, *when*, *how*, and *who* for addressing the outcome.

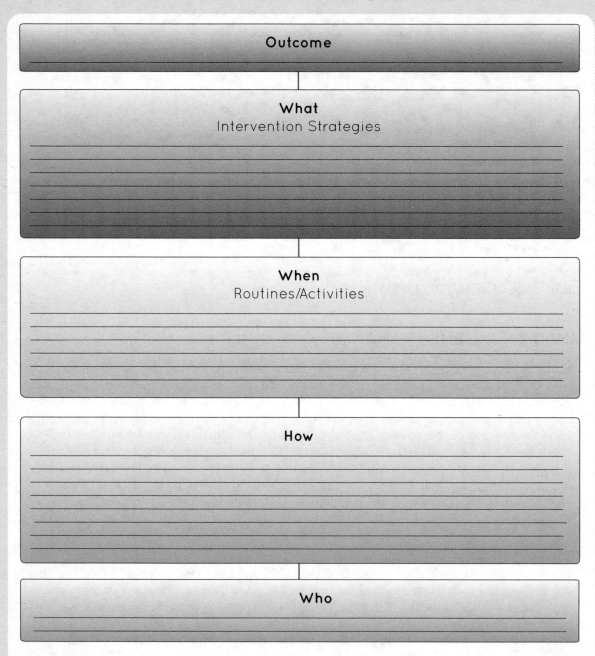

Outcome

What
Intervention Strategies

When
Routines/Activities

How

Who

helping their child grow, learn, and develop. The focus should be on the parent and parent–child dyad and not on the child alone or the child's interactions with the provider.

Readers are encouraged to review the highly regarded works of McWilliam (2010) on consultation and of Rush and Shelden (2011) on coaching, two very important ways of interacting with families also mentioned in Chapter 4. In addition to these approaches, we would like to highlight some specific behaviors that are not necessarily exclusive to these approaches but help to specifically define the mix of behaviors that providers actually use to facilitate adult learning and family engagement. The following provider-family interactions are drawn from the work of Friedman, Woods, and Salisbury (2012).

Within the context of IFSP-guided home visits, one service delivery interaction that providers engage parents in is information exchange. This includes a discussion on topics related to the IFSP outcomes and intervention. It may include discussing the status of progress toward outcomes or talking about how application of an intervention strategy is going. Another interaction that may occur is engaging in a problem-solving discussion with the family. This involves the provider and parent collaboratively discussing options for addressing a particular IFSP outcome. The problem-solving exchange is interactive, with the parents and providers all contributing to the discussion. Another approach is using practice with feedback. This involves the parent trying a specific strategy while the provider observes, and either during or immediately following the parents' actions, they discuss how it went and how to proceed. Two other interactions are indirect and direct teaching. In these cases, the focus of teaching is on the adult, not the child. Indirect teaching involves following the parent's lead, commenting or praising the action of the parent, and perhaps having a discussion of ways to expand or continue the action. In direct teaching, the provider suggests or recommends a strategy and, with parent agreement, uses demonstration or modeling. In doing so, the provider maintains an explicit focus on helping the parent learn a particular strategy and allows time for reflection. To illustrate how these interactions are actually applied in a home visit, let us take a closer look at an actual visit with Willie, Tasha, and Cyndi.

What Does This Look Like During a Home Visit?

On this visit, one of the outcomes addressed was, "Willie will understand signed directions at the park so that park outings are safe and enjoyable." As they began a dialogue, Tasha told Cyndi the biggest problem she was having was that she does not have a way to tell Willie how to be good and behave at the park. She always has to grab him to make him mind her. She cannot call to him or give verbal reminders like the other moms can with their children. Cyndi then asked Tasha to think about her last visit to the park with Willie and during what activities she had to physically grab him. Tasha described how he threw sand at a child, took another child's toy, and would not come off the slide. Cyndi and Tasha began problem solving to identify specific signed directions that would be helpful to teach Willie and that could be used in these situations. Tasha chose the signs for *stop* and *come here*. Cyndi showed Tasha the two signs, and they talked about how to use them in the situations Tasha described at the park. Cyndi demonstrated and Tasha practiced the signs with Cyndi's feedback and encouragement. Cyndi explained the importance of using the signs consistently, following through with a gentle physical prompt in order for Willie to gain understanding, and linking the signs and the verbal words. While they were talking in the living room, Willie started playing with the dog food in the kitchen, which presented an immediate opportunity to practice the strategies they were discussing. With Tasha's agreement, Cyndi prompted her to move in front of Willie and get down to his level to get his attention and use the sign *stop* before physically removing his hand from the dog food. Willie watched her but immediately went around her and returned to the dog food. Cyndi prompted Tasha to use the same strategy again. Willie pushed her hand away and went back to the dog food. Cyndi suggested that Tasha make a serious face and also shake her head no. On the third attempt, although unhappy, Willie left the dog food alone and Tasha took him by his hand over to his toy box and helped him choose a puzzle to do with her. Cyndi had not discussed redirection with Tasha and was very excited to see that Tasha had come up with this idea on her own. Cyndi praised Tasha for what she had added. She commented on how well Tasha directed him to a good activity and how it showed him what he could do in place of the thing they did not want him to do. Tasha said she could see many times at home with Willie that she could practice the signs and show him what he can do, but she was not ready to go to the park alone with Willie. Cyndi and Tasha planned for their next visit to be at the park. Cyndi would meet Tasha and Willie at their home, and together they would walk over to the park.

In this example, you can see elements of information exchange, problem solving, practice with feedback, indirect and direct teaching, as well as making a plan for what will happen between now and the next visit around this outcome. There was still time to address another outcome on the plan before Cyndi had to leave.

TIP   ✔

Conversation Starters About Outcomes

• How are things going?

• Which outcome would you like to start with?

• On our last visit, the ideas and activities we talked about were _____. How are they working?

• Would you like to brainstorm more about them?

• What do you think would help make them better?

• Tell me about other ideas you have tried.

• What worked and how?

• What did not work as you expected? Why do you think that?

• What should we add or change?

In the following example, read through an actual script of a provider-family interaction. What do you see the provider doing to engage and involve the family in the intervention decisions?

Outcome: Hannah will participate in meal time by eating what the rest of the family eats so that she can eat a greater variety of foods without needing special food prepared for her.
           We will know she can do this when she eats the dinner food that the rest of the family eats for 4 days in a week for 2 weeks.

Provider: How is it going with Hannah's eating?

Stephanie: Well, she is still a picky eater.
(Hannah's mother)

Provider: Is she eating any of the food the rest of you eat at dinner?

Stephanie: Well, I tried giving her what we were having, but she got really upset when I encouraged her. The other night we had meatloaf, and she pitched a royal fit when I wanted her to try it. So I gave her old faithful: the chicken nuggets that I knew she would eat. I didn't even try giving her the other food we were having.

Provider: It sounds like you've tried to give Hannah what you eat at meal times, but she does not try it, so you give her what you know she will eat. Is that accurate?

Stephanie: Yes, that's pretty much it. I wish she'd try the dinner. Sometimes I think she'd really like it if she just tried it. I hate to have to cook something different for her.

Provider: If it's okay with you, let's explore this a bit more.

Stephanie: Sure.

Provider: Would you tell me more about what you offer Hannah and how she responds?

Stephanie: I tell the girls about what's for dinner. Elle sometimes helps me hype it up. Anyway, I give Hannah a helping of what's for dinner. Then she starts to fuss or cry and does not try the food. So I give her something I know she will eat.

Provider: Hmm, it sounds like little Hannah is pretty strong willed about this.

Stephanie: Yes, that's for sure.

Provider: Are you still interested in having her eat what everyone else does?

Stephanie: Well, yes. I don't want to have to make her special meals all the time.

Provider: Hmm, let's think about this from Hannah's perspective, if we can. Remember when we talked about behaviors and how children learn things that are reinforced?

Stephanie: Yeah, we talked about how Hannah learned that she can come out and snuggle with me when I watch television at night, and then I had trouble having her stay in bed.

Provider: Could the idea of learning behaviors be applied to meal time and her holding out for her favorite food?

Stephanie: Sure, I guess so. She probably knows I'll give in. But if she gets the family meal only, she might not eat anything and have to go without if I really don't give her the favorite food.

Provider: How do you feel about that?

Stephanie: I talked to my mom about this, and she said I was the same way. She said that she had to let me go without a full dinner a few nights. I could give it another try, I guess. I know she is not starving.

Provider: So it sounds like you might want to persist with the plan we made earlier. That is to give Hannah what you're having, and after she tries a little, then she can have a bit of something else.

Stephanie: Yeah, I'll give it another try. I think I'll ask my mom about this again too, especially because she said I was that way too.

Provider: It seems that your mom is a good resource for you. I recall you saying that you talk to her almost daily.

Stephanie: Yes, I have a free calling plan. It's really nice. I don't have to always think about the cost when we have a longer chat.

Provider: Okay, do you want to brainstorm about this outcome more or do you feel like you've got a plan for the next week anyway?

Stephanie: I'm good on this one for now.

Provider: Okay, let's talk about the next outcome: using the potty. We haven't had a chance to talk about that one lately. Is that okay with you?

In this brief example, problem solving was the primary interaction used to address the outcome about Hannah's eating. (Complete Give It a Go! 7.2.)

GIVE IT A GO! 7.2.

Think of a home visit you made recently and answer the following questions.

What outcomes did you focus on?

_____

_____

_____

_____

What were the strategies you and the family discussed?

_____

_____

_____

_____

What were the intervention interactions that you used with the family?

_____

_____

_____

_____

PERIODIC CHANGES TO THE INDIVIDUALIZED FAMILY SERVICE PLAN

If the IFSP outcomes are the focal point of each home visit, it makes sense that the IFSP is looked over and reviewed during each visit. If necessary, it should be adapted, changed, or added to

Community of Practice Agreed-Upon
Practices: The Individualized Family Service Plan Review

- Prepare and assist with formal reviews and revisions of the IFSP.

- Review with the family questions, recommendations, and/or suggestions for change.

- Decide with the family the agenda for the meeting and their preferred role(s).

- Determine together who should be included and when and where the meeting should occur.

- Explain and provide prior notice and other required paper work.

- Conduct the review meeting.

- Make any agreed-upon changes to the IFSP as needed.

(Workgroup on Principles and Practices in Natural Environments, 2008)

whenever there is a need to make those adjustments. This is the family's document and should be an up-to-date record of what they are working on and who is helping them. If things need to be changed or have changed, update the IFSP to reflect those changes. The federal regulations and your state's policies will specify the necessary paperwork needed if changes are made.

The federal regulations guarantee that, at the least, there is a formal review of the IFSP every 6 months. You will assist the family as they prepare and participate in the review.

TIP

General Home Visiting Safety

- Let people know where you will be and when you expect to return.

- Schedule new visits or visits to questionable areas during daylight.

- Make sure you have correct addresses and phone numbers before leaving for the meeting.

- Call the family before the visit.

- Lock valuables in your car trunk before you leave the office or do not bring them if you do not need them.

- Carry your phone with you at all times. Have important numbers preprogrammed.

- Take only the items you need for the visits in a tote bag or briefcase.

- Dress appropriately and sensibly.

- Keep your car in good repair.

- Have your car keys in your hand when going to the car.

- Use common sense and be aware of your surroundings in any neighborhood or public place.

COMMON HOME VISITING CHALLENGES

Working in families' homes is not without challenges. During the majority of home visits, things go well, but it is important to think about situations that might be problematic before they occur. Many early intervention programs have developed specific policies around such things as safety. The guidelines provided here are not meant to replace procedures your agency has developed around these issues but, rather, serve as a point of reflection and future discussion with your team members.

What If the Family Home Feels Unsafe to Me?

Feeling safe and feeling comfortable in the family's home are two different issues. Cleanliness, clutter, smells, lack of furniture, different generations living together, bugs, animals, and loud music, for example, may be more of a comfort issue than a safety issue. It is important for you to consider if the situation is about not feeling physically or mentally safe or if it is a personal preference that is causing you to feel discomfort. Safety issues such as guns or other weapons lying around, visible drugs or drug sales, verbal or physical outbursts, sexually explicit behavior, negative comments directed toward you or other family members, unleashed snarling dogs, or people confronting you in a loud and angry manner can be safety issues. Trust your instincts if things truly do not feel right or safe. If this is a strong feeling, and you see or experience any of the mentioned conditions that are true safety issues, then you should politely and calmly leave the situation. Do not confront the family with your feelings. You can say you are not feeling well. Gather your things, tell them good-bye and that you will call the next day, and walk confidently and quickly to your car with keys in hand. If the environment is not safe for you, it most likely is not safe for the child. You are a mandatory reporter of child neglect and abuse, so if you feel the living conditions truly are impacting the child's heath, well-being, or safety, you need to talk with your supervisor and follow your agency guidelines about what to do. Issues with dogs can generally be addressed by asking the family members to restrain the dogs when you arrive. You can offer to meet the family in a nearby public space such as a library, school, or park, or you can take another person to the visit with you.

What If the Neighborhood Where I Need to Park Is a High-Crime Area?

Follow the general guidelines for safety in the earlier tip box, including always parking in a well-lit area that offers the safest way to the house. Leave nothing valuable in the car that can be seen, and be sure to lock the car. Park where you can leave quickly and where the car will not be blocked in. Do not block or take someone else's parking space. Be aware of your surroundings and the people around you. Use the middle of the sidewalk, walking confidently with a pleasant, self-assured posture. If you make eye contact or someone makes eye contact with you, acknowledge him or her with a simple hello and a smile. You can ask a family member to meet you at the door, watch you walk to the car, or walk back to the car with you if it is appropriate. If you are comfortable asking and feel the family would be receptive, ask them to tell their neighbors that you come visit their child and the color and make of your car. That way, you are a welcome visitor, not a suspicious one to the neighborhood environment.

What If a Family Member Gets Very Angry with Me During the Visit?

If a family member gets aggressive or angry with you, remain calm and respond quietly with an *I* message such as, "I know you are feeling angry about . . ." or "I see you are very upset." Keep your statement direct and simple. Never raise your voice or appear to be angry. Calmly back away from the person to allow for space and do not try to touch the upset person. Allow for some quiet space and time for the person to calm down without you continuing to talk. You can then try to change the subject to something not objectionable, such as a focus on the child (if that was not the anger button), or even ask for a glass of water, which has the person go do a physical task that may have a calming effect. If the anger subsides, then use active, reflective listening to calmly and logically address the issue. Do *not* argue your point or get defensive. If things escalate, then politely leave and call them the next day, either to reschedule or to try to resolve the issue over the phone.

Never get between two shouting or aggressive people during a home visit or take one person's side over the other's. Again, remain calm and try to refocus the situation. If you truly feel someone is in danger, then leave the house immediately and call 911 for help. Go to your car and remain until help arrives; do not simply flee, unless it is not safe to stay.

Always tell your supervisor about any instances and discuss the course of action for following up with the family. This might involve someone else visiting with you, someone visiting who is more able to deal with these types of issues, or referring the family to other appropriate services in addition to early intervention.

What Do I Do If the Family Keeps Demanding More Services?

Families want more for a variety of reasons, and it is important to understand the reasons behind their requests by considering the following questions: Which of the functional IFSP outcomes do they think could be improved if services were increased and how? Is there a new outcome that should be added to the IFSP? The service coordinator should then arrange for the early intervention team to meet with the family to discuss their concerns and not wait for the formal review. There may be a legitimate reason to increase services for a limited time. It should be clearly explained that early intervention does not regularly provide daily or three-times-a-week therapy or special instruction; however, the family is welcome to pursue these additional services outside of early intervention if they so desire. The service coordinator can assist the family with finding this type of service from a provider outside of early intervention if they do want to try the additional therapies. The service coordinator can add these to the IFSP as other non–early intervention services, and the family will have to arrange for payment of those services through insurance or other means. It is also the service coordinator's responsibility to share information about due process and family's rights as well as explain that, if the family is truly not satisfied with early intervention, then they can file a complaint.

When families ask for more, take the time to understand what they want from the increased services and help them to understand that it is the intervention that makes a difference, not the services alone. Intervention is what can happen every day as part of typical family routines and activities. In this discussion, address again how children learn and why early intervention is provided the way it is. If a family still desires more, remember to respect their perspective as well as help them see the other possibilities.

What Should I Do If the Television Is Always on and a Parent Is More Interested in It than Me?

We are surrounded throughout our day with sounds—people talking on their cell phones, music playing, and other environmental sounds—and most of the time we simply tune the noise out. Some stay-at-home parents find the sound of the television comforting and have particular programs they enjoy watching at certain times as a way of relaxing. If you are truly engaging the parent around a routine or activity in which they are interested, and they contributed to the plan, having the television on should not be an issue; it is simply background noise. However, if you are trying to teach something through verbal instruction alone or giving lots of information for which they do not feel a need to know, they may in fact be tuning you out, and the television may be more interesting. Examine the situation and your actions carefully. Never reach over and turn off the television. If, however, it truly is bothering you, then an honest *I* statement about your need, such as, "I'm having trouble hearing you" or "I keep watching the program, and I feel I'm not giving you my full attention" might be a reasonable request that the parent responds to by turning off the television. You might also plan a different time in the day for your next visit if this is a program the family member truly enjoys watching.

WRAP UP

In the introduction of this chapter, Tasha talks about her visits from early intervention and how she understood that Cyndi was there to help her help her son, not to only work with Willie. This is an important distinction that shows she understood the purpose of early intervention. In addition, Tasha felt that Cyndi listened to her, appreciated her, and acknowledged and built on her skills and abilities. Cyndi demonstrated many roles in her work with Tasha, Willie, and the family. She conveyed an understanding of family-centered practices, children's learning in natural environments, the use of the family's activities and routines as natural learning opportunities, adult learning principles, and teaming practices. Cyndi focused her visits on the provider-family interactions that built a trusting relationship and on using the IFSP outcomes to guide intervention while engaging the family in intervention decisions. A significant response from Tasha—and a true measure that early intervention was working—was the increased capacity and pride Tasha expressed. Tasha felt good about being able to help Willie and felt more confident and competent. She was even beginning to set some future goals for herself that would also benefit her son. None of this happened overnight, but it was the intentional focus of Cyndi's ongoing intervention over the year of home visiting interactions with Tasha, Willie, and their family. Willie and Tasha will continue to experience growth and meet outcomes as they continue to be in the early intervention program until Willie turns 3 and transitions to other services.

CHAPTER EIGHT

Transition Planning
Leaving Early Intervention

A Provider's Perspective

Cyndi left the office for her final visit with Daniel and his family. No matter how often she said good-bye to families, it was never easy. As she drove, she reflected on the past 2½ years she had worked with the Wagner family. Daniel had been referred to early intervention at 6 months by his physician, who suspected and later confirmed cerebral palsy. He was the smallest of the Wagner triplets and the only boy. His sisters, Dori and Dani, still outweighed him by several pounds and were developing typically.

The years seemed to go by so quickly. Visits with the family always involved Daniel's siblings, and most times Cyndi felt like she was also part of the family. She often worked with all the children, including the triplets, two older siblings, and of course their parents, Barbara and Steve. Cyndi smiled, thinking about the relief she sometimes felt when she left the house, knowing that the five children under 5 were not her own! She gave Barbara and Steve lots of credit for their ability to stay calm despite what she saw as chaos and what Barbara insisted was just their "normal" life.

From the beginning, Barbara had been clear that she had the same hopes and dreams for Daniel as she did for her other children. She understood Daniel had cerebral palsy that affected both his left arm and leg. As time went on, his speech was also affected. At first, Barbara was not convinced that having a primary provider (Cyndi) supported by the team members would meet Daniel's needs, and she continually demanded more services. Those beginning months were a challenge. Cyndi remembered how angry Barbara was at the 6 month review when she asked for PT to be provided at least three times a week in addition to Cyndi's weekly visit in order to "make Daniel be able to stand and cruise like his sisters. Something more needs to be done to help fix him!" Even though the program provided every other week covisits with PT and Cyndi, Barbara thought more therapy services would be better. After that meeting, Barbara began taking Daniel to private PT three times a week, which her insurance paid. When he was still not making the progress that Barbara expected after 3 months, she began to realize what the early intervention program was providing and how it was helping her, her husband, and their other children at home. She also saw that it was more beneficial than what the 30 minute private PT sessions did. As Barbara and Cyndi's relationship evolved, and with the support of the other team members, Cyndi began to enjoy the early intervention visits. Barbara and Steve came up with great ideas and helped the team know what was doable for their family. Through everyone's collaboration, Daniel gradually made progress in many ways, including actively playing with his sisters and letting others know what he did and did not like.

When Daniel turned 2, Barbara told Cyndi her goal was for him to be able to go to the same preschool that her older children had attended—the same one Dori and Dani would attend. The girls would be starting in a year. She wanted Daniel there with them and included in all the activities they would be doing. Cyndi and Barbara began to work toward this goal together. This outcome and the accompanying strategies were added to his IFSP during the transition planning conference and became part of his transition plan. The work culminated last week with a meeting with the local education agency that provides the 3- to 5-year-old special education services. During this meeting, the individualized education program (IEP) was written, and Daniel's placement at the private preschool was confirmed along with the necessary support services. All this would begin next month when Daniel turned 3. The meeting was attended by the director of the preschool, Daniel's future preschool teacher, representatives of the school system, Daniel's parents, and Cyndi. It was agreed that Daniel would attend the private preschool with his sisters, 5 half-days a week with weekly in-class physical and occupational therapy consultation provided by the public school system. Barbara also agreed to bring him twice a week to a speech group held at the local elementary school. The speech teacher would consult with the private preschool teacher twice a month. Cyndi was hopeful this arrangement would work and that Daniel would continue to make progress. She was happy that the children could be together at their favorite preschool.

Cyndi glanced at the "graduation booklet" she had completed for Daniel and his family. This was something she liked to do for all her families as they left early intervention. It contained pictures from their work, comments from Cyndi and the team members, and the IFSPs that documented his accomplishments. Even though she and the family knew this day was coming, it was not easy for the family or Cyndi to say good-bye. She liked to think the last visit was a type of celebration of the accomplishments they had made. That always helped her feel a little less sad as she and the family moved on to other things. As she pulled into the driveway, she spotted Daniel using his walker. Dani, the older sister who always seemed so tuned into him, was there right by his side. As Cyndi parked the car, Dori came out, yelling excitedly, "Ms. Cyndi, Ms. Cyndi! We got cupcakes for you!"

TRANSITION: PART OF THE EARLY INTERVENTION JOURNEY

Families in early intervention experience lots of changes before they transition from the program. These changes may be related to having a child with a disability, such as bringing the infant home from the NICU, learning about a diagnosis, early intervention providers coming and going, or outcome and service changes made to the IFSP. Change might also include life events, such as losing a job or starting a new one, moving to a new community, having more children, ending a marriage, beginning a new relationship, and the list goes on. Change is a natural part of life, but it is not always easy or welcomed.

> Transition is the difficult process of letting go of old situations, suffering the confusing nowhere of in-betweeness and launching forth again in a new situation . . . an ending followed by a period of confusion and even distress leading to a new beginning.
>
> —Bridges, 1991, p. 4

Whether the change is expected or unexpected, whether it is thought of as a good thing or not, a transition period always occurs. To make the transition easier, it is helpful to understand what to expect and acknowledge what is being left behind, a process that takes time and energy.

Life is full of change. It is not necessarily the event that presents the challenge; it is the associated transition. It takes time and effort to work through the feelings and actions needed to make transitions. Take Cyndi for example. Cyndi has worked in early intervention for 18 years. During this time, she has experienced many changes. She has had six different program directors, lost count of the team members that have come and gone, moved offices six times, implemented new and different procedures as a result of changes to the federal and state regulations, and said hello and good-bye to numerous families. Of course, Cyndi has experienced personal changes at home as well. Each of these changes was followed by a period of transition, and Cyndi, like others, does not always welcome having to end something that has become comfortable and familiar and move on to something that is new and different.

William Bridges (2004) provided the following suggestions for easing the transition process. It may be helpful for you and the families you work with to think about these general steps to ease transition. You should also think about how they apply to your work.

- Identify who is losing what.

- Accept the reality and importance of the subjective loss.

- Do not be surprised by overreactions.

- Acknowledge losses openly and sympathetically.

- Expect and accept the signs of grieving (anger, sadness, anxiety, disorientation, bargaining, depression, etc.).

- Give people information and repeat it often.

- Define what is truly over.

- Mark the endings.

- Treat the past with respect.

- Take a piece of the old way with you.

- Show how the ending ensures continuity of what is truly important. (p. 4)

As an early intervention provider you assist families as they experience many life changes and transitions. Your assistance may include directly helping a family—for example, finding a new early intervention program—or indirectly helping by providing emotional support and listening to them talk about a change or other upcoming events in their life. Helping families with life transitions is not necessarily part of your work, but listening and supporting families certainly is. You may provide information about the new situation, help them find needed resources, brainstorm solutions as they prepare for the change, and help them understand the feelings they may be experiencing. You will also help families transition out of early intervention, either as the child reaches 3 years of age or before, if necessary. (Complete Give It a Go! 8.1.)

GIVE IT A GO! 8.1.

Consider the following questions and statements related to your personal experience with transition. Write your responses in the space provided.

1. Think of a time in your life when a change was necessary (e.g., new boss, new job, a move, a child's birth)

   _____

   _____

2. What did you have to let go of?

   _____

   _____

3. Now think through what happened (i.e., what you did, how you felt) as you let those things go.

   _____

   _____

4. Now think about how long it was before you felt comfortable or things felt okay in the new situations.

   _____

   _____

EARLY INTERVENTION TRANSITIONS

In early intervention, *transition* is the name given to the process of preparing children and families as they leave the program with all the associated regulations and required timelines and procedures. There are two major types of transition. One occurs when a child leaves early intervention prior to age 3, and the other is transition out of early intervention as the child reaches 3 years of age. In this chapter, we explore both of these transitions. Regardless of the type of transition or the reason for it, it is essential for you to help the family prepare and understand the options available for their child and for themselves.

 CONVERSATION STARTER

I would like to talk about some transitions that might occur while we work together and how we might assist, if you would like us to. One type of transition is moving out of the area our program serves. In that case, I would help you find the early intervention program where you are moving to and link you with resources in that area.

Another transition is when a child turns 3 years of age. As we talked about before, early intervention goes up to a child's third birthday. We always want to be thinking about types of support a family may need as they prepare to leave early intervention. When it comes to this type of transition, we will help you gather resources and information you need to make a smooth transition. Are there any changes and transitions you see happening for Carmen or your family in the near future?

TRANSITIONING PRIOR TO AGE 3

Families leave early intervention for a variety of reasons; some may be planned and others happen unexpectedly. Reasons for transitions out of early intervention before a child's third birthday may include a family moving, a family deciding to discontinue services, or a child making considerable progress and no longer needing early intervention—to name a few. In some states, eligibility for early intervention must be reestablished each year, and children who have made good progress and have no known disability may be discharged, often at an annual IFSP meeting. In rare instances, the reason may be that the child has died as a result of their condition. No matter the reason, as families leave early intervention, providers should make every effort to ensure their transition is as smooth as possible.

Providers and service coordinators should talk with families about possible transitions and make plans as early as possible in order to support the child and family through the process. If a family moves, you can get the family connected with new services at another location. If a child progresses and is no longer eligible, you can assist the family with finding other programs if they are interested. If a family elects to discontinue services, you can give them the information they need to get back in contact with early intervention if they have further questions, including who to contact after the child turns 3. The conversations and actions to prepare for the transition may take several visits, but ensuring the family is informed and prepared is time well spent. Abruptly discontinuing contact without offering help with the transition process can set families back in providing the best for their children. Sometimes, however, exit from early intervention happens suddenly. It may be that the family has moved and not told you. When making a prescheduled home visit, you may find out the family is clearly not living there anymore. Changes can happen quickly, and the family may not see a need or have time to contact you. Other times, the family may call the office and say they are no longer interested in continuing services. At a minimum, in these unplanned situations, an attempt to contact the family should be made by either e-mail, mail, or phone call. The purpose of this contact is to thank them for their participation in the program, get a forwarding address in case it is needed, and to offer any last assistance they might need. Information about how to get back in touch with the early intervention program or preschool services should be included as well as how to obtain their child's records.

When possible, a last visit to give the necessary information and say good-bye helps the relationship end on a positive note. When families leave abruptly, providers may wonder if they did something wrong or feel the family does not care, both of which are likely not true. The family may be able to provide some useful information to the program if a program evaluation is made available to them on or before this last visit. The evaluation can also be given via mail, e-mail, a social media venue, or a phone call from the program. Getting feedback from families as they exit early intervention helps the program support future families.

Sometimes a family may leave early intervention because their child has died. Although this is not common, it does happen. Children enrolled may be medically fragile or their disability may present health challenges. How you respond is impacted by your relationship with the family, your feelings, circumstances around the death, and any guidelines your program has. Possible responses may include sending a card, attending the funeral as a team or individual provider, or calling the family. In some circumstances, you may even make a few visits after the child's death, assisting the family with grief resources or simply being a good listener. The passing of a child is difficult, and the way providers working with the family to gain closure is just as individual as the provider, child, and family are.

CONVERSATION STARTER

Hi, Maria. Thanks for calling yesterday to cancel next week's appointment. I also want to thank you for letting us know about your family moving to Georgia in 2 weeks. I will miss visiting with you and José, but it is great that Manuel got a job! I can imagine this will be a very busy time getting everything in order to leave. Is there anything you can think of that Early Care can do to help you? (Parent asks if she knows about early intervention in Georgia.)

I can definitely help with that. Do you know where in Georgia you will be living? No? Okay, then it would work better if I can give you the contact information for the state early intervention office and you can call once you get settled and have an address. They will be able to tell you how to contact the local program for that area of the state. (Great!)

May I also prepare copies of José's IFSP and other records like his last evaluation and assessment for you to give to the program after you are settled? It might help you get into the new program more quickly. (Okay.) I can mail those to you now before you leave or I would be happy to drop them by. Sure, I can mail them. I will put the contact information for the Georgia programs in the envelope as well as my name and number for the program here, just in case after you are settled you need anything. Is there anything else you need or would like to talk about? Well, I do wish you and your family all the best, and thank you for being in our program. It was a pleasure to work with you and José. If anything comes up in the next 2 weeks—or even after you move—you can call me. Good-bye.

Federal Regulations

- Transition conference to discuss services (§ 303.209)

- Notification to the SEA and LEA (§ 303.209[b])

- Transition Plan (§ 303.209[d])

- IFSP requirements for transition (§ 303.344[h])

Providers are encouraged to seek support from managers, colleagues, or others during such difficult times.

TRANSITION FROM EARLY INTERVENTION TO PRESCHOOL SERVICES: FEDERAL REGULATIONS

Children who transition from early intervention to preschool special education services at 3 years of age experience a series of transition steps. Included in these steps are those regulated by the IDEA (listed in the following box) to ensure a smooth transition with little or no interruption in services once the child has turned 3. This is the transition that Cyndi assisted Daniel and his family with in the earlier scenario. The regulations guiding the transition of children from early intervention to preschool special education are found in section 303.209.

Community of Practice
Agreed-Upon Practices: Transition at Age 3

PREPARE FAMILIES FOR TRANSITION OUT OF PART C SERVICES

- Early in the relationship, have conversations about what they think their child's future may look like.

- At formal IFSP reviews, share written information about the transition process and options when early intervention services end at age 3.

- By no later than the child's second birthday, have conversations about the types of programs, places, and activities the family would like their child to participate in at age 3.

- Discuss and share written information about *all* options available to children and families when the child turns 3.

- Assist the family as needed to explore and visit these options.

- Develop a transition plan that includes the outcomes and activities to prepare the child and family for success after early intervention.

EXPLAIN AND FOLLOW THE REGULATIONS, TIMELINES, AND PROCEDURES FOR TRANSITION PLANS, PLANNING CONFERENCES, AND DATA COLLECTION.

- Help the family prepare for any formal evaluations.

- Assist in arranging the formal transition meeting.

- Assist the family with finding ongoing family support, if needed.

- Acknowledge feelings about ending the relationship.

- Celebrate with the family or caregiver the accomplishments and joys they have experienced with their child.

(Workgroup on Principles and Practices in Natural Environments, 2008)

States also have policies and procedures for implementing the federal regulations you need to know as you help families with this type of transition. For example, some states transition children who will turn 3 at the beginning of the school year even though they are not yet 3. Other states wait until the child's third birthday to make the move to preschool. Both states are fulfilling the obligations of the law, but each has set different policies with the specifics of when a child begins preschool services and has an IEP in place by the third birthday. Although service coordinators are often the staff most involved in the transition paperwork requirements, such as sending notifications and planning meetings, it is important for all early intervention providers to be aware of the transition process, as they also help prepare the child and family for a successful transition.

The formal and required transition process, spelled out in the federal statute and regulations, must begin no fewer than 90 days before the child's third birthday and, at the discretion of parents and providers, no more than 9 months before the child turns 3. It also includes specific activities. The timeline for transition activities that must be completed follows this paragraph. Please note that the timeline may vary depending on your state's transition policies and procedures.

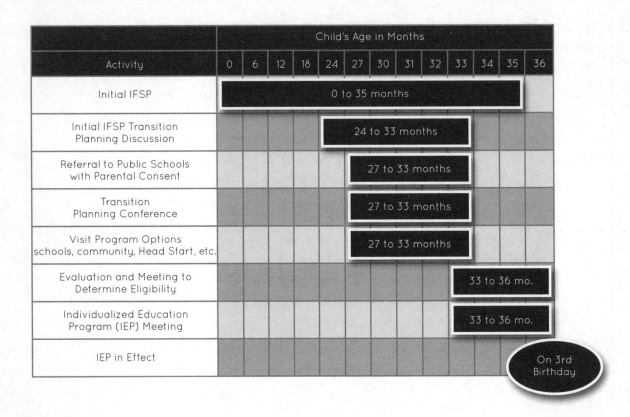

Activity	Child's Age in Months												
	0	6	12	18	24	27	30	31	32	33	34	35	36
Initial IFSP	0 to 35 months												
Initial IFSP Transition Planning Discussion					24 to 33 months							
Referral to Public Schools with Parental Consent						27 to 33 months						
Transition Planning Conference						27 to 33 months						
Visit Program Options schools, community, Head Start, etc.						27 to 33 months						
Evaluation and Meeting to Determine Eligibility										33 to 36 mo.		
Individualized Education Program (IEP) Meeting										33 to 36 mo.		
IEP in Effect													On 3rd Birthday

Figure 8.1. Sample Transition Timeline (From Georgia Department of Education, Division for Exceptional Students, and Georgia Department of Human Resources, Babies Can't Wait. [2004, October]. *Transition at age 3—Steps for success: A guide for Georgia children with disabilities, their families, Babies Can't Wait early intervention services, schools, and community programs.* Atlanta: Georgia Department of Education.)

EARLY TRANSITION DISCUSSIONS

Conversations about what will happen once a child turns 3 can happen at any time in the early intervention journey. Families may ask questions early on or share their hopes about what they want for their child long before the required transition process begins. This is what Barbara and Steve shared with Cyndi when Daniel was 18 months old. As part of ongoing intervention, you will be listening for what the family says about their hopes and goals for their child's future. Even if you feel what they are sharing may not seem *realistic*, it is important to acknowledge and respect those ideas as you help them work toward their dreams. Daniel's mom shared with Cyndi in an early conversation, "Why would I even be in early intervention if I did not think that Daniel will have the same opportunities as his sisters! I look to you to help me make this happen for Daniel!"

Just as family dreams are individual, so too is the transition process unique for every family. Key elements of the transition process include consideration of what is happening now as well as what needs to happen to help the child be successful in the new setting or program and to prepare the parents for the change. Children react differently to changes in their routines. Some children adjust easily, but others have a difficult time separating from parents and navigating a new experience. Anticipating adjustment challenges and implementing strategies to minimize adjustment struggles are essential ingredients in transition planning. As highlighted earlier, this transition is a major change for parents too. Parents may be concerned about being away from their child for the first time, putting their child on a bus, building a trusting relationship with a new teacher, learning policies and practices of a new program, adjusting schedules, or saying good-bye to providers they have known since they first learned about their child's condition. Addressing parents' concerns and developing strategies to help them work through these concerns are also key elements in transition planning and can occur at any time.

An important early conversation that must occur is about the federal requirement to notify the state and local education agency about the transition. After the child turns 2, and the team is considering a transition to Part B preschool special education, a formal notification must be sent to the Local Education Agency (LEA) and the State Education Agency (SEA). Early intervention notifies the LEA for the area where the child resides that they are working with a child who will soon be 3 and who may be eligible for preschool special education services. The notification should include the child's name, the child's date of birth, and the parents' contact information. Parents have the option to give or not give permission to share this information, but the reasons for and the consequence of what happens if the notification is not sent need to be carefully explained. If the parent chooses to not have the notification sent, then an "opt out" form and parent signature must be documented. If informal discussions about transition have not already occurred, the parents would understandably be unprepared and perhaps even surprised about a notice to the school about special education. They may still be hopeful that their child will continue to improve and not need special education. It is important to assure the family that this is a step to be taken if it is anticipated that their child will need continued support, to help prepare everyone, and to facilitate a timely process without undue delays. Although special education is being considered, other community options can also be considered.

TRANSITION CONFERENCE TO DISCUSS PRESCHOOL SERVICES

For children who may be eligible for Part B preschool services, a meeting called the *transition conference* is held to discuss service options available for a child once they turn 3, and to

CHECKLIST FOR FAMILIES

❑ Find out about the preschool options available for the child and make visits.

❑ Ask about activities to help the child make the transition and be "ready" for preschool services.

❑ Meet with other parents who have made similar transitions.

❑ Make a list of questions about the preschool services.

❑ Participate in all transition meetings and be confident about your knowledge about your child.

develop the written plan for the transition. This conference is *required*, with family approval for any child thought to be eligible for Part B services. At the request of the family, a similar conference to discuss options and make plans *may* be held for children potentially not eligible for Part B services. The transition conference can occur as early as 9 months before a child's third birthday, but not later than 90 days before the child turns 3. The conference includes the family, anyone they wish to attend, applicable early intervention staff working with the family (e.g., service coordinator, primary provider, other providers), and representatives from the LEA. It includes a discussion about the potential supports and services the child may need as well as potential locations for such services. Other discussion topics may include the similarities and differences of Part B and early intervention, eligibility requirements for Part B, consideration of community preschool options, what might be needed to help the child adjust to a preschool setting or any other new services, and resources the family needs for a successful transition.

It is important to note that the transition conference does not determine a child's eligibility for Part B or obligate the LEA to provide the services discussed. Rather, this is a planning meeting to review options and determine the next steps that must be taken to facilitate the transition.

THE TRANSITION PLAN

A transition plan is included in the IFSP. Because state and local programs might have different-looking IFSP forms, there may be some variation in where the transition plan appears in the actual IFSP form. Because the plan is written to reflect the individual child and family needs and concerns, what is written will also vary from child to child. A plan should be developed for any child leaving early intervention, regardless of how, when, or where the child will transition. However, a transition plan *must* be developed for those children potentially eligible for preschool services under Part B of IDEA. The transition plan should define the steps and activities needed to ensure a timely and smooth transition. The required content of the transition plan is defined in the federal regulations in section 303.343(h).

As the team develops the plan, the family may express concerns or questions about service delivery changes and their child's adjustment. Some concerns might include worries about their child riding a school bus when the child is small; how the school handles toileting training; their son having not had many opportunities to play with other children and learn to share toys; or their daughter's speech difficulties and how the teacher will understand her wants and needs. The transition plan should include activities that address family concerns and the steps needed to facilitate a smooth transition.

For example, a plan that addresses a concern about riding a bus to preschool might include activities that allow the family and child to visit the bus at school and let the child climb up and sit in a seat. The parent and driver may have a conversation to explore what kind of adaptive seating is used for younger children and to talk about any special needs the child might have. The family might check out books from the library and read about riding the school bus and going to school. The parent may decide to take the child to preschool for several weeks so that only one adjustment at a time is necessary. (Complete Give It a Go! 8.2.)

GIVE IT A GO! 8.2.

(True/False) Circle *True* or *False* after the following transition-related statements (answers on page 148).

1.	The transition plan helps the family know and understand what will be happening over the next few months.	True	False
2.	Early intervention stops once the transition plan is developed.	True	False
3.	The transition plan includes activities for the child to help adjust to a new service setting.	True	False
4.	The transition plan spells out specific activities the parent and team will do as they explore transition options.	True	False
5.	The transition plan identifies the IEP services the child will receive from the LEA once he or she turns 3.	True	False
6.	The transition plan is written by the LEA staff.	True	False
7.	The transition plan helps assure continuity of services.	True	False
8.	Developing a transition plan is required for children approaching their 3rd birthday who are potentially eligible for Part B.	True	False
9.	The family is involved in developing the transition plan.	True	False
10.	The transition plan can include how the team will conduct updated evaluations to assist the LEA with determining a child's eligibility for Part B.	True	False

PARTS B AND C: SIMILARITIES AND DIFFERENCES

In preparation for transition to Part B, information about the similarities and differences between the two programs should be shared with the family. Families should know how the referral process works in Part B, including how eligibility for Part B is determined, and that not all children who have participated in early intervention qualify for Part B services. In addition to materials describing the transition process, many state Part C and Part B programs have materials explaining the program similarities and differences. When available, early intervention staff should share these materials with families. As discussed earlier in this book, when sharing written materials, do not only give them to the family. Take the time to review the material, highlight information particularly pertinent to the family, and respond to their questions.

As you facilitate the transition process for families, it is important that you have a good understanding of similarities and differences between Part C and Part B. Just as early intervention has procedures and required paperwork, so too does Part B. By understanding their requirements, you can help ease the transition process for all involved. Table 8.1 highlights information about both Part C and Part B programs. After reviewing Table 8.1, complete Give It a Go! 8.3.

Table 8.1. Part C – Part B Comparison

	Part C	Part B
Ages served	0–3	3–21
Individualized plans	Individualized Family Service Plan (IFSP)	Individualized Edication Program (IEP)
Plan reviews	IFSPs are reviewed/revised at least every 6 months and more frequently as needed.	IEPs are reviewed annually and changed more frequently, if needed.
Program focus	The family and the child	The child's educational needs
Services	Services for the child and family to meet the developmental needs of the child and increase the family's capacity to meet the needs of their child	Special education and related services needed to meet the educational needs of the child in order to enable the child to participate in the general education curriculum
Family involvement	Participate as a full member of the team making decisions about the individualized plan for services. Participate in and receive services to enhance the family's confidence and competence in meeting the needs of their child and family.	Participate as a full team member making decisions about the child's individualized plan for services.
Eligibility	Eligibility is state-defined and includes developmental delays based on state criteria as well as conditions that have a high probability of resulting in developmental delays if early intervention is not provided.	Eligibility is determined by state special education definitions of disability. A part of the determination is that the child needs the special education services to be successful in the general education curriculum.
Location of services	Natural environment, to the maximum extent appropriate Services are provided in locations the child would typically be in if not for his or her delay or disability. Most often, this is the home, child care facility, or other community settings.	Least restrictive environment (LRE) to the maximum extent appropriate Students receive services and participate in the general curriculum alongside their peers without disabilities. This may be in a school or community preschool.
Service coordination	Service coordination is a required service and is provided at no cost to the family.	No service coordination is required, but the IEP is managed by the LEA to ensure provision of appropriate services.
Cost	Depending on state guidelines, parents may be asked to pay family fees and copays or have public or private insurance billed for some services, with parental consent, as long as it does not negatively impact the use of the insurance for the family.	Free Appropriate Public Education (FAPE); services included in the IEP are provided at no cost to the family under FAPE.
Service provision	Services are provided year-round (12 months)	Services are provided on a school calendar unless special circumstances require extended school-year services.

Source: Beach Center on Disability (2008).

GIVE IT A GO! 8.3.

Imagine you are preparing to explain Part B services to a family getting ready for their child to transition out of Part C. Fill in your responses in the space provided.

List the materials your program uses to explain transition.

Write a script that explains the major differences between early intervention and Part B services. Be careful in your selection of words to not imply that school services are inferior to early intervention services.

Who is eligible?
_____
_____

What is the purpose of Part B?
_____
_____

How is Part B eligibility determined?
_____
_____

How are goals and services decided?
_____
_____

What might services look like?
_____
_____

Where do services occur?
_____
_____

How are families involved?
_____
_____

CONVERSATION STARTER

Although there are similarities between early intervention and preschool special education services, there are differences as well. The focus of early intervention is on the needs of Mia and your family. The focus of the preschool services is on Mia's educational needs. The location of services might be different as well. In early intervention, we have worked with you and Mia in your home. Preschool services often occur in school settings. And just like early intervention, preschool special education has a process for gathering of information, establishing eligibility, and if eligible, writing a plan for Mia called an *individualized education program* (an IEP).

EVALUATION AND ASSESSMENT TO
DETERMINE ELIGIBILITY FOR PART B SERVICES

The evaluation and assessment to determine Part B eligibility is the responsibility of the LEA. They may use information from the early intervention to help establish eligibility and to develop the IEP. The transition conference is a good time to discuss what the LEA will need to do to determine a child's eligibility for Part B and to share information with the family about the process. If further evaluation is needed and the LEA will be conducting it, they are responsible for getting parental consent beforehand and for explaining parental rights and due process procedures under Part B.

Although you may not participate with the family in an LEA evaluation, you can assist the family by talking with them about their child's skills, behaviors, and learning style, as the LEA finds this information helpful. You can answer questions or help them identify who can best answer their questions. You may also help them prepare a list of questions to ask the LEA. It is important that the family is well informed and comfortable with the transition steps as they are implemented.

ELIGIBILITY

Following the evaluation and after reviewing other information provided, an LEA meeting is held to determine the child's eligibility for Part B services. This meeting includes LEA representatives, the family, and anyone they wish to invite, which might include early intervention staff. If the child is eligible for Part B, the next step is developing the IEP. If the child is not eligible, then the LEA may inform the family of other services if the family is interested. If a family does not agree with the eligibility decision, then they can apply their procedural safeguards and work with the LEA to resolve the conflict.

During the evaluation, eligibility, and IEP meetings, the family may still participate in early intervention and may want to talk with you about these processes and associated decisions. If a child is determined not eligible you might help the family locate community preschools or other services. Some families might feel a sense of relief that their child does not need special education. Others might be concerned about no longer receiving services. Helping families through these decisions is all part of your work as the family and child transition out of early intervention when the child turns 3.

THE IEP

By the time the child turns 3, eligibility for Part B should have been determined. If eligible, an IEP must be written by the child's third birthday in order to begin Part B services. If a child turns 3 during the school's summer break, the child's IEP team identifies the date when services will begin, which is no later than the beginning of the school year following the child's third birthday. State policies spell out the specific timelines for children who turn 3 in the spring or over the summer and for children who are referred to Part C after 33 months of age.

To assist families with the IEP process, it is helpful to be familiar with the LEA's IEP. Many state and parent training centers have developed materials for families that explain the IEP process. Sharing and reviewing these with the family can help ease the process for the family. Depending on the transition plan, these materials may be shared by the LEA, early intervention, or collaboratively at a shared meeting with the family. Given the differences between the IFSP and IEP, it is important that families have a good understanding of the IEP as they participate in the IEP development process.

You do not have to be an expert on the IEP, but you should have a general understanding of how the process works, what IEP goals might look like, the family's role in the meeting, and who the family can contact if they have questions or need further assistance. The family may also invite the service coordinator or other providers to their IEP meeting if they desire. If you are asked to attend, you may lend emotional support or contribute if asked by the family. At this point, you are helping the family develop a new relationship with their next service providers. If you have done a good job empowering the family, you will have a very minor role at this point in their journey.

FINAL PART C RESPONSIBILITIES

As the child exits the early intervention program, follow your local policies for closing the family's record and making any final entries in your local database. This includes ensuring that the required child and family outcome measures were collected. Each state and early intervention program collects child and family outcomes, but the way they do this varies from state to state. Your program may also have agreements to share child outcome exit information with the receiving Part B program because they will also be collecting child outcome data. As explained in Chapters 4 and 5, the child and family outcomes are not the same as IFSP functional outcomes. They are the outcomes that are reported by each state in their annual performance report and used to measure results of Part C for children and families.

As the family and child leave and you say good-bye, remember that a measure of your success is the confidence and competence the family has in meeting the needs of their child and family now and in the future. If your practices have truly been supported by the pillars and practices discussed throughout this book, then you have also helped the family know their rights, effectively communicate their child's needs, and help their child develop and learn. These are the three family outcomes all early intervention programs strive to attain for all the families they work with. They are also the indicators reported as part of federal requirements. These are more than measures of satisfaction with you or the program; they are the optimal results a family experiences by participating in the program. Helping families feel competent, gain confidence, and enjoy their child are important goals that can yield lifelong positive results for the child and the family.

As Cyndi drove away after the final visit, she thought about her last hugs from Daniel and his family, and the fact that there will be many years and many new adventures ahead for the Wagners. As they travel down the path with Daniel into school and beyond, she felt sure that Barbara, Steve, and the children were all going to be fine.

GIVE IT A GO! 8.2. ANSWER KEY

1. True
2. False
3. True
4. True
5. False

6. False
7. True
8. True
9. True
10. True

PART THREE

Agreed-Upon Practices in Action

CHAPTER NINE

Identifying Questionable Practices

In this chapter, you meet the Thomas family: Dorthea, Paul, and their daughter Kendra. This is a working chapter for you to apply what you have learned from reading this book and completing its activities.

This case study is organized around the steps of the early intervention journey, including referral, intake/screening, evaluation/eligibility, assessment, IFSP development, and ongoing intervention. In the description of each step are actions that align with quality practices you have read about in the previous chapters. In each section of the case study, there are also examples of questionable practices. These are things that stand out as not recommended practice. Your task is to identify the questionable practices in each step of the journey. The *red flags* space provided at the end of each section identifies the number of questionable practices you will look to identify. As you find each, briefly describe what is questionable and what you might have done differently that would be more aligned with recommended practices. The answer key at the end of the chapter highlights the questionable practices and why they are not recommended practice. There may be other examples of behaviors and statements you think could be improved on, but they are not the very obvious examples of poor practice. Discuss the best and questionable practices as well as what you would do differently with a colleague or your team members.

Note that this case study does not include all the positive behaviors that should be present. As an early intervention provider, you know that every minute of every home visit does not always go perfectly. However, by reflecting on what happens during home visits, you can learn from what goes well and what does not. This case study is a snapshot of some of the many possible examples, both positive and negative. There is so much to do in each step of the early intervention journey for families and for providers!

THE THOMAS FAMILY: DORTHEA (MOM), PAUL (DAD), AND KENDRA (17 MONTHS OLD)

Referral

Today was Dorthea's 25th birthday. In the morning, she received the call from early intervention that she had anxiously been waiting for all week. It was a happy day because it was her birthday and her husband, Paul, a long-distance truck driver, was coming home for the weekend. It was also a sad time because she worried about their daughter, Kendra. Kendra was almost 17 months old and not yet walking on her own. Dorthea had worried for several months. Just last week, Dr. Paddi, the pediatrician, confirmed Dorthea's concerns about Kendra. He told Dorthea he would make a referral to early intervention so that a physical therapist from the early intervention program.could help get her walking. He handed Dorthea a prescription for PT two times a week and told her to give it to someone from the program.

As Dorthea answered the phone, the caller introduced herself as Amanda Hausen from early intervention. She asked Dorthea if this was a good time to talk. It was, so Amanda proceeded to explain how her program had received a referral from Dr. Paddi due to concerns about Kendra not walking. Amanda then asked if Dorthea had the same concern about her daughter's development. Dorthea did not expect that question but liked that Amanda took time to ask what she thought. Dorthea confirmed that Kendra was not yet walking and that she was worried about this. She said she also worried that Kendra did not seem to do all the things that her neighbor's children were doing, and they were 2 months younger and twins. Amanda acknowledged Kendra's concerns and talked a bit about the early intervention program. She explained how early intervention works with families to help them help their children. Dorthea said she had been given a prescription for PT two times a week. Amanda explained that the program would look at Kendra's overall development including walking, and if she was behind developmentally, they would provide assistance—but it might not be a physical therapist who actually worked with her. She explained how children learn best in their home or in other familiar places through things they do every day. An early intervention provider would help find activities that Kendra enjoyed that would also encourage her to walk. If needed, a physical therapist could come and evaluate Kendra and then see how best to help. Amanda explained a bit more, and Dorthea expressed her understanding. Amanda offered to mail a brochure that explained the program, provided a link to a video about the program, and said during their visits that they would certainly talk more about how the program worked with families.

The next step would be scheduling a time to do a developmental screening to get an overall picture of Kendra's development if Dorthea was interested. Amanda explained what a screening was and that, after the screening, they would decide together if further evaluation was needed and who should be involved in the evaluation—for example, a physical therapist. Amanda mentioned that they typically do the screenings in the family's home. Dorthea questioned having people come into her home. Amanda assured Dorthea that they were not coming to judge her home or housekeeping skills but that children simply did better where they were most comfortable. This made sense to Dorthea. She shared with Amanda that Kendra was sometimes shy around people she did not know. Although she did not say this to Amanda, she knew she would be spending extra time making sure the house was extra clean for the visit. The only time Amanda had available in the next 2 weeks was next Thursday at 2 p.m. She offered this time to Dorthea. Dorthea knew that she would have to wake Kendra early from her nap. She mentioned this and asked if there was another time in the morning that would work. Amanda said that, if that time did not work, it would be 5 weeks before she had a morning slot open. Dorthea agreed to the time, as she did not want to wait any longer. It had already been more than a week since the doctor said he made the referral. She just hoped Kendra would be in good mood and not too tired if she had not had a nap.

Later that weekend, Dorthea talked to Paul about her concerns with Kendra and the upcoming appointment she had made. Paul was not concerned. He knew his baby girl was perfect and that she would be walking on her own in no time. Paul's work was taking him away again for the next 2 weeks. He encouraged Dorthea to cancel the appointment, but in the end, he said it was okay, as he saw how concerned his wife was. As Dorthea tried to enjoy the weekend, in the back of her mind she wondered what would happen at the appointment. She spent a lot of time watching Kendra and Paul play and wondering more about the things she was not doing.

Questionable practices (Identify 2):

1. _____
   _____
   _____
   _____

2. _____
   _____
   _____
   _____

How would you have done these questionable practices differently?

1. _____
   _____
   _____
   _____
   _____

2. _____
   _____
   _____
   _____
   _____

Intake/Screening

Thursday finally came. Dorthea cleaned the house, still concerned that the person coming would judge her parenting and housekeeping skills. The doorbell rang, and Dorthea answered the door. On the porch stood a woman with a large bag of toys slung over her shoulder. The woman introduced herself as Amanda and said that she was the service coordinator for the early intervention program. She warmly greeted Dorthea and asked if this was still a good time for the visit. Dorthea liked her; she was pleasant and had a nice smile. Dorthea invited her in and introduced her to Kendra, who was sitting on the floor in front of the television. A penguin movie was on, and Kendra was quite engaged in it. Amanda sat on the floor near Kendra and directed Dorthea to sit on the floor nearby. Dorthea, a bit embarrassed, replied that sitting on the floor was very uncomfortable for her, and she would rather sit on the couch. Amanda seemed surprised. Dorthea, who knew she was overweight and had a bad back, was also 3 months pregnant, but she did not want to tell Amanda about the pregnancy yet, and her weight issue was always an embarrassment for her when meeting new people.

Amanda commented on what how charming Kendra was and then reached in her bag and took out a toy for Kendra, trying to divert her attention from the television. Dorthea wondered if maybe she did not have the right toys or if maybe the television was not a good idea, but she did not dwell on it. Amanda tried for a few minutes to get Kendra to play with the toy, but Kendra was not interested. Amanda then started to explain a bit more about early intervention and took out a copy of the brochure Dorthea had received yesterday. Amanda used it to talk about the program and how early intervention worked. She briefly explained what her job as a service coordinator was all about. She asked if Dorthea had any questions. Dorthea asked again about physical therapy, as that is what the doctor had said Kendra needed. Did early intervention provide physical therapy? Amanda took time to explain how there were teams of people who worked together from different disciplines and training and that, yes, one of them was a physical therapist. She explained how, if Kendra was eligible, the program used a primary provider that would be someone who could assist a family with the goals they selected. She explained who the other team members were and how they would help the primary provider, the one who would be doing most of the visits. The other members could do visits to when needed. Amanda provided more details, including how eligibility was determined and how having one main person would keep the family from having more people coming into their home and that a service coordinator would visit them regularly and help coordinate the entire plan. It would be the goals they decide to work on as well as information from the screening and the later evaluation that would help the team determine who the main or primary provider would be and how the others would help. That actually made sense to Dorthea, as long as the person would help Kendra.

Amanda began explaining the screening. She showed the protocol to Dorthea. If a child did well with the screening, they usually did not need an evaluation, which would take more time and involves more team members. However, if a parent requested an evaluation, it would be done even if the child did fine on the screening. If Kendra did not pass the screening or Dorthea requested it, then with the family's permission, a full evaluation would be scheduled. It was the evaluation and assessment information that determined if a child was eligible for early intervention and what early intervention would provide to help meet the family's goals. As Amanda began to explain more about the assessment process, she could tell from Dorthea's body language that this was too much information right now and that she was losing Dorthea's attention.

Kendra's movie was over, and she crawled to the sofa and pulled herself up. Dorthea lifted Kendra to her lap, where Kendra then sat sucking her thumb and watching Amanda. This gave Dorthea a little break to think about all the information. After Kendra was settled, Amanda asked if she had any questions. Dorthea said, "Not right now. It's a lot to think about." Amanda said she understood and that there were only few more things to cover. Dorthea agreed, and they continued.

Amanda explained that every family had rights in early intervention and briefly discussed each one listed in the brochure. Amanda highlighted the ones that were particularly pertinent to what they would do that day. After this, Amanda asked Dorthea to sign a permission form for the screening. Dorthea commented again that this was a lot of information to take in, and Amanda assured her that they would go over this information many times if needed. She stated again that family rights and family involvement were very important.

Together they proceeded to read the elements of the screening, and Dorthea shared information about what Kendra did about what Kendra did. They engaged Kendra in several activities in order to complete the questionnaire. Kendra cooperated and seemed to enjoy some of the things she was asked to do. She even got off Dorthea's lap and crawled over to Amanda.

Once they had completed the screening, Amanda explained the scoring process and then showed Dorthea how Kendra did. The screening showed delays in gross motor skills, as expected, but also in talking and doing things like feeding herself and following simple directions. Dorthea had mixed feelings; she did not want Kendra to be behind, but she also wanted to know that her concerns were real. Although Dorthea expected a delay in walking, she was surprised that Kendra scored poorly in the self-help and communication sections. Amanda explained that the screening was a snapshot that gave them good information, and because of these low scores, further evaluation must be done to get Kendra in the program. She repeated in a firm voice that Kendra would benefit from early intervention and was probably eligible based on the low screening scores. Amanda told Dorthea that the evaluation to determine her eligibility would be done on another visit with two other providers, including a physical therapist.

Finally, they spent time talking about Kendra's birth and that she had horrible trouble with reflux as an infant. Dorthea was happy to report that Kendra was doing much better and was eating and gaining weight as she should be, according to Dr. Paddi. Amanda explained that they would like to review Kendra's health records as part of evaluation and assessment for eligibility. She asked Dorthea to sign a paper to allow that release and to give permission for the program to let Dr. Paddi know that early intervention had followed up on his referral. Dorthea agreed and signed the form.

Dorthea agreed to go ahead with the evaluation, but in the back of her mind, she wondered what her husband might say. Amanda and Dorthea talked a bit more about the evaluation, what would happen, and how the results would be used to help determine if Kendra was eligible for the program. Amanda stated that she would call to schedule the appointment after she checked with her team members' schedules. She reassured Dorthea that she would be calling back in the next 2 days. As Amanda picked up her items and put them in her bag, she commented again on how happy she was to meet the family and how lucky Kendra was to have such a loving family. This made Dorthea feel good, but she still had lots of questions that she was not ready to ask.

After Amanda left, Dorthea realized they had spent an hour and a half together. She felt overwhelmed and tired. She was glad that Amanda had left her things to read. Kendra was very ready for a nap. As Dorthea rocked her and watched her fall asleep, she wondered how these delays in Kendra's development happened and what had she done wrong. She also wondered how she would tell Paul. As she laid Kendra in her crib, she decided to call her aunt, which always seemed to help. Her aunt was very reassuring, saying that Dorthea had done the right thing by getting help for Kendra. After talking to her aunt, Dorthea called her husband. Much to her surprise and relief, Paul was very supportive. He told her he too had been thinking a lot about the things Kendra was not doing. After she hung up, she started to cry, feeling alone with her two closest friends so far away.

It was a week after the screening; Amanda called Dorthea to set up a time for the evaluation. Dorthea had told herself that if she had not heard from Amanda by 5 p.m., she was going to call the next day. Amanda gave several dates and times, all of which were 10 days to 2 weeks away. Amanda wanted the physical therapist, Jerry, to be involved in the evaluation, and he was not free until then. Fortunately, there were morning times available. Even though Dorthea was eager to get things going, she agreed to a later date, thinking it was important for the physical therapist to be there. They made arrangements for the evaluation in 10 days.

Amanda apologized for the delay in calling, saying Jerry had been out and his schedule had not been available until that day when he came back from sick leave. She thanked Dorthea for her understanding and asked if she had any more questions or concerns since the prior visit. Amanda added that an advantage to waiting was that Paul might be able to arrange his schedule so he could be home for the evaluation. Dorthea had mentioned this to Amanda on the first visit, and she was impressed that Amanda had remembered. She thought she would ask Paul when he called tonight to see if that was a possibility.

Questionable practices (Identify 4):

1. _____
   _____
   _____
   _____

2. _____
   _____
   _____
   _____

3. _____
   _____
   _____
   _____

4. _____
   _____
   _____
   _____

How would you have done these questionable practices differently?

1. _____
   _____
   _____
   _____

2. _____
   _____
   _____
   _____

3. _____
   _____
   _____
   _____

4. _____
   _____
   _____
   _____

Evaluation

Evaluation day finally came. Unfortunately, Paul was gone again, so Dorthea was on her own. Dorthea was happy to see Amanda again because she felt comfortable with her. Amanda introduced Dorthea to Jerry, the physical therapist, and Emma, the early child-hood specialist. Amanda mentioned that she was sorry Paul could not be there, but she understood. Jerry carried in a small bench like one Dorthea had in the bathroom. Emma had what looked like a fishing tackle box with her. Dorthea invited them into the living room and introduced them to Kendra, who was sitting and jumping in her exerciser jumpy seat. When Kendra saw all the people, she got quiet and looked at Dorthea, ready to cry. Dorthea responded by picking her up, and then Kendra looked at the visitors from the safety of her mother's arms and smiled shyly.

As Dorthea held Kendra, Amanda reviewed the information about the evaluation she had shared on the last visit and explained that the evaluation would involve asking Dorthea some questions and watching to see what Kendra would do with a variety of activities. At the end, they would talk about what they saw, score the evaluation, and decide together if Kendra met the eligibility requirements for early intervention or, if needed, make arrange-ments to gather more information. Dorthea sat on the sofa still holding Kendra, and Amanda sat next to her. The mother and daughter both watched as Jerry and Emma started to take out their papers and open their "tool kits." Jerry asked Dorthea if it was okay for Kendra to sit on the floor so they could get started. Dorthea put Kendra on the floor, but she crawled back over to Dorthea. Jerry offered Kendra a toy from the tool kit, and she slowly started to play with it. Kendra crawled over to him much to Dorthea's surprise.

Emma began asking Dorthea questions about how Kendra did with things like eating, dressing, and interacting with others. Dorthea was trying to respond to the questions while watching and wondering what Jerry was seeing Kendra do or not do. She was having trou-ble listening and answering Emma at the same time. At some point, it seemed like Emma understood that Dorthea was trying to attend to both, so she said, "Let me pause for a while so that we can see what Kendra is doing with Jerry." That made Dorthea feel a bit better, as she really wanted to know what Jerry was doing. He had put Kendra into different posi-tions, like standing, kneeling, and sitting on the bench he brought, and she was starting to get fussy.

As Jerry saw he had Dorthea's attention, he asked her questions about Kendra such as how she did on her tummy and how often she was in the jumpy seat. Dorthea responded to the questions but felt a bit like she was not giving the responses Jerry wanted to hear. At one point, Dorthea thought she heard Jerry mumble that she should get rid of the jumpy seat. She felt he was talking to her like a lecturer in school when he began talking about muscle tone, sensory input, and hip something or other. Dorthea did not really understand what he was saying and felt like she would sound dumb if she questioned him; he appeared very smart. While he was talking about getting rid of the jumpy seat, Dorthea was also thinking that Kendra really enjoyed it. It was also a safe place for Kendra when Dorthea was busy doing housework or taking a shower. At first, she got irritated with Jerry, and then she quickly began to feel guilty, thinking maybe she caused Kendra's problems. She kept her feelings to herself.

After Jerry was finished talking, Emma took over with some questions. She asked about what things Kendra liked to do. Dorthea explained that Kendra had favorite books, and Emma asked if it would be okay to see them. Dorthea got out two of Kendra's favorite books. She began to read them with Kendra. Kendra turned the pages and Dorthea named the pictures while Kendra looked. On two different pages, Dorthea asked Kendra, "Where is the dog?" and "Where is the cat?" Both times, Kendra pointed to the correct animal and then looked up at Dorthea with a big smile. Emma commented on what a great job Dorthea was doing labeling the pictures in the book for Kendra. This was an important way for Kendra to learn the names of objects and to follow directions. After finishing with the books, Emma presented a few more toys to Kendra from her tackle box. With each toy she explained what she was looking at Kendra doing. Dorthea understood what Emma was saying and liked that each time Emma did something, she would tell Dorthea what she was looking for. When Emma gave Kendra a small bottle with Cheerios, she explained she was looking to see Kendra's thinking and problem-solving skills as she tried to get the Cheerios out and how persistent she was. Dorthea thought Emma was smart too, but she did not feel as intimidated by her as she was by Jerry.

After about an hour, Emma and Jerry said that they had the information they needed and that they wanted to take a few minutes to score their evaluations. During this time, Amanda talked with Dorthea about questions Dorthea had about early intervention. Dorthea asked her to explain again about the primary person and how that person could help if he or she was not a physical therapist. Amanda carefully explained again how the program worked with families, and Dorthea felt like she was beginning to understand.

Jerry and Emma then took some time to review how Kendra did on the evaluations. Emma explained that Kendra was doing well socially; she warmed up to them quickly and was friendly and curious. In the area of communication and self-care, Kendra was behind, and Emma shared more information about these domains and the delays they saw. In the area of thinking and problem solving, Kendra was at her age level, but she might benefit from more experiences with pretend play activities. Emma commented how great it was to see her interest in books and that Dorthea followed Kendra's lead when looking at books, which was a great way to help Kendra learn more words. Dorthea thought Emma described Kendra's skills pretty accurately. She was happy to hear Emma talk about the good things Kendra was doing.

Next, Jerry shared his observations. They were less positive. He started by saying that Kendra should have spent more time on her tummy when she was little, and again he said the jumpy seat was not good for her and should no longer be used. Dorthea started to feel a bit defensive. She had tried to explain earlier that Kendra had reflux and absolutely hated being on her tummy, but he did not seem to listen. He went on to say that Kendra was delayed in her motor skills and gave some number that he did not explain. Dorthea did understand when he said that Kendra was delayed approximately 5 months. He said the good news was he did not see anything physically wrong with her muscle tone or bone structure; just stop using the jumpy seat and give her lots of practice pulling herself up, standing, and walking with assistance.

Everyone on the team agreed that Kendra met the program's eligibility criteria so the family could receive early intervention services. Amanda explained that parents did not directly pay for services but that their insurance could be billed. Dorthea asked a few questions about payment, and Amanda carefully explained the process and offered her a paper that explained the insurance billing. Dorthea stated she was interested in the services.

With the eligibility established, assessment was the next step. This involved talking more about how a typical day went for the family, what times during the day went well or were difficult for Kendra, and what the family felt they wanted to work on with early

Questionable practices (Identify 3):

1. _____
   _____
   _____
   _____
   _____
   _____

2. _____
   _____
   _____
   _____
   _____
   _____

3. _____
   _____
   _____
   _____
   _____

How would you have done these questionable practices differently?

1. _____
   _____
   _____
   _____
   _____
   _____

2. _____
   _____
   _____
   _____
   _____
   _____

3. _____
   _____
   _____
   _____
   _____
   _____

intervention. What concerns, hopes, and dreams did Paul and Dorthea have for Kendra and for their family. At that point, Emma suggested making an appointment for the family assessment and another one to develop the IFSP. Amanda reminded everyone that the IFSP had to be developed within 45 days from when the referral was received and that this was quickly approaching. Both dates were set: one at the end of that week and the other early in the next week. Dorthea asked what an IFSP was, and Emma briefly explained it and assured her that they would talk more about it when she came back. Dorthea agreed that she was ready to get started.

Assessment

For the family assessment, Emma came alone. It was a beautiful day and Kendra was in her jump-up airplane that hung from the porch roof. Dorthea was sitting on the porch swing. She asked if they could stay outside because Kendra was so happy. Emma agreed and took a seat in the rocking chair. She opened a folder and began to ask questions. Although Dorthea had some idea from the conversation last week with Amanda that the questions were to help Dorthea decide what she wanted to work on with early intervention, she felt a bit bombarded with the questions at first and was not sure why she was being asked the first group of questions. Emma asked things about who helped Dorthea while Paul was on the road; what activities in the community the family liked to do; what organizations, groups, or programs they belonged to; and which family and friends Dorthea thought were helpful to them. Gradually, the questions turned into a conversation, which was more comfortable for Dorthea. Emma asked Dorthea to describe what the family's day was like from waking up in the morning to bedtime. For this round of questions, Emma explained the purpose of asking about their day and invited Dorthea to share only what she wanted. Dorthea talked about what it was like without Paul at home and what it was like when he was there. As they talked, Emma took notes, sometimes checking with Dorthea to see if she understood Dorthea's responses correctly. Dorthea mentioned that a major difficulty was at wake-up and nap times, when she has to carry Kendra up and down the steps. Dorthea explained that it was difficult because Kendra was getting heavier and because she was 3 months pregnant and "getting more pregnant every day." Both women laughed at the remark, and Emma congratulated Dorthea and waited to see if she would say anything else about the pregnancy. She did not, so Emma did not pry.

Dorthea said that, when playing with the neighbor twins, Kendra was not able to keep up with them unless they were sitting and playing. When the twins took off walking, Kendra either tried to crawl after or just sat by herself and watched them. Kendra not being able to walk was also an issue when running errands such as going to the grocery store, especially if Paul was away. Dorthea had to carry Kendra from the car to the store to put her in the cart.

When they talked about meal time, Dorthea said that Kendra screeched or threw things on the floor that she did not want. Dorthea wanted Kendra to have some way to tell her what she actually wanted. Was it a drink or a bite of something or was she finished eating? Kendra was not using a spoon much at meal time, and when she tried, she was very messy. Kendra had a way of tipping the spoon over before putting it in her mouth. Dorthea said this was upsetting mostly for Paul and especially if they all went out to eat. Dorthea thought Kendra was still young to use a spoon or fork, so she had been feeding her at most meal times.

Emma listened, wrote things down, and sometimes asked for more examples of what Dorthea wanted Kendra to do. They also talked about things Kendra could do and seemed to enjoy. Dorthea found it was easy to talk about their day. She was a bit surprised with herself that there were many things she was worried about or found hard to do that she had never spoken about with anyone. Emma's listening to her made it easy to talk.

Dorthea mentioned that Kendra had used the potty three nights last week before her bath. She thought Kendra was ready for potty training. Emma responded by saying that Dorthea must have caught her at just the right time, because Kendra was clearly not ready for potty training and that they should focus on other things right now. Dorthea felt that Emma did not quite believe her, but she knew that Kendra used the potty. Potty training was important to Dorthea, especially with the new baby coming and the cost of two children in diapers. She kept her feelings to herself at this point in the conversation and figured she would simply keep putting Kendra on the potty before bath time. The conversation continued, and Dorthea mentioned another concern she had: preparing Kendra for the new baby. About then, Kendra began to get fussy, so they all went inside.

Emma shared her notes with Dorthea and highlighted the things Dorthea had mentioned that sounded like she might want to work on with early intervention. Dorthea identified the things she wanted to work on in the coming months. They were for Kendra to be able to walk, especially when playing with the neighbors and when out shopping; to find ways to help prepare Kendra for the new baby; to help Kendra go up and down the steps at wake-up, nap, and bed time; to have Kendra use words to say what she wanted at meal time; for Kendra to learn to use her spoon on her own; and to potty train Kendra. Dorthea mentioned the last one even though Emma did not think Kendra was ready. Emma thought this was a great list of priorities and explained how these ideas would be used to develop "outcomes" and would be part of the IFSP. Emma explained the IFSP meeting and that Amanda would get the meeting started but that all the team members would participate. She told Dorthea that, as Kendra's mother, she was one of the most important team members. If she did not understand something, she was encouraged to ask questions. The meeting would be at the house, and Dorthea was free to invite anyone she wanted. Emma checked if Dorthea had any questions about the meeting. Dorthea did not but did share that Paul would be home that day and that she hoped he would participate.

Questionable practices (Identify 2):

1. _____

2. _____

How would you have done these questionable practices differently?

1. _____

2. _____

Individualized Family Service Plan Meeting

For the IFSP meeting, Dorthea planned to have everyone sit at the large kitchen table, and when Emma and Amanda arrived they thought that was a great idea. They explained that Jerry would not be able to attend but that he had written all the necessary information in his report. Amanda gave Dorthea the written report from the evaluation. Although they had shared information with her after the evaluation, they had not given her the actual report until now. Dorthea wanted to look it over, but it was quite long, and Amanda asked if Paul would be able to join them. Dorthea said he had decided to entertain Kendra in the living room so she would not be in the way. He did come into the kitchen and meet everyone. Even after gentle encouragement from Amanda to participate in the meeting, he still declined, saying that Dorthea was better able to handle it.

Emma started off by briefly reviewing the evaluation results that Jerry, Emma, and Amanda had written in the report. Amanda went on to explain again that the focus of intervention was not just on Kendra but on the whole family and that the team would be working with Dorthea and Paul to help Kendra. Emma then reviewed the concerns that Dorthea had identified the previous week and asked if she had any others to add. Dorthea said that she and Paul reviewed the list and agreed that they wanted to work on the ones she and Emma had talked about. Emma said, "Great!" and then introduced one more: for Kendra to learn pretend play skills. Dorthea was surprised, as that was not something she remembered saying and said that she had not said that. Emma replied that she thought it was something important to include. Not knowing she could counter Emma, Dorthea said okay.

Emma gave Dorthea a copy of the IFSP form and time to look it over as they talked about it being a plan to guide their work and that it was the family's document. It would also be used and referred to at each visit. With the parents' permission, portions of it could be changed or added to at any time. There would be a formal review of the plan every 6 months. Nothing could be changed without first notifying a parent. Dorthea said she did not have any questions at that time. Amanda had a laptop they were typing on, so she suggested that Dorthea sit beside her so she could see what was being written on the IFSP form. She said the step they would complete next was to take the priorities that Dorthea had identified last week and write them as *functional outcomes*. Emma said a functional outcome meant that it was something useful and meaningful to Dorthea and Paul that they wanted to work on with the early intervention team to help Kendra and their family. Once the outcomes were written, they would identify ideas or activities that could help with achieving the outcomes. After that was done, they would talk about who on the early intervention team would assist Dorthea and Paul to help Kendra.

As Amanda pulled up the IFSP, Dorthea saw the first outcome filled in. This was the one about pretend play that she was not interested in. It read,

Outcome 1: Kendra will increase her pretend play skills. **Criteria:** We will know she can do this when she has age-expected pretend play abilities.

Even though Dorthea did not understand what this outcome meant or why it was important, she still did not say anything. Amanda and the team went on to write the other outcomes from the list that Emma and Dorthea had generated the week earlier. Together they talked about each outcome, and Amanda typed them into the IFSP form. Dorthea asked what the criteria meant. Emma explained it as a measure to see progress and to know when the outcome was achieved. Amanda said that Paul and Dorthea were really the final ones to say when the outcome was achieved to their satisfaction. That seemed to make sense to Dorthea, and she liked the idea that it was she and Paul who would help decide. The remaining outcomes were as follows:

Outcome 2: Kendra will participate in play with the neighbors by walking on her own so that she does not need to be carried. **Criteria:** We will know she can do this when she walks independently across the yard twice a week for 3 weeks.

Outcome 3: Dorthea and Paul will have information on how to prepare Kendra for her new brother or sister. **Criteria:** We will know this is met when the family has the information to their satisfaction.

Outcome 4: Kendra will walk up and down the hall steps at nap and bed time so that she does not have to be carried. **Criteria:** We will know she can do this when she walks up and down holding the hand rail 2 times per day for 2 weeks.

Outcome 5: Kendra will participate in meal times by using words to say what she wants or does not want. **Criteria:** We will know she can do this when she uses two words at each meal time to request something.

Outcome 6: Kendra's parents will have information to help Kendra use the potty. **Criteria:** We will know this is met when the family has information and a plan for potty training by the time the new baby arrives.

Outcome 7: Kendra will use her spoon to feed herself at meal times so that she is less messy. **Criteria:** We will know she can do this when she uses her spoon independently with minimal spilling each meal for a week.

Once they were done writing the outcomes in the IFSP, Dorthea spent several minutes reading over them. She commented about Outcome 6, the one about potty training. She said that her hope was to have Kendra using the potty regularly but agreed that a plan was a good place to start. She also questioned the pretend play outcome. She did not understand it and did not know what age-expected pretend play skills were. Emma explained a bit more, and Amanda asked if it was something that Dorthea truly wanted on the plan. In a quiet voice, Dorthea said that she thought Kendra did well with playing and that it was not a concern of hers. Together they decided to take this one off the plan. Amanda also reminded the team that things could be added or changed later.

After the outcomes were agreed upon, they talked about ideas—called *strategies*—to help accomplish the outcomes. As they started talking about and writing strategies for Outcomes 2 and 4, it seemed that Emma and Amanda were talking between themselves and looking over Jerry's notes without including Dorthea. Dorthea did not feel involved in their conversation, so she decided to go check in on Paul and Kendra in the other room. She found that Paul had been listening to them talk after all but that he still did not want to join them. Dorthea returned with drinks of water for everyone and then was more involved with writing the strategies for the other outcomes. She was pleased that Emma remembered so much of their conversation from the other day about things the family did together and the things Kendra liked to do. These were included in some of the strategies.

They were almost done. The next step was to decide services. After some discussion, the team agreed that Emma would be the primary provider, coming once a week, and

Jerry would join her for the first three sessions. After that, he would come once a month, but Emma would keep him up to date on how things were going. A speech therapist would consult with Emma and come with her on visits once a quarter. Amanda would be the service coordinator, and she too would call or visit at least once a month. She would also be the person who was going to help find information, or even a class that Dorthea could attend at the hospital, about siblings and new babies. As they finished the meeting, Dorthea felt good that she was going to get help to work on things that were really important to her and Paul.

Questionable practices (Identify 3):

1. _____
   _____
   _____
   _____
   _____

2. _____
   _____
   _____
   _____
   _____

3. _____
   _____
   _____
   _____

How would you have done these questionable practices differently?

1. _____
   _____
   _____
   _____
   _____

2. _____
   _____
   _____
   _____
   _____

3. _____
   _____
   _____
   _____

Ongoing Intervention

It had been 10 weeks since services began, and Kendra was making nice progress. She was almost 20 months old now. During this time, Jerry had kindly explained why the jumpy seats were not a good choice for Kendra, and Dorthea agreed to put them away. Jerry also showed her pictures of toys from a local store that would be more appropriate if she was interested in replacing them with something else. They were cute things that Kendra could stand behind, hold on to, and push forward. They also had lots of fun gadgets on the front for her to play with. Dorthea remembered that the twins had something similar. Paul actually surprised Kendra with one when he came home right after Jerry's first visit. Kendra learned to push it around and enjoyed standing up tall behind it and playing with the gadgets on it. She was walking better but continued to rely on the push toys or her parents' hands for support. Kendra could now go backward down the steps on her tummy, which was a safe way so she would not fall.

Over the past 10 weeks, they had tried several ideas to help Kendra go up stairs by walking. Together they brainstormed some ways to do this, and Dorthea's idea was the best. It was to make a game of it by putting a favored toy up a few steps and encouraging Kendra to go up and get it. It seemed that she was too tired to go up on her own at sleep times, so the game was a workable alternative. During play, Dorthea put one of Kendra's favored toys a couple of steps up and encouraged her to walk up to get it. After a few weeks, Kendra would step up one step with Dorthea holding her hand.

Kendra started using words for *drink* ("deek") and *eat* ("tea") at meal time, and they were working on saying *more* and *all done*. She was also doing better with using her spoon. Dorthea and Emma spent quite a bit of time talking about how children learn to use utensils and that practice was essential. They also talked about the kinds of foods that were easier to eat with a spoon, like mashed potatoes, oatmeal, and other foods that easily stuck to the spoon. Dorthea started with those so they would be easier for Kendra. Kendra was not ready for soup yet, but she was making progress. Dorthea's interest in potty training Kendra continued, and she was very consistent with putting Kendra on the potty after waking up, after breakfast, and before bath time. Kendra went in the potty a few times and appeared most consistent after breakfast. Dorthea was pleased with the progress Kendra had made and the plan she and Paul had developed for helping Kendra learn to use the potty, so the team agreed to mark that outcome as met. They also added a new one: Kendra would participate in potty times by going pee in the potty so she could wear regular panties. The outcome was met when Kendra peed in the potty two times a day for 3 consecutive weeks. Paul and Dorthea saw that Kendra was making progress, but they also knew that Kendra was behind other children her age. They kept wondering why and hoped the new baby would not have similar problems.

When Amanda called the family after 3 weeks of services, Dorthea reported that she was pleased with how things were going and really liked how Jerry and Emma did not give her "homework" to do. Rather, they brainstormed, tried things, and were very careful to be sure that Dorthea had a plan of what she wanted to try from week to week. Sometimes the plans worked, other times they did not. When they did not work, like the idea to try a special spoon, Dorthea felt comfortable explaining what happened, and together they thought of new things to try.

Dorthea had to cancel the appointment last week, so it had been 2 weeks since she had seen Emma. This day's visit began like all the previous ones. They first talked about how things were going, how the pregnancy was going, and how and where Paul was. Dorthea was so excited to tell Emma that, just in the last week, Kendra seemed to be walking all the time on her own. She was still a bit unstable, and when her legs seemed tired she sometimes reverted to crawling but would then stand herself right back up and toddle off. She still had work to do, but she was using walking as her way to move around without the push toy. This was a big celebration, and Emma shared the joy with Dorthea.

Emma suggested starting with this outcome, and Dorthea agreed. Emma asked Dorthea what she thought might help Kendra be steadier in walking. Dorthea replied that the practice Jerry encouraged is probably what she needs. She and Paul had moved the kitchen and the coffee tables so Kendra had more room to walk longer distances. Emma remarked, "What a great idea." They talked about safety, and Dorthea showed Emma how Paul had taped a towel to the corners of the table that stood out a bit in Kendra's walk space. They talked about other practice opportunities for Kendra, including going outside on the playground, to where there was lots of space on the cushy tiles, and after church, when the hallway from the Sunday School classroom was clear of other people. Emma agreed that practice was a good idea and asked Dorthea if she wanted to set that as the plan for this outcome for the next week or if she wanted to talk more about it. Dorthea agreed on the plan to give Kendra more practice opportunities and said, "Let's move on to the next outcome." Dorthea knew the home visits were organized around her outcomes and felt comfortable directing the focus on to the next outcome. Emma was quite happy about this.

The next outcome was about going up and down the steps. Emma asked how the step game was going. Dorthea reported that Kendra was still going up one step with help, but not much more than that. Emma asked if they could give it a try today, and Dorthea agreed. As Dorthea showed Emma how she was helping Kendra go up the stairs, Emma noticed that it seemed awkward and maybe uncomfortable for Dorthea. When Emma asked, Dorthea concurred that it was hard for her to bend over and help Kendra. Emma had a suggestion, and asked Dorthea what she thought about having Kendra hold the railing instead of her hand and then follow behind her just in case she were to lose her footing. Dorthea gave Emma a questioning look, and Emma asked if Dorthea would like her to demonstrate. Dorthea said yes; she liked to see things being done before jumping in and giving them a try. As Emma helped Kendra hold the hand rail, she got behind her and encouraged her to go up the steps. It did not work at first because Kendra did not want to go up the steps. Just then, Dorthea saw the same thing and said, "I'll go up the steps. Then she'll have a reason to go up." Emma responded, "Great idea! You're right. She has to have a reason to go up the steps." The second time they tried it, Kendra went up four steps before reverting to crawling. This was a great success, as she had never taken more than one step. Emma asked if Dorthea wanted to try. As Dorthea gave it a try, Emma reminded her to stay closely behind Kendra. This time Kendra went up three steps. Dorthea and Emma agreed that this was a huge accomplishment and that they had better give Kendra a rest, as she was clearly losing interest. Emma asked Dorthea how it felt helping Kendra this way, and she said it was easier. Dorthea asked about doing the same to help Kendra go down the steps. In response, Emma said that going up steps was easier than going down and that, when going down, Dorthea should be in front of Kendra rather than behind her. That made sense to Dorthea, and she said, "Maybe I'll just stick with going up this week, and we can tackle going down next week." Emma responded, "That sounds like a good plan." As they finished their discussion about this outcome, they agreed that Dorthea would show Paul what they had talked about and that they would help Kendra use the hand rail and spot her from behind when going up the stairs. Emma wrote their plan down on the home visit note, and they moved on to the next outcome.

Dorthea suggested they talk about the outcome for Kendra to talk at meal times because Kendra was ready for her snack. During previous visits, Emma discussed and demonstrated how to give Kendra two choices, saying the name of each item and then waiting for Kendra to request one by saying the word or something that sounded like it. Emma asked how the choice-making strategy was working, and Dorthea said that she had been trying it but that Kendra was not saying the word. Emma asked if she could try it again with Kendra, and Dorthea agreed. As Kendra started her snack, Emma seemed to take over. She jumped in, picked up the two things Dorthea put out, and offered Kendra the choices, saying *apple* and *cracker*. When Kendra said something and looked at her desired item, Emma gave it to her and praised her effort. Emma did this several times, showing Dorthea that Kendra could do it even if the word was not clear. As Emma demonstrated, Dorthea wondered what she was doing different and said to Emma that she would have to come for snack more often to get Kendra to talk. Emma laughed and said, "You can do it!" but did not give any real guidance on what she was doing. When Emma asked Dorthea to try, Kendra was getting fussy and was done with her snack. They talked about the outcome some more, and Dorthea said that she would try the choices again over the next week, and then they could revisit it.

Before ending the visit, Dorthea wanted to talk about preparing Kendra for the baby. She wanted to show Emma the baby doll they had gotten Kendra and to talk about how and when to give it to her. Emma agreed with Dorthea that the baby doll they had picked out was perfect. As they discussed when to give Kendra the doll, Emma asked Dorthea what she thought, and they began exploring the pros and cons of giving her the doll now or waiting until the baby comes home. In the end, Dorthea decided that she would wait a bit longer but give Kendra the doll before the baby arrives. They had also gotten some information from the hospital that Amanda had shared about a "sib-shop" for children 2 to 4 that the hospital held each month for a few hours on Saturday mornings. They thought they would wait until right before the baby was born to attend so that Kendra would be a little older. Amanda had also shared the names of several books and even a video about being a big sister. Paul and Dorthea had watched the video and talked about some of the ideas. Emma asked if they had enough information or if they wanted more. Dorthea wanted to ask about having Kendra touch her belly and look at the ultrasound pictures they had, but she saw Emma was starting to put her papers in the bag.

Emma looked at her watch and saw that their hour was up. She said she had to leave. She apologized for being so abrupt but that she had so many other visits to do that day she could not run over. They had not reviewed their plan for the next week, but she promised to call later in the week.

As she walked to the door she waved good-bye to Kendra, who waved back and said bye-bye. Dorthea hoped that Emma noticed Kendra saying bye-bye. She did, and with a big smile, she said bye-bye again.

At the door, Emma turned around and said she that she would like for Dorthea to arrange that the next visit be outside with the neighbors if the weather was nice. She thought it would be good to see how Kendra was doing playing with the twins. Dorthea said she would check, but in the back of her mind, knew she could not schedule the neighbors, as their lives were so busy and play time between the kids just happened spontaneously. Emma had already gotten to her car, so there was no time to talk more. Emma waved as she started the car, and Dorthea closed the door and went over to Kendra, who was holding her favorite book. Sitting on the sofa to snuggle and look at books together seemed like a very good idea for now.

Questionable practices (Identify 3):

1. _____
   _____
   _____
   _____
   _____

2. _____
   _____
   _____
   _____

3. _____
   _____
   _____
   _____

How would you have done these questionable practices differently?

1. _____
   _____
   _____
   _____

2. _____
   _____
   _____
   _____

3. _____
   _____
   _____
   _____

WRAP UP: SO HOW DID YOU DO? ANSWER KEY

Now that you have reviewed a snapshot of the Thomases' early intervention journey and identified what you believe are both the best and the questionable practices, let us see how you did. In this section, we comment on the recommended practices and highlight the main questionable practices that were demonstrated in each step of the Thomases' story. You will also find the recommended practices identified by the Workgroup on Principles and Practices in Natural Environments' (2008) Community of Practice. These practices were illustrated in the preceding chapters and are included here as a final reminder. As you have the opportunity to discuss this case study further with your colleagues, you may identify additional quality and questionable practices as well as variations that might occur in a family's early intervention journey due to unique characteristics and needs of the specific family you are discussing.

REFERRAL

Recommended Practices from the Thomas Family's Story

- When the early interventionist, Amanda, called the family, she explained how her program received the referral and then asked Dorthea if she had the same concerns. Asking this informs the family about the referral and invites them to share their concerns and clarify if they are the same or different from the referring provider's.

- Amanda addressed how early intervention looks at children's overall development and helps families help their children. When asked about the prescription for PT, Amanda reassured Dorthea that, if Kendra was behind in her development, the program would assist but that it might not specifically be a PT that would work with the family. At the referral point in the early intervention process, it is too early to determine the actual services needed.

- Amanda invited Dorthea to decide if she wanted to proceed with the referral and explained that, after the screening, they would decide together how to proceed.

- Amanda shared information with Dorthea (e.g., descriptive information over the phone, a video link, and a brochure) to help Dorthea understand the program and prepare for their first visit.

Questionable Practices

1. The doctor stated that early intervention would provide physical therapy and gave a prescription. Early intervention services are decided on with the family and are not based on referring physician prescriptions. Referral agencies should have correct information about early intervention and share it with families. Early intervention programs must work closely and regularly with referral agencies to avoid this type of confusion for families.

2. The timeline for the screening was 2 weeks from the referral, and the time offered was in the middle of Kendra's nap. The next available appointment was in 5 weeks. Families should not have such a long time to wait for an appointment. More screening times should be available.

Community of Practice Agreed-Upon Practices: Referral

- Ask what language the family usually speaks and if any family members may want an interpreter.

- Balance the time listening to the family with sharing information.

- Engage in a conversation to find out why the family is contacting early intervention and to identify the next appropriate step in the referral process.

- Use open-ended questions and/or comments such as, "What are your questions or concerns about Michael's health and development?"; "I understand [insert referrer's name] suggested that you call us. What were his or her concerns?"; and "What kind of information would be most useful to you?"

- Explain the general purpose of the early intervention program and how children and families are eligible. Provide public awareness materials.

INTAKE/SCREENING

Recommended Practices from the Thomas Family's Story

- Upon arriving at the family's home, Amanda, the service coordinator, introduced herself and confirmed if it was still a good time for the visit. This allowed the family the chance to respond if something unexpected had occurred, as is often the case in family life, which might result in a need to reschedule. Amanda's tone and appearance was pleasant and friendly, and by introducing herself by name and title, she clarified for the family who they were inviting in. Amanda did not assume the family would remember the name given over the phone.

- Amanda referred to the brochure she had sent Dorthea, used it to talk about the program, and asked if Dorthea had any questions. This also allowed the family to have something to look back to after the visit, or perhaps they could use it to share about the program with other caregivers who were not able to be at the visit.

- Amanda took time to address Dorthea's questions about PT and explained their primary provider model. In doing so, she did not make it appear that the doctor was incorrect or wrong. Her explanation included how Kendra's motor needs and strategies to address them would be determined by the team with the family. The physical therapist would be part of this decision. The physical therapist would also determine how best to help Kendra through everyday family activities. At this point the information shared should be clear and not complicated.

- Amanda showed Dorthea the screening protocol (instrument) to help ease any fears Dorthea might have about what was going to be tested. This sharing also opened up communication for Dorthea to share what she saw as her daughter's strengths and needs. Providing information about the difference between screening and evaluation helps Dorthea to make an informed choice if she preferred to go straight to evaluation and not do a screening.

- Amanda read Dorthea's body language and realized she was losing Dorthea's interest as she detailed out the evaluation process. At this point, she made a simple summary statement and moved on.

- Amanda explained the family's rights and highlighted those immediately pertinent to what they would do during this visit and did not overwhelm Dorthea with *all* the family rights that could be explained at later visits.

- Amanda involved Dorthea in the screening by reading the screening questions together and trying what was needed with Kendra. Dorthea was an equal partner in this process, helping Kendra display the skills and behaviors that were typical.

- Amanda finished the visit on a positive note, genuinely saying what a pleasure it was to meet both Dorthea and Kendra.

Questionable Practices

1. The service coordinator, Amanda, came in and took her spot on the floor. She directed the parent, Dorthea, to join her on the floor. Amanda should have followed the family's lead and asked where to sit. Amanda should remember that she is a guest in the family's home. Many adults—for a variety of reasons—do not feel comfortable sitting on the floor.

2. Amanda pulled a toy out of her toy bag without explaining what she was doing. This left Dorthea wondering. Early interventionists should explain their actions and interactions with the parents to facilitate the parents' understanding and involvement in the session.

3. Amanda stated that further evaluation was needed without involving the parent in the decision. She went on to state that Kendra's eligibility was probable, based on the screening scores. The decision to go on to further evaluation should be done *with* not *for* the parent. Stating probable eligibility based on screening results alone is wrong.

4. Amanda did not get back in touch with the family until almost a week after the screening, yet she had said she would call back in 2 days.

Community of Practice Agreed-Upon Practices: Intake and Screening

- If the child has a diagnosis, ask questions such as, "What has your doctor/nurse told you about Michael's diagnosis?" and "What questions do you have about the diagnosis?"

- Listen for developmental *red flags* indicating an appropriate referral or a diagnosis that would make a child automatically eligible.

- Consider whether a child's development sounds typical enough that a screening may be a good idea before the full evaluation and assessment.

- If a decision is made that early intervention is not appropriate at this time, explain that the family can contact the early intervention program any time up until the child turns 3 years old.

- Share with the family other appropriate community resources or services.

Describe early intervention as a system of supports and services for families to assist them in helping their children develop and learn.

- Discover family members' personal preferences for sharing and receiving information.

- Offer information in multiple formats.

- Explain how children learn best through everyday experiences and interactions with familiar people in familiar contexts. Explain how services work to support caregivers in making the most of the many learning opportunities.

- Explain how family members are experts in understanding their child, family circumstances, and interests.

- Use the family's interests and concerns to offer concrete examples of how a service provider might work with the child and family.

- Explain that the early intervention program has rules and procedures that providers must follow.

- Show the family the location of the procedural safeguards written in the program materials and take time to explain them and how they apply to the current step in the process. Tell them that you will review these at different points in the process.

- Describe the kinds of information that will be important in the assessment process. Explain confidentiality. Make sure that the family knows that they should only share information they are comfortable sharing.

As applicable, conduct a developmental screening.

- Follow state and local procedures about providing written prior notice and obtaining consent for screening. Always explain the meaning and intent of pertinent procedural safeguards.

- Ask engaging questions that invite the family to share their thoughts and concerns about their child's development.

- Explain that there is an age range when children learn certain skills and abilities and that screening is a quick way to determine how a child is doing.

- When implementing a screening protocol, clearly describe the process with the family.

- Talk with families about what the screening is showing and ask for their observations of their child's behavior or other information they want to share.

- Come to agreement on the results of the screening and what the next steps should be.

- If the screening shows no concerns and the family does not want their child to be evaluated, describe other available community resources, as appropriate.

- Leave the family with necessary information, such as how to contact the early intervention program, resources on developmental milestones, and information about other community resources.

- Follow state and local protocols about notifying the referral source about action taken on referral.

EVALUATION

Recommended Practices from the Thomas Family's Story

- Amanda introduced everyone to Dorthea and acknowledged that Paul was not able to be there. This helped Dorthea know who was who and their roles on the team. Her acknowledgement of Paul's absence indicated that she realized he too would be important to include in helping Kendra but was simply not available for that day.

- Amanda briefly reviewed information from the last visit and explained again what would happen on that day's visit. This served two purposes: 1) to make sure the team also had important information and 2) to allow Dorthea to elaborate on or correct information. Amanda explaining the visit and what the team would to do next set a verbal agenda for the time together so all were clear on what to expect.

- Jerry asked if it was okay for Kendra to sit on the floor rather than putting her on the floor himself. He did not impose his ideas and allowed Kendra to get comfortable with him before beginning.

- Emma (although a bit late) tuned into the reality that she and Jerry were essentially conducting separate evaluations and not effectively involving Dorthea.

- Emma commented on how Dorthea naturally read books with Kendra and how this could help Kendra learn. She pointed out a real strength and acknowledged a competency Dorthea already had and how it could be used as they all worked together.

- With each item Emma presented to Kendra, she explained what she was seeing and looking for Kendra to do and why.

- Amanda took the time to respond to Dorthea's questions about early intervention.

- The team set the next appointments with Dorthea before leaving.

Questionable Practices

1. The educator, Emma, and physical therapist, Jerry, were doing simultaneous evaluations, making it difficult for Dorthea to fully participate in either part. To ensure family understanding and participation, evaluation should be one event with evaluators explaining what they are doing and what they are seeing.

2. Jerry did not explain information in a way that was understandable to Dorthea. He did not check to see if she understood him. He made suggestions to get rid of the jumpy seats without a clear explanation or understanding from the parent's perspective. He also did not describe why he brought the bench rather than use something similar in the family's home.

3. Jerry did not actively listen to Dorthea.

Community of Practice Agreed-Upon Practices: Evaluation

These practices are included after the following section on assessment. The CoP members combined the practices into evaluation/assessment because there are many overlapping practices applicable to both evaluation and assessment.

ASSESSMENT

Recommended Practices from the Thomas Family's Story

- Emma actively listened and sought clarification when needed during their conversation about a typical day for Dorthea, Paul, and Kendra and shared what she had written down for Dorthea to review.

- A routines-based interview with open-ended questions was used to identify family priorities for what they wanted to work on with early intervention.

Questionable Practices

1. Initially, the educator, Emma, started asking questions without an introduction about the purpose of the questions and how the information would be used. Dorthea felt bombarded.

2. Emma questioned Dorthea about her interest in having Kendra potty trained. She even questioned the parent's report of what she had seen her daughter doing. This sent the message, "I don't believe you," yet we know parents are valid reporters of their children's abilities and behaviors.

Community of Practice Agreed-Upon Practices: Assessment

For children proceeding to evaluation/assessment, explain the purpose and process, including the importance of gathering information about family concerns, priorities, and resources.

- Plan with the family how to address relevant individual, cultural, and linguistic characteristics that may influence assessment.

- Explain how family information can be used to know who to involve and how to conduct an appropriate evaluation/assessment.

Begin gathering information about the family's everyday routines and activities and the child's behavior and interactions with others in those contexts.

- Ask open-ended questions such as, "What happens during a typical day for your family and child?"

- Ask strengths- and interest-based questions such as, "What activities go very well?"; "What do you like to do together?"; and "Is there anything you wish you could do together? Tell me about that."

- Ask questions about activities the family might find challenging such as, "What is a tough time of the day or activity for you?" and "How does your child behave and interact with others in these challenging activities?"

- Use prompts and observations to encourage the family to describe their child's engagement, participation, independence, and social interaction in various routines and activities.

Discuss with the family the formal and informal supports they use or would like to use.

- Ask open-ended questions such as, "Who is important to your child and other members of your family?"; "Who do you call on for help?"; "Who do you see regularly?"; and "If something really good (or bad) happens, who do you contact?"

- Ask the family members if they would like to be put in contact with other families in early intervention or family organizations that offer support.

- Inquire about formal services and other community programs the family uses or may wish to use (e.g., medical, social services, Medicaid, recreation, place of worship).

Explore and identify the roles the family may want to play in their child's evaluation and assessment process.

- Describe and discuss the evaluation and assessment process.

- Discuss who the family would like to include in the evaluation and assessment process.

- Use screening and family information to identify the team members and assessment styles to fit the needs and interests of the child and family.

- Schedule times and locations that are convenient to the family.

- Make a list with the family of specific questions they would like to have answered.

- Provide written prior notice along with the procedural safeguards and ask the family to sign consent for evaluation and assessment and release of medical or other records.

- Explain that, just as the early intervention program cannot share information about the family without permission, it also needs the family's permission to ask other programs for information about their child and the family.

- Explain prior notice and review all the rights and procedural safeguards with the family, asking if they have any questions.

Evaluate and assess the functional needs and strengths of the child.

- Use assessment procedures that ensure collaboration among the family and providers, including supporting the family to participate in the way they choose.

- Identify the child's skills that seem to be emerging.

- Observe the child's authentic behaviors in typical routines and activities.

- Use assessments that capture information about the child's interests, engagement, social relationships, and independence.

- Give equal weight to the family's observations and reports about their child's behaviors, learning, and development.

- Throughout the assessment process, reflect with the family about observations of the child's behaviors, summarize results, clarify and confirm that the family understands the process and results, and record the findings.

Throughout the assessment process, observe and ask the family about their teaching and learning strategies with their child.

- Observe and discuss with the family how they help their child learn.

- Offer compliments about how the family uses specific strategies that support the child's learning. Use concrete examples of how the family supported the child's skills during assessments.

Determine if the child is eligible.

- Describe and discuss eligibility for the program.

- In order to make the eligibility decision, review and summarize findings, sharing perspectives among the team, which includes the family.

- If the team determines that the child is eligible, provide written prior notice for both the eligibility decision and the IFSP meeting.

- If the child is not eligible, explain the team decision, provide written notice for the eligibility decision—including procedural safeguards—and explain the process for filing a complaint if the family disagrees with the decision.

- If the child is not eligible, discuss and give information about available community resources, developmental milestones, and contacting the early intervention program in the future.

INDIVIDUALIZED FAMILY SERVICE PLAN MEETING

Recommended Practices from the Thomas Family's Story

- Dorthea had an opportunity to review the list of priorities with her husband before the meeting, which allowed for both of them to talk together and feel they were working together toward similar goals and outcomes.

- Amanda shared a copy of the IFSP form with Dorthea so she could refer to it as they filled in the document. She also invited Dorthea to sit beside her as they completed the form on the computer. Working on it together and communicating that it was really her family's document helped convey the message that Dorthea was a valuable part of the team.

- Time was given for Dorthea to review the outcomes once they were written, and her questions were responded to by the other team members. She did not feel forced to sign something she had not had time to review.

Questionable Practices

1. Amanda did not grant Dorthea time to review the evaluation. Rather, she pushed the meeting along. The evaluation report could have been shared before the meeting, either in writing or even through a phone call.

2. Emma introduced an outcome that was not a concern of the family. The unwanted outcome was already in the IFSP prior to the meeting, and the way it was written was not functional. It should not have been in the IFSP.

3. Emma and Amanda excluded Dorthea from the conversation as they went over Jerry's notes. Sidebar conversations among providers should not occur. It may have been better if Jerry could have participated over the phone if he was not able to attend the meeting in person.

Community of Practice Agreed-Upon Practices: Individualized Family Service Plan Meeting

Establish a welcoming and respectful climate for family members and caregivers as equal members of the IFSP team.

- Introduce all present as equal team members with essential input to share throughout the meeting.

- Clarify roles; for example, service coordinator, facilitator, and note-taker.

- Encourage all team members to learn together, share observations, raise questions, and develop a functional plan.

- Avoid the use of jargon or explain what it means so that everyone at the meeting understands terms that are used.

- Tailor interactions to the unique learning preferences and modes of communication of each adult.

Review the purpose and process (agenda) of the IFSP meeting. Review the IFSP document as a dynamic plan that will guide the provision of supports and services.

- Explain the meeting process thoroughly.

- Emphasize the family's role as an equal team member in developing the IFSP and in implementing, evaluating, and revising it over time.

- Explain the pertinent rights and procedural safeguards and explain that the team will revisit these rights and safeguards throughout the IFSP process.

Collaboratively review information collected during early contacts regarding family concerns, priorities, and resources.

- Review and update family concerns, priorities, and resources in the context of the family's day-to-day life.

- Allow time for all the team members to understand concerns from the family's perspective.

- Determine if there are any additional family needs or interests that the IFSP should address.

Collaboratively review information gathered previously about the child's health, development, and learning.

- Review and update health information pertinent to the child and the provision of early intervention support and services.

- Assure that the synthesis (report) of present levels of the child's development across all domains is functional and focused on skills, strengths, and behaviors, rather than a rote recap of test scores.

- Review the child's unique abilities, emerging skills, and engagement or participation in various routines and activities.

Consider preliteracy and language skills that are developmentally appropriate for the child.

- Talk with the family about the many ways they support language (preliteracy) development through their daily activities.

- Consider outcomes or strategies to further support preliteracy interests.

Collaboratively identify and write functional outcomes to be achieved for the child and the family.

- Discuss the outcomes the family wants to work on to enhance the child's development, engagement, social relationships, and independence in family and community routines and activities.

- Prioritize potential outcomes and choose which to work on first.

- Discuss what can be reasonably achieved in an agreed-upon time frame.

- Write outcomes using active language that describes a desired and measurable end result, including what the routine/activity/behavior should look like and where/when/with whom it should occur.

Collaboratively plan and write strategies/activities, services, and supports to address outcomes and enhance participation and learning in natural environments.

- When developing strategies, activities, and methods, reinforce the positive, emphasize how caregivers and providers will work together, and indicate who will do what.

- Avoid the use of jargon or explain what it means, so that everyone at the meeting understands terms that are used.

- Tailor interactions to the unique learning preferences and modes of communication of each adult.

If the team decides that a specific child outcome cannot be met in a natural environment, write a sufficient justification.

- Make sure the justification includes a plan for how to move the child from the non-natural environment back into other settings at home or in the community once the specific outcome that could not be met in the natural environment is achieved.

- If services are provided in an exclusive/restricted environment, discuss plans for moving services to a natural environment.

Identify the team member who will provide ongoing service coordination.

- Assign the service coordinator, based on the state and local models of service coordination.

- Assure that the family has appropriate contact information and a good understanding of service coordination.

- Explain how the family may ask for a change in service coordinator, if state policy and procedures address this issue.

Ensure that the family understands relevant procedural safeguards and next steps.

- Review procedural safeguards related to providing consent for services and obtaining written consent for IFSP services.

- Discuss the timely initiation of services.

- Make sure the family understands that changes can be made to the IFSP as needed.

- Give the family reports, records, and copies of the IFSP.

- Discuss confidentiality and family access to educational records.

- Agree upon the next steps for all team members to begin services in a timely manner.

ONGOING INTERVENTION

Recommended Practices from the Thomas Family's Story

- The team included Dorthea as a partner, coming up with strategies to address the family's IFSP outcomes. This emphasized the importance of the strategies and activities needing to be part of family life and not additional things the family was being asked to do between visits.

- Emma started the visit by asking about how things have been going and used the IFSP outcomes to guide the early intervention visit. Asking how things are going opens up the conversation for both to talk about anything new, things that may not be working well, or things that might need to be considered and planned for. It also reminds the family that it is their visit with the providers. Focusing on the IFSP provides some structure for the visit and allows for the ongoing evaluation of progress as well as adjustment of activities to reach the outcomes. The IFSP guides the visit as a working document.

Questionable Practices

1. Emma took over the snack and did not involve Dorthea, undermining her sense of competence.

2. Emma ended the session abruptly, making it feel that Dorthea was not important.

3. Emma directed Dorthea to have the next session with the twins, not allowing Dorthea a choice of what she felt they should work on. There was no explanation or conversation as to why having the twins would be a useful strategy.

Community of Practice Agreed-Upon Practices: Ongoing Intervention

During the first visit after the IFSP meeting, review the IFSP and plan together how the time can be spent.

- Describe the practical aspects of a visit and what the family or caregiver can expect. For example, the length of the typical visit, that other people are always welcome at the family's invitation, the variety of places in which visits can occur, the program's cancellation policy, and so forth.

- Describe examples of visits in various home and community settings where the family participates.

- Invite the family to reflect on their experience with the IFSP process to date and share any concerns or questions.

- Review the IFSP document and assessment information.

- Consider each agreed-upon outcome: Is it what the family is still interested in? Prioritize again, if necessary, where to begin; change wording, if needed; provide any explanations to help family understand purpose, and so forth.

- Discuss how outcomes, activities, and strategies can be starting places for each home visit.

- Talk about community activities and events that can be used to support practice and mastery for specific outcomes.

- If not previously done, ask the family to sign the IFSP, consent forms, and any other necessary documentation.

- Provide information about family-to-family support and parent groups that are available.

FOR ONGOING VISITS

Use the IFSP as a guide to plan how to spend the time together.

- Begin each visit by asking open-ended questions to identify any significant family events or activities and how well the planned routines and activities have been going.

- Ask if there are any new issues and concerns the family wants to talk about. Explore if these concerns need to be addressed as new outcomes; if so, plan an IFSP review.

- Decide which outcomes and activities to focus on during the visit.

Participate with the family or other caregivers and the child in the activity and/or routine as the context for promoting new skills and behaviors.

- Offer a variety of options to families for receiving new information or refining their routines and activities, such as face-to-face demonstrations, videos, conversations, written information, CDs, diaries, and so forth.

- Listen, observe, model, teach, coach, and/or join the ongoing interactions of the family and child.

- Encourage the family to observe and assess the child's skills, behaviors, and interests (a continual part of ongoing functional assessment). For example, ask the family if behaviors have been typical, if they have seen new behaviors (suggesting emerging skills), or how much the child seems to enjoy the activity.

- Use a variety of consulting or coaching strategies throughout the activity, including observing, listening, attending, acknowledging, expanding, responding, probing, summarizing, and so forth.

- Reflect with the family on what went well, what they want to continue doing, and what they would like to do differently at the next visit.

Jointly revise, expand, or create strategies, activities, or routines to continue progress toward achieving outcomes and to address any new family concerns

- Having listened throughout the visit, reflect on what you have heard that may suggest new outcomes or activities; explore with the family if this is something they want to address soon.

- Support and encourage family decisions.

- Focus recommendations on promoting the child's participation in everyday family and community life.

- Explain the *why* behind recommendations that you make so the family understands what to look for and do.

- Together, plan next steps and/or revise activities and strategies to build on the child's and family's interests, culture, enjoyment, and strengths.

- Consider any adaptations and augmentations to toys, materials, or environments that are necessary for success.

- Try out new strategies or activities to be sure family members or caregivers can do them on their own.

- Determine if and what type of support from other team members is needed for the next steps (consultation, information, covisit, etc.).

Modify services and supports to reflect the changing strategies, activities, or routines.

- Identify community activities and informal supports that will assist the outcomes and activities to be achieved.

- Facilitate referrals and provide any needed assistance, adaptations, or support for the family and the child to participate in desired community activities.

- Plan what early intervention and other services and supports are needed to help the child succeed and make progress.

- Add to or modify the IFSP as appropriate. If changes are significant (adding outcomes or changing services, frequency, or intensity), a team review of the IFSP is necessary.

Prepare and assist with formal reviews and revisions of the IFSP during ongoing visits.

- Minimally, every 6 months and any other time the family or provider team wants to make significant changes to the IFSP, plan a formal review meeting with the family.

- Review with the family questions, recommendations, or suggestions they wish to discuss with other service providers.

- Decide with the family the agenda for the meeting and their preferred role(s), including who should facilitate.

- Determine together who should be included in the formal review meeting as well as when and where the meeting should occur.

- Explain and provide written prior notice for the review meeting.

- Conduct the review meeting and evaluate progress toward outcomes. Ensure all outcomes, services, and supports are still needed, current, and accurate. Make additions and revisions as needed.

CHAPTER TEN

The Significance of Personal and Organizational Change

This final chapter discusses implications for personal and organizational change. Without reviewing the extensive literature on change and change models, the chapter highlights some of the positive and negative factors that affect practice changes early intervention programs and providers might be required to implement as advances in research, policy, and practice occur in the field of early intervention.

Change is both complex and dynamic. It involves moving or transforming from something familiar to something new and possibly unfamiliar. It might be broad, affecting multiple practices or aspects of the program, or it might be narrow, affecting fewer practices and elements of the program. Regardless of the scale, change is an active process rather than a single event. A change process means there is a relationship among various elements and that each aspect and phase of the change process is related to every other piece (Robinson, 2011). Change is "a highly personal experience and entails developmental growth in feelings and skills" (Hord, Rutherford, Huling-Austin, & Hall, 1998, p. 152). Individuals experiencing a change will have different feelings about the change. They have different skill sets, individual values and beliefs, as well as unique experiences, and they form their own perceptions about the change, what it entails, and what impact it will have. (Complete Give It a Go! 10.1.)

GIVE IT A GO! 10.1.

Think of a change you have recently gone through and jot down the words that come to your mind when you think about this experience.

_____

_____

_____

_____

_____

_____

_____

The words you wrote down may have been positive, such as *necessary, timely, visionary, energizing,* or *welcome.* You may have written down more negative words, such as *unwanted, frustrating, feared, not necessary,* or *chaotic.* You may also have included words that fit on both ends of the continuum from positive to negative. Whatever words came to mind were likely influenced by changes you are involved in right now and the circumstances associated with those changes. As American journalist Sydney J. Harris remarked in Lara (2003), "Our dilemma is that we hate change and love it at the same time; what we want is for things to remain the same but get better!" (p. 46). In our lives, we sometimes struggle with change; it is hard to give up what we have and what we believe we have (Farson, 1996). Although we often say we welcome change, we also can still remain fearful about the unknown future change creates.

In Chapter 8, we highlighted some of the changes Cyndi faced working as an early intervention provider for 18 years. Some of those changes Cyndi made on her own, perhaps after attending a workshop or reading a book such as this and applying it to what she was currently doing. Some of the changes were handed down to her from a new agency director, resulted from a reorganization of team structures and responsibilities, or were associated with the introduction of a new form or process. Other times, the changes she experienced came from actions above her agency, such as when the state-led agency adopted new policies and procedures or when new federal statutes and regulation were enacted to guide and support how early intervention components were implemented at the regional and local levels. As you read and work through this book, there might be ideas and practices that you want to implement. You might be motivated to try something because it makes sense to you, it matches what you believe about families and the purpose of early intervention, or it is a resource or tool that might make something you already do a bit easier.

Other changes might need support from your agency. Perhaps there is a group that would like to try something like the primary provider approach or that feels the teams could be better organized. A learning community might be established to explore different ways to gather useful information about families and their day-to-day routines in order to assist in writing functional IFSP outcomes. The IFSP process and the form itself might need revisions to help reduce paperwork or facilitate other changes. The agency might want to establish a mentoring system made up of providers who have the skills and knowledge that effectively build family relationships and facilitate family capacity. These mentors could then assist other staff members who are struggling a bit in this area.

The state may adopt a primary service provider approach, which will require changes throughout the system. This system-wide change effort might include articulation of a new state-wide vision and mission for early intervention through state-wide public awareness messages. State-wide training on the many *how to* aspects of implementing the new practices will need to be provided through different venues. Necessary funds will need to be aligned to support both training and reimbursement for a new practice, such as doing covisits and having time for teaming. The comprehensive system of personal development will need to focus efforts to support a long-term series of trainings for providers to understand and embrace the system-wide change. Large systemic changes have a cascading impact on many smaller practices and activities. Innovations that are critical in supporting system-wide range changes in practices will take careful planning to ensure the changes are implemented effectively and sustained over time.

Some changes are an individual effort; others take the combined efforts and support from different levels of your system. The push to change can come from any level of the organization, including the provider level. Regardless of where the initial push comes from, it is essential that the change effort is carefully thought through, effectively planned, respectful of what is needed at all levels within the system, and considerate of what the change will mean to others including families, partner organizations, and other stakeholders. (Complete Give It a Go! 10.2.)

GIVE IT A GO! 10.2.

Part 1: Think about what you have read in this book and list four things you would like to do differently with the families you are currently working with or with families you might work with in the future.

1. _____
   _____
2. _____
   _____
3. _____
   _____
4. _____
   _____

Part 2: Now take two of your ideas and think about what agency leadership might need to do to help support you and other providers to make and sustain your desired changes.

_____
_____
_____
_____
_____
_____
_____

TYPES OF CHANGE

Change can be thought of in two large categories: change that is anticipated and change that is reactive. *Anticipated change* has been talked about, planned for, and has a date or event that will bring it about. *Reactive change* happens without a preparation period involving the individuals impacted by the change. Both types of change can cause strong feelings and reactions. The difference is that personal reactions, during an anticipatory change, occur during the period before the change event; in reactive change, these feelings/reactions occur as the change is happening and in its immediate aftermath. Many negative reactions to change come from prior experiences or perceived notions that the change is defined and initiated by someone other than the person who is expected to do the change and it is done in a judgmental context that fosters resistance, self-doubt, and a fear of failure (Gallwey, 2000). Of course, it does not need to be this way.

On the other hand, there are individuals who thrive on change. They are energized by new ideas and by putting them into practice. They view new ideas as self-improvement and seek out opportunities that allow for change. They get bored when things remain the same. These individuals are often the first to volunteer for something new or are the front-line staff that has suggestions for improvements they continually bring to management. They like discussing new ideas and figuring out how these ideas fit within what they currently do or how these ideas could change the way things are done. Organizational change actually needs both types of reactions to successfully implement change. Listening carefully to the objections or concerns of a seemingly critical or cautious person often helps identify where the real issues are, what problems need action, and what skill sets and steps need to be defined. People who are enthusiastic and/or more receptive to change help to lead others, but they sometimes fall short of realizing and planning for the details necessary for sustaining the change over time.

Within the two broad categories of change are two subtypes called *incremental* and *discontinuous*. Incremental change involves a tuning up or an adaption of something. This change is limited in scope and is often reversible (Quinn, 1996). Incremental change can be thought of as a first-order change. It can happen without a change in the existing relationships among people, job roles, or responsibilities. No new skills or abilities are needed. Incremental changes are often better received by individuals who will be using them, as they do not require a major shift from what they believe, know about, and do each day. Examples of incremental change in early intervention include the use of a simply revised intake form that only moved two boxes and added one new piece of information to gather or a new piece of data to collect using the same procedures already in place to get the information.

Discontinuous change requires a more complex and complicated reorientation or even a re-creation of something. It may consist of a number of smaller innovations or changes within the larger scope of the change (Smale, 1998). Discontinuous change may be thought of as second-order change or radical change, where the rules and boundaries of the system change and the relationships and roles of the staff are impacted by the change (Marzano, Waters, & McNulty, 2003).

An example of discontinuous change in early intervention is implementing Robin McWilliam's Routines-Based Interview (RBI). It is a semistructured interviewing process

Reasons for Change

- A newly defined vision or direction
- A crisis
- A new mandate
- Data that supports the needed change; the right data at the right time
- Changing resources
- New information or ideas
- Old ways are not getting the needed or desired outcomes
- New leadership bringing different practices

with providers and family members that leads to the systematic development of functional IFSP outcomes. This change to use the RBI with fidelity is discontinuous because it involves a reorientation in the assessment process, including who will do it, how they will be trained, how proficiency will be reviewed, as well as how it will be used to guide the development of functional outcomes and subsequent intervention support and services. Families will need an explanation of what the RBI process involves. Because the RBI is tied to understanding a family's daily routines and activities as a way to determine useful and meaningful IFSP outcomes, based on family priorities, staff will need to understand why family routines are an important focus, what functional outcomes are, and how to write them. This will involve training and ongoing support to ensure implementation with fidelity and effectiveness. This may require changes in values, thinking, or learning new skills. There are other procedures and processes the staff has used previously in their work that will need to change as well to support use of the RBI as part of assessment with families.

Discontinuous change can also be thought of as systemic change, which needs leadership to move it along. Incremental change may only need a management decision and can then be easily implemented by individuals with a small amount of new instruction or support. Incremental change is often a management issue, whereas discontinuous change takes a stronger form of leadership to bring about the systemic, long-term, and complex changes.

POSSIBLE MISTAKES REGARDING CHANGE

One common mistake is not understanding the type of change needed for the task at hand. When thinking about a change and what support is needed, it is important to think about what is currently occurring, including what individuals believe, know, and do. Then think about what the desired future—with the change—will look like. How different is it from what is happening now? If the change involves reorientation or re-creation and is discontinuous, all the incremental changes in the world will not work in that situation. However, large change events can be broken down into smaller steps or tasks, some of which might be incremental in nature. This type of overall change will take time, energy, and leadership to support the envisioned future. In 1987, when IDEA law and regulations required that services to families be provided in home and community settings, as opposed to a clinic or segregated program settings, reorientation and re-creation as part of discontinuous change were necessary. There was an array of steps and activities required at many levels within the services system to effectively have providers working with families in homes and other community settings. Providers needed to drive to families rather than have families or buses transporting children. This alone resulted in adjustments to insurance rates, reimbursement rates for providers, and adjustments in the number of children that could be seen. The use of the physical space of the center or program that already existed needed to be reenvisioned. Each provider needed to learn new skills to focus on family members and not just on the child, as was often done in the clinic or center-based programs. Some of the new skills essential for effective implementation of the change conflicted with prior training and provider values. Each identified change seemed to cascade and uncover even more necessary change steps and activities.

Many people feel overwhelmed by the time and energy needed to bring about systemic change. They get lost spending time and energy on small tasks or pieces that do not really impact the whole picture. Some people might avoid the complex or more complicated tasks and do *anything* in order to feel like they are doing *something*, when in fact the *some things* may make the situation worse. For example, after listening to a workshop about gathering useful information from families, a provider might jump in and make up her own list of questions to ask the family and simply start using that without consulting other team members. However, without thoughtful consideration of the impact on team members and families, the well-intended change may result in team conflict and family confusion. The team members might not understand or embrace the importance of gathering information about family routines and activities. Families may also be confused with the reason for the questions and how the information they share will be used. Doing without applying careful thought to the system impact can essentially be a waste of time or, worse yet, disrupt coordinated efforts to implement change. Interestingly, the more changes leadership attempt to make that involve reorientation or re-creation, the less likely that leadership will be viewed as effective by the people directly affected by the change (Smale, 1998). This supports the personal nature of change in which people have a hard time implementing or doing things differently and often *blame* others who are *in charge* of the change. We continue to want things to get better but, at the same time, want them to remain the same.

A second mistake agency administration/leadership may make as they bring about any type of change is underestimating or not understanding the range of personal feelings and reactions from staff who will be affected by the changes. To be truly successful at implementing change, we need to remember that change does not happen without the *people* who are expected to do something in a new or different way. As an example, here is Sharon's experience.

> Sharon is the professional development coordinator and technical assistance provider for her agency. Nine months ago, the agency created two pilot teams to adopt a primary service provider approach with an emphasis on family coaching. They are now moving from two to four pilot implementation teams. Leadership has supported this initiative, training is in place, and some adaptations have been made based on feedback from the providers in the first two teams. During a training activity, one particular provider in the new group, Darcy, began constantly challenging Sharon, demanding more research and then adamantly demanding to know "who says this is a good idea." Sharon responded to the many questions with research and even examples of how positively things were working with the initial pilot teams. Darcy also had opportunities to talk with members of the initial pilot teams, yet she clearly continued to disapprove of the change. She shared her feelings with other members of her team and complained to the regional and state administration about how this approach would not work and how Sharon was a very poor trainer. Surprised by the amount of negative resistance, Sharon spoke to the program administrator about her concerns with Darcy. The program administrator invited Darcy for an informal conversation to find out her perspective. She invited Darcy to share what she was currently doing with families during home visits that she liked and asked probing but nonjudgmental questions such as, "What do you feel you are losing or being asked to give up?" and "What are you afraid of not being able to do once this new model is implemented?" This conversation revealed that Darcy felt she only knew how to provide direct therapy to the child and did not feel she had the skills to work effectively with families. She was afraid the rest of the team would see this and was afraid of losing their respect if she asked for help. This provider's negative energy was actually a way of hiding behind personal fear. This allowed the program administrator to explain Sharon's role and how Sharon could help her gain the necessary skills to feel competent and confident in her job. The administrator agreed that it was not more training Darcy needed but a safe environment with a family she had a good relationship with and one other team member she trusted to try out some of these ideas. Sharon would act as a coach to assist Darcy and the other team member. Even though this was not easy for Darcy, she began trying—with Sharon's assistance—new ideas and methods that had been presented. Gradually Darcy became successful with one family, and then after a few more months, she applied the new strategies with more families and began feeling more comfortable with the approach. The negativity stopped, and at team meetings, Darcy was supportive of others, shared her successes, and began to openly ask for help.

> ## Change Gets Personal:
> ## Common Reasons for Resisting Change
>
> 1. The change is not needed; I like it the way it is.
> 2. The change will make it more difficult; I will have to work harder.
> 3. The risks and efforts outweigh the benefits; I do not see any advantages to the change.
> 4. There is no basis for change; it is not based on what I know.
> 5. Change is pushed down; people advocating for the change do not have to do it.
> 6. We will likely end up back where we started; the change will not work here.
> 7. I do not have the skills they are talking about; I will look foolish.
>
> (Petrini & Hultman, 1995)

CONCERNS-BASED ADOPTION MODEL

Concerns-Based Adoption Model (CBAM) developed by Gene Hall, Shirley Horde, Susan Locks-Horsley, and Leslie Huling in the late 1970s was a series of stages with specific questions and a checklist to assess a teacher's readiness for adapting to changes in using new curriculum. The stages and questions are widely used today to help people understand the personal side of adapting to change. The seven stages of concern explain the experiences people deal with as they accept and invest themselves in the change effort. It serves as a framework for understanding—from a personal level—what a person might experience while adjusting to change as well as what the leadership level should anticipate and how they can help individuals move forward.

The seven stages of concern include awareness, information, personal, management, consequences, collaboration, and refocusing (Hall & Loucks, 1978). There is not always a simple linear progress from one stage to the next. More often, people go back and forth between stages or even get stuck in one particular stage for a while. As most change efforts, such as those in early intervention, involve more than one person, various people may be at different stages. For some people, they are thinking about the information for the first time, and some may have read and digested a lot of information and have a good working understanding of the details of the change itself. Others may be willing to jump in and try. Personality and preferred learning style also play a role in which stages might become sticking points, as certain individuals need more time at a particular stage than others. Looking closer at the seven stages defined by Hall and Loucks (1978), the following lists include comments or behaviors that help us understand where people might be in their process of understanding, strategies someone might use to help facilitate new levels of understanding, and a brief review of each stage.

1. AWARENESS

Comments

- What issue?

- I did not know we had a problem with [insert problem idea].

- I have never heard of this idea.

- I am not interested; I don't see a need this fits.

- I am too busy to think about this.

Strategies for Leadership

- Allow people time and an open environment for expression of feelings.

- Use active listening skills to hear and understand where a person is coming from.

- Provide information in an open, nonthreatening way.

- Try to find a real match between what a person does and how the change will improve the situation.

- State things in a simple and positive manner.

- Model new skills.

From a personal vantage point, this stage might better be described as *unawareness*. At this stage, it is important to acknowledge feelings and express them with respect. Keep an open mind and ask for more information—or a clarification—and a reason behind the proposed change. Listen as others explain. Ask for the kinds of information you feel you need.

2. INFORMATION

Comments

- I would like to know more about this.

- Tell me more.

- Describe this for me.

- What is the research?

- Whose idea is this and where is it coming from?

- What can we read (or see)?

- Who is already doing this?

Strategies for Leadership

- Be clear about what the change is and is not.

- Have a consistent message.

- Share information in a variety of ways.

- Use adult learning methods to give and share information.

- Do not overwhelm people with too much too soon.

- Involve staff in discussions.

- Create some learning communities in which people read written information or look at videos and can talk together about the information.

In the information stage, people are trying to listen and learn what the change means and truly is. They are trying to gather, learn, and explore what the change is, what it is not, and what it involves. Acknowledging adult learning styles is important at this step in order to recognize the way information should be provided. A one-shot workshop in which an expert is brought in to help staff understand what a change is will not be enough. Staff will need time and a variety of resources to explore the change, talk about it, learn about it, and share ideas and feelings. Providing staff with the necessary information does not necessarily mean everyone will "buy in." In fact, it is now that the next stage begins to emerge.

3. PERSONAL

Comments

- Wait! How will this impact me?
- What will my role be?
- I already have too much to do.
- I cannot do this.
- Why do we always change things?
- Families will not like this.
- Great idea!
- I really think this will work.
- How will we do this?
- Can I help?

Strategies for Leadership

- Allow time to listen to feelings without comment.
- Acknowledge the issues that may be identified.
- Acknowledge past strengths of individuals.
- Clarify how the change builds on what they already know and do.
- Talk about what will remain the same, not only what is changing.
- Form work teams to address issues.

At this stage, it is important to identify the real issues that need to be addressed. These can be discovered as people begin to talk. This stage is full of feelings and reactions, some of which may be negative. Anger, guilt, frustration, and worry about what others may think of them if they do or do not agree are common. On the other hand, there may be people who are enthusiastic, think it is a great idea, and want to jump right in. Leadership needs to be supportive and positive. By identifying the real issues, they can help move the group toward the next stage: *management*. Fear of not looking competent, fear of failure, or fear of being taken out of personal comfort zones may be a real factor behind personal reactions. As leaders move toward management, the ego support and group building of what they have accomplished in the past as well as building on individual personal strengths are important strategies to use.

4. MANAGEMENT

Comments

- How will I manage to do this?

- How does it fit with what I already do?

- What will I have to give up?

- What are you adding?

- Who will help me learn to do this?

- What kind of support will I get?

- Will my [team, schedule, families, job description] change? How?

- When does it start?

Strategies for Leadership

- Provide emotional support and listen.

- Suggest concrete ideas and alternatives.

- Answer questions as honestly as you can.

- If there is no answer yet, then allow staff to suggest ideas.

- Continue to provide information focused on some of their specific questions.

- Have learning communities continue and begin to discuss and suggest options for the details.

In the management stage, individuals are trying to figure out how they will manage—or implement—a new idea along with their other (already existing) responsibilities. For leaders, it may often seem like staff are focusing on little details. They are! Remember, it is important to involve staff in making at least some of the decisions. They may need to be provided with more information or shown the *how*. As a leader, if you do not have all the answers yet, it is vital to let staff know their questions will be addressed. Reassure them that you are listening and will allow them to help make appropriate decisions.

5. CONSEQUENCES

Comments

- Who says we have to do this?

- What happens if I wait it out?

- Who will actually supervise me and how will they see if I am doing this or not?

- The old way is better.

- Who is responsible?

- I am not convinced it is worth it.

Strategies for Leadership

- Listen to and acknowledge all feelings.

- Be clear about who is in charge.

- Explain timelines and expectations of what and when changes will happen.

- Calmly state the consequences, both positive and negative, of the implementation of the change.

- Explain who is there to help, mentor, and supervise.

The consequences stage is often when road blocks surface. Individuals weigh the repercussions of what will happen if they do change with the benefits of remaining the same. "I'll just wait it out" and "It seems like they always talk about something but never do it" are real feelings that may or may not be expressed out loud. Individuals may defend the old way as better and ask the leader why the change is necessary and why the new way is better. Sometimes staff may try to sabotage the effort by speaking poorly about the person they see as the change agent to colleagues. They may also divert time and energy away from the change effort by bringing up other issues or problems or sticking to one detail they do not like. If individuals decide the consequences of the change are not important enough or are too hard, they may try to convince others to join their "nonchange" camp. This is when people often sort themselves into the early adaptors or later adaptors, the laggards or the opponents (Smale, 1996). It is important for leadership to think positively about people but be prepared to help them immediately if road blocks appear. Addressing personal issues individually and as quickly as possible often prevents negativity from taking over. Negativity spreads faster than enthusiasm; when systemic change is on the table, it is certain to shake up the status quo.

6. COLLABORATION

Comments

- Who can work with me on this?

- I would like to try this but will need help.

- Can I watch someone who knows how to do this?

- Can the team meet more often so we can see how this is working?

- What else can we read (or who else can we talk to) from people who have done this before?

Strategies for Leadership

- Be on the ground with the people who are trying to do the change.

- Acknowledge strengths and partnerships of people working together.

- Give real, everyday examples of what you see as working.

- Teach, model, and suggest new skills and actions that can be used.

- Use consultation and coaching to build staff confidence.

- Provide feedback loops to allow people to talk, identify issues, and work on solutions together.

In the collaboration stage, individuals are trying things out and beginning to implement some of the defined changes as they make the change happen for themselves and for the groups they work with. As the name suggests, the people who are implementing the change are working together with leadership, trainers, coaches, and other team members. It is important to keep communication lines open between all groups so that training needs and other issues can be identified and addressed as soon as possible.

7. REFOCUSING

Comments

- Things are going pretty well.

- This might improve what we thought would work.

- Here is a new idea.

- This seems to work better in this situation.

- I see a new issue we need to look at.

Strategies for Leadership

- Keep a focus on the change efforts and innovations.

- Acknowledge what is working, letting staff share their successes.

- Use a variety of data to document what is working.

- Facilitate discussion to identify new needs and potential solutions.

- Continue to provide updated information, training, and support for the change efforts.

- Make sure adequate resources are in place to sustain the changes.

Refocusing may be necessary to help adapt ideas to fit both the individual and the agency, and it will involve honest discussion, collected data, reflection, feedback, and trying again. If the change is to be sustained and not be simply a few "pilot efforts" or only happen with an initial group, then the importance of time spent in collaboration and refocusing is critical and cannot be stressed enough. While holding on to the original vision, mission, and the necessary practices implicit in the approach, day-to-day operations of a specific practice may need to be reexamined and then adjusted to make it fit for a particular provider, family, or program. We talk more about implementation a bit later in this chapter. (Now complete Give It a Go! 10.3.)

ORGANIZATIONAL SUPPORT FOR CHANGE

Many of the changes suggested in this book will need leadership and support from the organization if they are to be implemented and sustained over time. Some organizations are more nurturing and supportive of continuous learning and improvement than others. These organizations will often have the best outcomes when implementing and sustaining systemic change. Organizations that have open communication channels between staff and administration and that have a stated vision or clear purpose that is understood and

GIVE IT A GO! 10.3.

Think about a change you have been asked to make in your early intervention program and write it here.

_____
_____
_____

Identify the stages that you experienced. List those stages here.

_____
_____
_____

Were there particular stages that were more difficult for you than others? Which ones and why?

_____
_____
_____

How did you (or did you not) move forward? What did you need and how was it provided?

_____
_____
_____
_____

followed are often in a better position to implement and sustain change. Another helpful strategy is demonstrating respect for everyone at all levels of the organization, seeing work as collaborative rather than competitive, and encouraging innovations and change. Other characteristics of organizations that are successful in helping new ideas to be explored and implemented include having built-in structures for continuous learning, allowing equal sharing of ideas, providing supervision as a personal growth opportunity (not as punitive feedback), and using relationship-based practices that build on trust and support.

Individuals who work for an organization and are going to learn to do something new need a work environment in which they feel supported and not judged or belittled for what they do not know or try. They need an environment that is motivating and has a "can do" mentality. They need to feel valued in what they are currently doing. They need a basic understanding of all new tasks and responsibilities and how the changes impact their current work. They will need to see progress in incremental steps and activities of change and to be involved in discussions and decisions that will directly impact their work. They also need to know who will answer questions, who will help them with practical applications, and who will provide them with support and help in all their endeavors.

For systemic change, organized leadership needs to emerge. "In education readiness for change is something that needs to be developed, nurtured and sustained. Readiness is not a preexisting condition waiting to be found or an enduring characteristic of a person, organization or system" (Fixsen, Blasé, Horner, & Sugai, 2009, p. 1). Leaders need to know the elements of their system and think in whole pictures as well as be able to identify the smaller, critical aspects of the system. Included here is a list of other necessary leadership responsibilities associated with change (Scholtes, 1998):

Actions Leaders Take that Promote Change

- Have a clear vision of the desired end state
- Understand the variability of the work needed to bring about the desired change in planning and problem solving
- Understand adult learning styles
- Establish true learning communities
- Know their staff
- Give vision, direction, and focus to the work at hand
- Be an excellent communicator

If one particular person in a leadership capacity does not have all the skills necessary, then leadership can be shared among the staff that have one or more of the desired skills for leading systematic change. The leadership team can be charged with the responsibility to lead the entire change initiative. Leadership for a particular change—such as those indicated in this book—does not have to be the sole responsibility of one person, such as the agency director or the regional or state Part C coordinator. However, these individuals do need to support the change effort and certainly be part of the team. Leadership can also emerge from a group of committed stakeholders who together share the skills and abilities needed to bring the change about and support it. (Complete Give It a Go! 10.4.)

Actions Leaders Take that Stifle Change

- Regard any idea or suggestion from below with suspicion
- Insist that people must have your approval before starting anything
- Set up layers of management for individuals to go through before they can act
- Treat identified problems as a sign of failure
- Control everything carefully
- Do not ask for staff input about reorganization that will affect them, just tell them
- Make decisions alone and then spring these on staff
- Keep communication open only to higher management
- Believe that he or she already knows everything important

GIVE IT A GO! 10.4.

Considering the information you have read so far, describe the following:

1. Your agency's ability to foster change

   Describe the climate.

   _____
   _____
   _____

   What does it do to support change?

   _____
   _____
   _____

   Where might it improve?

   _____
   _____
   _____

2. The leadership at all levels within your organization

   Are they the people hired into this position or someone else you see with influence and skills?

   _____
   _____
   _____

   What do these leaders do or not do that supports change?

   _____
   _____
   _____

3. Think of yourself

   How do you rate yourself in accepting change and doing things differently?

   _____
   _____
   _____

   Do you see yourself as a leader?

   _____
   _____
   _____

   What is it that you personally need to make some of this book's ideas happen for you?

   _____
   _____
   _____

ADOPTING A PARTICULAR APPROACH
WITHIN A PROGRAM, REGION, OR STATE

If you are adopting the mission, vision, and foundational principles in this book and its many applied practices or are adopting a particular approach within an agency, regional program, or throughout an entire state, there are a number of helpful resources available. The work of Dean Fixsen, Karen Blasé, and colleagues at the National Implementation Research Network (NIRN) as well as the Center for State Implementation and the State Implementation and Scaling-Up of Evidence-Based Practices (SISEP) Center provide the field with valuable resources to help leadership understand, plan, and address the many challenges faced at the program, regional, or state level. These can be found on their web sites at http://nirn .fpg.unc.edu and http://sisep.fpg.unc.edu. Accountability for creating readiness rests with the leadership/implementation team, not with those who are expected or invited to change.

This chapter concludes with a description of two important frameworks from the work of SISEP. These are *implementation stages* and *implementation drivers*. As technical assistance staff began assisting states with putting new service delivery systems in place and the many new practices that come with that change, they realized that state teams needed more information about the implementation stages and drivers as well as how to organize the change efforts to get the work done and sustain it over time.

National Early Childhood Technical Assistance Center staff, Pletcher and Hurth, in collaboration with Karen Blasé of SISEP, developed a document that has been used by many of the states implementing change in their service delivery approach. The document of the stages outlines some implementation considerations, steps, and important tasks that need to be done.

1. Explore service delivery approaches with stakeholders
   ◦ Articulate desired mission
   ◦ Compare approaches
   ◦ Describe the desired changes for the state
   ◦ Begin discussions about how to implement, evaluate, and sustain

2. Build support and commitment, and advocate for change with a clear message
   ◦ Secure leadership support
   ◦ Develop communication plan
   ◦ Develop message and public materials

3. Develop an implementation (change) plan
   ◦ Build an implementation team
   ◦ Determine systems support
   ◦ Build training and TA capacity
   ◦ Determine how to begin . . . (pilots, regions, all programs)
   ◦ Draft implementation (change) plan

4. Put plan into action
   ◦ Adapt or adjust infrastructure
   ◦ Begin training and TA activities
   ◦ Begin the service delivery changes with determined groups
   ◦ Fully implement
   ◦ Provide adequate oversight and ongoing support

5. Assure sustainability
   ◦ Maintain and expand support base
   ◦ Continue infrastructure and fiscal support
   ◦ Continue TA for fidelity to the approach
   ◦ Evaluate for fidelity and quality
   (Pletcher & Hurth, 2011)

The full document can be found at http://ectacenter.org/waproject/splash.asp.

Implementation drivers are the basic components of the infrastructure needed to support the practice, organization, and systems undergoing change. Of course, to drive the change, all aspects of *what* the change is have to be clearly defined and understood, hence the exploration support-building aspects of the implementation stages. The drivers have been defined based on research of the commonalities among successful program implementation (Fixsen, Naoom, Blasé, Friedman, & Wallace, 2005; Fixsen, Blasé, Duda, Naoom, & Wallace, 2009). The drivers include structures at all levels of the system, from local up through state, needed to support the change in provider practices. They are represented in Figure 10.1.

Organizational drivers intentionally develop support and sustain the new practices. These include features such as data systems that support decisions and facilitative leadership to use the data to make decisions and adjustments, address challenges, and create solutions. Organizational drivers also address systems intervention, which includes strategies to make sure that both fiscal and human resources are available to support the work of the new practices. In Part C, some system components such as data systems, general supervision, memorandums of agreement, lead agency structures, fiscal practices, work of the interagency coordinating councils' policies and procedures, and comprehensive systems of personal development might need to be better aligned to address the changes.

Competency drivers are the components used to develop, improve, and sustain the practices. They also make sure these practices have the desired effect for families and

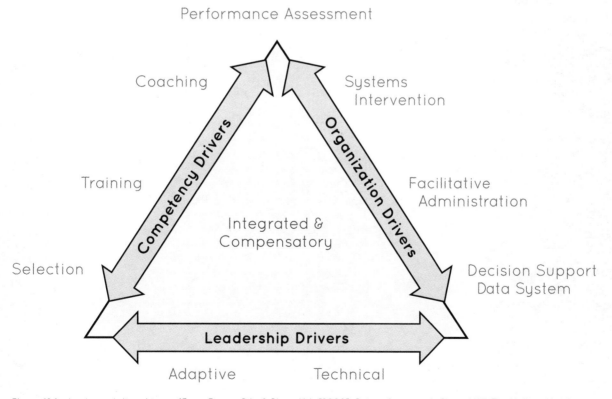

Figure 10.1.   Implementation drivers. (From Fixsen, D.L., & Blase, K.A. [2008]. *Drivers framework*. Chapel Hill: The National Implementation Research Network, Frank Porter Graham Child Development Institute, University of North Carolina; adapted by permission.)

children. The competency drivers include selection of staff that has the needed skills, training of staff that does not, coaching and consulting of staff as they begin the implementation, mentoring over time, and performance assessment.

The third driver is the leadership driver, which was discussed previously. These are all the qualities, climates, and skills needed by both adaptive and technical leaders and leadership teams to shepherd the various systems through multiple years of work. The three drivers support the performance fidelity of the staff to implement the chosen practices so that there are improved outcomes for children and families.

This complex work takes time and energy at the program, regional, or state level. Is it worth it to support local providers, like Cyndi, to use more current evidence-based practices such as those this book describes? Perhaps the ultimate value of changing a state-wide service delivery approach can best be summarized by the Part C state coordinator for Missouri, Pam Thomas, who has worked for more than 5 years now, through the implementation stages and through redesigning her system of support, as her state adopted a particular approach to delivering services to infants and toddlers with disabilities and their families. When she spoke at an OSEP National Early Childhood Meeting to her own colleagues in 2009, she challenged the group with these words:

> This is no easy task to implement change in practice consistently across the state. This will take years. You must plan carefully and make that plan known throughout the state to a variety of people. It is hard but exciting work that really is never finished. To know we will have service providers using practices that have years of research and evidence supporting them, based on values and beliefs we feel are fundamental and that all families across our state will receive services and supports consistently no matter where they live, will be worth it in the end.

References

Annual Performance Plan. (2011). In NECTAC, Part C, SPP/APR, Indicator Analyses (FFY 2009). Retrieved from http://www.nectac.org/~pdfs/partc/part-c_sppapr_11.pdf#page=12

Bagnato, S.J., Neisworth, J.T., & Munson, S.M. (1997). *Linking assessment and early intervention: An authentic curriculum-based approach.* Baltimore, MD: Paul H. Brookes Publishing Co.

Bailey, D.B., Raspa, M., & Fox, L. (2012). What is the future of family outcomes and family-centered services? *Topics in Early Childhood Special Education, 31*(1), 216–223.

Barr, D., & Cochran, M. (1992, June). Understanding and supporting empowerment: Redefining the professional role. *Networking Bulletin: Empowerment and Family Support, 2*(3), 1–8.

Barrera, I., & Corso, R.M. (2002). Cultural competence as skilled dialog. *Topics in Early Childhood Special Education, 22*(2), 103–113.

Beach Center on Disability. (2008, February). *Policy advisory: Comparison of IDEA Part C and Part B.* Lawrence: The University of Kansas Beach Center on Disability. Retrieved from http://www.beachcenter.org/Wisdom/ParentRights/Wisdom_PolicyAdvisory1Comparison_Feb08.pdf

Bernheimer, L.P., & Keogh, B.K. (1995). Weaving interventions into the fabric of everyday life: An approach to family assessment. *Topics in Early Childhood Special Education, 15*(4), 415–433.

Beverly, C.L., & Thomas, S.B. (1999). Family assessment and collaboration building: Conjoined process. *International Journal of Disability, Development and Education, 46*(2), 179–197.

Bridges, W. (1991). *Managing transitions: Making the most of change.* Reading, MA: Addison-Wesley Publishing Company.

Bridges, W. (2004). *Transitions: Making sense of life's changes* (2nd ed.). Cambridge, MA: First Da Capo Press.

Bronfenbrenner, U. (1975). Is early intervention effective? In G.B. Friedlander, G. Sterritt, & G. Kirk (Eds.), *Exceptional infant: Assessment and intervention* (Vol. 3, pp. 449–475). New York, NY: Brunner/Mazel.

Bronfenbrenner, U. (1979). *The ecology of human development.* Cambridge, MA: Harvard University Press.

Bronfenbrenner, U. (1992). Ecological systems theory. In R. Vasta (Ed.), *Six theories of child development: Revised formulations and current issues* (pp. 187–249). Philadelphia, PA: Jessica Kingsley.

Brookfield, S.D. (1986). *Understanding and facilitating adult learning.* San Francisco, CA: Jossey-Bass.

Campbell, P.H. (1997). *Services for young children and their families in their homes and communities.* Philadelphia, PA: Temple University Press.

Campbell, P.H., Sawyer, B., & Muhlenhapt, M. (2009). The meaning of natural environments for parents and professionals. *Infants and Young Children, 22*(4), 264–278.

Department of the Army, Educational and Developmental Intervention Services and Comprehensive System of Personnel Development. (2013). *Individualized family service plan process document: Linking early intervention processes.* Retrieved from http://projects.fpg.unc.edu/~eco/assets/pdfs/IFSPPDHandbook5May2013finaldraft.pdf

Dinnebeil, L.A., Hale, L., & Rule, S. (1999). Early intervention program practices that support collaboration. *Topics in Early Childhood Special Education, 19*(4), 225–235.

Dunst, C.J. (2000). Everyday children's learning opportunities: Characteristics and consequences. *Children's Learning Opportunities Report, 2*(1). Retrieved from http://www.everydaylearning.info/reports/lov2-1.pdf

Dunst, C.J. (2004). An integrated framework for practicing early childhood intervention and family support. *Perspectives in Education, 22*(2), 1–16.

Dunst, C.J. (2006). Parent-mediated everyday child learning opportunities: Foundations and operations. *CASEinPoint, 2*(2). Retrieved from http://www.fippcase.org/caseinpoint/caseinpoint_vol2_no2.pdf

Dunst, C.J., & Bruder, M.B. (1999, December/2000, January). Expanding learning opportunities for infants and toddlers in natural environments: A chance to reconceptualize early intervention. *ZERO TO THREE, 20*(3), pp. 34–36.

Dunst, C.J., Bruder, M.B., Trivette, C.M., Hamby, D., Raab, M., & McLean, M. (2001). Characteristics and consequences of everyday natural learning opportunities. *Topics in Early Childhood Special Education, 21*(2), 68–92.

Dunst, C.J., Johanson, C., Trivette, C.M., & Hamby, D. (1991). Family-oriented early intervention policies and practices: Family-centered or not? *Exceptional Children, 58*(2), 115–126.

Dunst, C.J., Raab, M., Trivette, C., & Swanson, J. (2010). Community-based everyday child learning opportunities. In R.A. McWilliams (Ed.), *Working with families of young children with special needs* (pp. 60–92). New York, NY: Guilford Press.

Dunst, C.J., & Trivette, C.M. (1994). What is effective helping? In C.J. Dunst, C.M. Trivette, & A.G. Deal (Eds.), *Supporting and strengthening families: Methods, strategies and practice* (pp. 162–170). Cambridge, MA: Brookline Books.

Dunst, C.J., & Trivette C.M. (1996). Empowerment, effective helping practices and family-centered care. *Pediatric Nursing, 22,* 334–337.

Dunst, C.J., & Trivette, C.M. (2005). Characteristics and consequences of family-centered helping practices. *CASEMakers, 1*(6). Retrieved from http://www.fipp.org/Collateral/casemakers/casemakers_vol1_no6.pdf

Dunst, C.J., & Trivette, C.M. (2009). Capacity-building family systems intervention practice. *Journal of Family Social Work, 12,* 119–143.

Dunst, C.J., Trivette, C.M., & Deal, A.G. (1988). *Enabling and empowering families: Principles and guidelines for practice.* Cambridge, MA: Brookline Books.

Dunst, C.J., Trivette, C.M., & Hamby, D. (2008). *Research synthesis and meta-analysis of studies of family-centered practice.* Ashville, NC: Winterberry Press.

Dunst, C.J., Trivette, C.M., & Johanson, C. (1994). Parent professional collaboration and partnership. In C.J. Dunst, C.M. Trivette, & A.G. Deal (Eds.), *Supporting and strengthening families: Methods, strategies, and practice* (pp. 197–211). Cambridge, MA: Brookline Books.

Farson, R. (1996). *Management of the absurd.* New York, NY: Touchstone Books.

Federal Register of September 28, 2011, 76–188, Rules and Regulations, 34 CFR §§ 303.26, 303.321.

Fixsen, D.L., & Blasé, K.A. (2008). *Drivers framework.* Chapel Hill, NC: The National Implementation Research Network, Frank Porter Graham Child Development Institute, University of North Carolina.

Fixsen, D.L., Blasé, K., Duda, M., Naoom, S., & Wallace, F. (2009). Core implementation components. *Research on Social Work Practice, 19,* 531–540.

Fixsen, D.L., Blasé, K., Horner, R., & Sugai, G. (2009). Scaling-up brief: Readiness for change. *FPG Child Development Institute, 3.* Chapel Hill, NC: State Implementation & Scaling-Up of Evidence-Based Practices, University of North Carolina, Chapel Hill.

Fixsen, D.L., Naoom, S.F., Blasé, K.A., Friedman, R.M., & Wallace, F. (2005). *Implementation research: A synthesis of the literature.* Tampa, FL: National Implementation Research Network, Louis de la Parte Florida Mental Health Institute, University of South Florida.

Friedman, M., Woods, J., & Salisbury, C. (2012). Caregiver coaching strategies for early intervention providers: Moving toward operational definitions. *Infants and Young Children, 25*(1), 62–82.

Gallagher, J.J., Danaher, J.C., & Clifford, R.M. (2009). The evolution of the national early childhood technical assistance center. *Topics in Early Childhood Special Education, 29*(1), 7–23.

Gallwey, T. (2000). *The inner game of work.* New York, NY: Random House.

Garguilo, R.M., & Kilgo, J.L. (2000). *Young children with special needs.* Albany, NY: Delmar Thompson Learning.

Garmston, R., & Wellman, B. (1998). *The adaptive schools: Developing and facilitating collaborative groups.* El Dorado, CA: Four Hats Seminars.

Hagan, J.F., Shaw, J.S., & Duncan, P.M. (Eds.). (2008). *Bright futures: Guidelines for health supervision of infants, children, and adolescents* (3rd ed.). Elk Grove Village, IL: American Academy of Pediatrics. Retrieved from http://brightfutures.aap.org/pdfs/Guidelines_PDF/1-BF-Introduction.pdf

Hall, G., & Loucks, S. (1978). Teacher concerns as a basis for facilitating and personalizing staff development. *Teacher College Record, 80*(1), 36–53.

Hanft, B.E., & Pilkington, K.O. (2000). Therapy in natural environments: The means or end goal for early intervention? *Infants and Young Children, 12*(4), 1–13.

Hanft, B.E., Rush, D.D., & Shelden, M.L. (2004). *Coaching families and colleagues in early childhood.* Baltimore, MD: Paul H. Brookes Publishing Co.

Harrower, J.K., Fox, L., Dunlap, G., & Kincaid, D. (2001). Functional assessment and comprehensive early intervention. *Exceptionality, 8*(3), 189–204.

Hobbs, N., Dokecki, P.R., Hoover-Dempsey, K.V., Moroney, R.M., Shayne, M.W., & Weeks, K.H. (1984). *Strengthening families.* San Francisco, CA: Jossey-Bass.

Hord, S., Rutherford, W., Huling-Austin, L., & Hall, G. (1998). *Taking charge of change.* Austin, TX: Southwest Educational Development Laboratory.

Hurth, J., & Goff, P. (2002). *Assuring the family's role on the early intervention team: Explaining rights and safeguards.* Chapel Hill, NC: The National Early Childhood Technical Assistance Center. Retrieved from http://www.nectac.org/~pdfs/pubs/assuring.pdf

Individuals with Disabilities Education Improvement Act (IDEA) of 1990, PL 101-476.

Individuals with Disabilities Education Improvement Act (IDEA) of 2004, PL 108-446, 20 U.S.C. §§ 1400 et seq.

Jung, L.A. (2003). More is better: Maximizing natural learning opportunities. *Young Exceptional Children, 6*(3), 21–26.

Jung, L.A. (2007). Writing individualized family service plan strategies that fit into the ROUTINE. *Young Exceptional Children, 10,* 2–9.

Keilty, B. (2010). *The early intervention guidebook for families and professionals: Partnering for success.* New York, NY: Teachers College Press.

Kelly, J.F., & Barnard, K.E. (1999). Parent education within a relationship-focused model. *Topics in Early Childhood Education, 19*(3), 151–157.

Knowles, M. (1980). *The modern practice of adult education* (rev. ed.). Chicago, IL: Association Press/Follett.

Knowles, M.S., Holton, E.F., & Swanson, R.A. (1998). *The adult learner: The definitive classic in adult education and human resource development* (5th ed.). Woburn, MA: Butterworth-Heinemann.

Lara, A. (2003). *How to stay motivated during difficult times* (p. 46). The Cuban Guy.com. Retrieved from http://www.scribd.com/doc/22812562/How-to-Stay-Motivated-During-Difficult-Times

Lucas, A., Gillaspy, K., Peters, M.L., & Hurth, J. (2012). *Enhancing recognition of high-quality, functional IFSP outcomes and IEP goals: A training activity for infant and toddler service providers and ECSE teachers.* Retrieved from http://www.ectacenter.org/~pdfs/pubs/rating-ifsp-iep-training.pdf

Lynch, E.L., & Hanson, M.J. (Eds.). (2004). *Developing cross-cultural competence: A guide for working with children and their families* (3rd ed.). Baltimore, MD: Paul H. Brookes Publishing Co.

Markova, D. (1996). *The open mind.* San Francisco, CA: Conari Press.

Martini, M. (2002, February/March). How mothers in four American cultural groups shape infant learning during mealtimes. *ZERO TO THREE, 22*(4), pp. 14–20.

Marzano, R.J., Waters, T., & McNulty, B. (2003). *School leadership that works: From research to results.* Alexandria, VA: Association for Supervision and Curriculum Development.

Mayhew, L., Scott, S., & McWilliam, R.A. (1999). Project INTEGRATE: A training and resource guide for speech language pathologists. Chapel Hill, NC: Frank Porter Graham Child Development Center University of North Carolina at Chapel Hill.

McWilliam, R.A. (2004). *Enhancing service in natural environments.* Retrieved from http://ectacenter.org/~pdfs/calls/2004/partcsettings/mcwilliam.pdf

McWilliam, R.A. (2010a). Assessing families' needs with the routines-based interview. In R.A. McWilliam (Ed.), *Working with families of young children with special needs* (pp. 27–59). New York, NY: Guilford Press.

McWilliam, R.A. (2010b). *Routines-based early intervention: Supporting young children and their families.* Baltimore, MD: Paul H. Brookes Publishing Co.

National Center for Family-Centered Care. (1998). *Family-centered care for children with special health care needs.* Bethesda, MD: Association for the Care of Children's Health. Retrieved from http://www.familyvoices.org/admin/work_family_centered/files/FCCare.pdf

National Early Childhood Technical Assistance Center (NECTAC). (2011). Part C, SPP/APR, Indicator Analyses (FFY 2009). Retrieved from http://www.nectac.org/~pdfs/partc/part-c_sppapr_11.pdf

National Scientific Council on the Developing Child. (2004). *Young children develop in an environment of relationships.* Waltham, MA: Heller School for Social Policy and Management, Brandeis University.

National Scientific Council on the Developing Child. (2010). *Early experiences can alter gene expression and affect long-term development.* (Unpublished paper, no. 10). Retrieved from http://www.developingchild.net

Norman-Murch, T. (1996, October/November). Reflective supervision as a vehicle for individual and organizational development. *ZERO TO THREE, 17*(2), pp. 1–7.

Office of Special Education and Rehabilitative Services Department of Education. (2008, October 28). Early intervention program for infants and toddlers with disabilities. 34 CFR, Part 303.

Parlakian, R. (2001). *Look, listen, and learn: Reflective supervision and relationship-based work.* Washington, DC: ZERO TO THREE Press.

Pawl, J.H., & Milburn, L.A. (2006). Family- and relationship-centered principles and practices. In G.M. Foley & J.D. Hochman (Eds.), *Mental health in early intervention achieving unity in principles and practice* (pp. 191–226). Baltimore, MD: Paul H. Brookes Publishing Co.

Petrini, C., & Hultman, K.E. (1995). Scaling the wall of resistance. *Training & Development, 49,* 15–18.

Pletcher, L.C. (1997). *Family-centered practices: A training guide.* Chapel Hill, NC: ARCH National Resource Center.

Pletcher, L., & Hurth, J. (2011, December). *Implementing and sustaining an effective service delivery approach: Steps and stages.* NECTAC. Retrieved from http://www.nectac.org/effectiveservicedelivery/splash.asp

Pletcher, L.C., & McBride, S. (2000). *Family-centered services: Guiding principles and practices for delivery of family-centered services.* Des Moines, IA: Iowa Department of Education.

Quinn, R. (1996). *Discovering the leader within.* San Francisco, CA: Jossey-Bass.

Robinson, K. (2011). *Out of our minds: Learning to be creative.* London, UK: Capstone Press.

RRCP-NECTAC-ITCA-OSEP Orientation Committee. (2009, November 13). *At-a-glance introduction to IDEA Part C for new Part C coordinators.* Retrieved from http://www.tadnet.org/uploads/File/At-A-Glance.doc

Rush, D., & Shelden, M.L. (2005). Evidence-based definition of coaching practices. *CASEinPoint, 1*(6), 1–6. Retrieved from http://www.fipp.org/Collateral/caseinpoint/caseinpoint_vol1_no6.pdf

Rush, D.R., & Shelden, M.L. (2011). *The early childhood coaching handbook.* Baltimore, MD: Paul H. Brookes Publishing Co.

Sanchez, S., & Thorp, E. (2008). Teaching to transform: Infusing cultural and linguistic diversity. In P. Winton, J. McCollum, & C. Catlett (Eds.), *Practical approaches to early childhood professional development: Evidence, strategies and resources* (pp. 81–97). Washington, DC: ZERO TO THREE Press.

Scholtes, P.R. (1998). *The leader's handbook: A guide to inspiring your people and managing the daily workflow.* New York, NY: McGraw-Hill.

Senge, P.M. (1990). *The fifth discipline: The art and practice of the learning organization.* New York, NY: Doubleday Currency.

Shelden, M.L., & Rush, D.D. (2009). Practical applications of early childhood and family support practices. *Family, Infant and Preschool Program (FIPP) BriefCase, 2*(1). Retrieved from http://eipd.vcu.edu/html/tips_techniques-IFSP_BC_V2_N1.html

Shelden, M.L., & Rush, D.D. (2010). A primary-coach approach to teaming and supporting families in early childhood intervention. In R.A. McWilliams (Ed.), *Working with families of young children with special needs* (pp. 175–202). New York, NY: Guilford Press.

Shonkoff, J.P., & Phillips, D.A. (Eds.). (2000). *From neurons to neighborhoods: The science of early childhood development.* Washington, DC: National Academy Press.

Smale, G. (1996). *Mapping change and innovation.* London, UK: HMSO Publications Centre.

Smale, G. (1998). *Managing change through innovation.* London, UK: Stationery Office.

Smith, J.D., & Polloway, E.A. (1995). Patterns of deinstitutionalization and community placement: A dream deferred or lost? *Education and Training in Mental Retardation and Developmental Disabilities 30*(4), 321–328.

Thomas, P. (2009, December). Presentation at OSEP National Early Childhood Meeting, Arlington, VA.

Vacca, J.J. (2001). Promoting positive infant-caregiver attachment: The role of early interventionist and recommendations for parent training. *Infants and Young Children, 13*(4), 1–10.

Wasik, B.H., Bryant, D.M., & Lyons, C.M. (1990). *Home visiting: Procedures for helping families.* Newbury Park, CA: Sage Publications.

Westby, C., Burda, A., & Mehta, Z. (2003, April 29). Asking the right questions in the right ways: Strategies for ethnographic interviewing. *The ASHA Leader.* Retrieved from http://asha.org/Publications/leader/2003/030429/f030429b.htm

Whitmore, E., & Kerans, P. (1988). Participation, empowerment and welfare. *Canadian Review of Social Policy, 22,* 51–60.

Wilson, L.L., & Dunst, C.J. (2005). Checklist for assessing adherence to family-centered practices. *CASEtools, 1*(1). Center for the Advanced Study of Excellence in Early Childhood and Family Support Practices, Morganton, NC. Retrieved from http://www.fippcase.org/casetools/casetools_vol1_no1.pdf

Woodruff, G., & McGonigel, M.J. (1988). Early intervention team approaches: The transdisciplinary model. In J. Jordan, J. Gallagher, P. Hutinger, & M. Karnes (Eds.), *Early childhood special education: Birth to three* (pp. 163–182). Reston, VA: Council for Exceptional Children.

Workgroup on Principles and Practices in Natural Environments. (2007). *Mission and principles for providing services in natural environments.* OSEP TA Community of Practices-Part C Settings. Retrieved from http://www.nectac.org/topics/families/famctrprin.asp

Workgroup on Principles and Practices in Natural Environments. (2008, February). Agreed-upon practices for providing services in natural environments. OSEP TA Community of Practice-Part C Settings. Retrieved from http://www.ectacenter.org/~pdfs/topics/families/AgreedUponPractices_FinalDraft2_01_08.pdf

Zhang, C., & Bennett, T. (2003). Facilitating the meaningful participation of culturally and linguistically diverse families in the IFSP and IEP process. *Focus on Autism and Other Developmental Disabilities, 18*(1), 51–59.

Helpful Resources

BOOKS

Hall, G.E., & Hord, S.M. (2011). *Implementing change: Patterns, principles and potholes* (3rd ed.). Upper Saddle River, NJ: Pearson.

Hanft, B.E., Rush, D.D., & Shelden, M.L. (2004). *Coaching families and colleagues in early childhood.* Baltimore, MD: Paul H. Brookes Publishing Co.

Halle, T., Mertz, A., & Martinez-Beck, I. (2013). *Applying implementation science in early childhood programs and systems.* Baltimore, MD: Paul H. Brookes Publishing Co.

Keilty, B. (2010). *The early intervention guidebook for families and professionals.* New York, NY: Teachers College Press.

McWilliam, R.A. (2010). *Routines-based early intervention: Supporting young children and their families.* Baltimore, MD: Paul H. Brookes Publishing Co.

McWilliam, R.A. (Ed.). (2010). *Working with families of young children with special needs.* New York, NY: Guilford Press.

Rush, D.R., & Shelden, M.L. (2011). *The early childhood coaching handbook.* Baltimore, MD: Paul H. Brookes Publishing Co.

Shelden, M.L., & Rush, D.D. (2013). *The early intervention teaming handbook: The primary service provider approach.* Baltimore, MD: Paul H. Brookes Publishing Co.

ON THE WEB

Model/Approach Developers

Carl Dunst and Carol Trivette

- http://www.puckett.org/index.php
- http://www.evidencebasedpractices.org
- http://www.ceecenc.org
- http://www.innovativepractices.org
- http://www.communitylinkages.org
- http://www.practicalevaluation.org

Dathan Rush and M'Lisa Shelden

- http://www.coachinginearlychildhood.org/coaches.php
- http://www.fipp.org
- http://www.fipp.org/Collateral/casetools/casetools_vol2_no1.pdf
  - Checklist for Promoting Parent-Mediated Everyday Child Learning Opportunities

- http://www.fipp.org/Collateral/casetools/casetools_vol2_no4.pdf
  - Assets-Based Context Matrix: An Assessment Tool for Developing Contextually Based Child Outcomes
- http://www.fipp.org/Collateral/briefcase/briefcase_vol2_no1.pdf
  - Tips and Techniques for Developing Participation-Based IFSP Outcome Statements (2009)

Juliann Woods

- http://tactics.fsu.edu
- http://facets.lsi.ku.edu
- http://fgrbi.fsu.edu

On these sites, look for resources to use with families, including "Meet the Family: A One-Page Tool to Help Families Know What to Expect during the Initial Home Visit" (FGRBI), "Do the Math: Who Practices Speech More?" (FGRBI), and "Routine-Based Assessment in the Child's Natural Environments."

Pip Campbell

- http://jeffline.jefferson.edu/cfsrp

Robin McWilliam

- http://www.siskin.org/www/docs/4/research
- http://naturalenvironments.blogspot.com
- http://www.youtube.com/watch?v=zUwcRFgbdYk
- http://www.siskin.org/downloads/Ecomap_Development_Checklist.pdf
  - Ecomapping checklist
- http://www.siskin.org/downloads/RBIImplementationChecklistCriticalItemsBOLD.pdf
  - Routines-based interview checklist
- http://www.siskin.org/downloads/RBI_Report_Form.pdf
  - RBI report form
- http://www.siskin.org/downloads/Examples_of_Functional_Child_Outcomes.pdf
  - Examples of functional outcomes

Center Resources

Center for the Advanced Study of Excellence (CASE). The following list includes the Family Infant Preschool Program (FIPP) bibliography of research articles and briefs regarding effective practices that support positive outcomes for young children and their families.

- http://www.fipp.org/case/caseinpoint.html

- http://www.fipp.org/case/casemakers.html
- http://www.fipp.org/case/casetools.html
- http://www.fipp.org/case/briefcase.html
- http://www.fipp.org/case/casecollections.html

The Division for Early Childhood (DEC) is a part of the Council for Exceptional Children (CEC). The DEC is especially for individuals who work with or on behalf of children with disabilities—birth through age 8—and their families. Their site includes information and resources for families, policy makers, professionals, students, and other interested browsers. The DEC's recommended practices will be revised and made public in 2013.

- http://www.dec-sped.org

The Early Childhood Technical Assistance (ECTA) Center. Formerly known as NECTAC, ECTA provides many topical resources, state contact information, regulatory guidance, and state training materials. The seven key principles and the agreed-upon practices for providing early intervention services in natural environments—as well as a variety of state resources used for training—are listed here.

- http://ectacenter.org
- http://ectacenter.org/topics/natenv/natenv.asp
- http://www.nectac.org/knowledgepath/ifspoutcomes-iepgoals/ifspoutcomes-iepgoals .asp
  - Developing High-Quality Functional IFSP and IEP Outcomes and Goals: A Training Package (2013)
- http://ectacenter.org/search/natenvbibfinder.asp
  - ECTA's annotated bibliographic database of the literature that supports the seven key principles and agreed-upon practices for providing early intervention services in natural environments

The Early Childhood Outcomes Center (ECO) provides information and resources for state and local administrators, technical assistance providers, families, teachers, and other direct service providers about implementing high-quality outcome systems for early intervention and early childhood special education programs. Included on this web site is a video that describes and illustrates the three child outcomes adopted by the Office of Special Education Programs (OSEP) and reported on by all state early intervention (Part C) and preschool special education (Part B/619) programs as part of their annual performance report.

- http://projects.fpg.unc.edu/~eco
- http://projects.fpg.unc.edu/~eco/pages/videos.cfm

The Individuals with Disabilities Education Act (IDEA) is the U.S. federal law that governs how states and public agencies provide early intervention, special education, and related services to children with disabilities. Part C of this law addresses the provision of early intervention services. Their site includes the statute, regulations, questions and answers, as well as training materials.

* http://idea.ed.gov

The Technical Assistance and Dissemination Network (TA&D) is a network of numerous centers funded by OSEP. The TA&D web sites include information about the various centers and links to the centers. See those listed as *Early Childhood Centers*.

* http://www.tadnet.org

* http://www.tadnet.org/pages/526-find-a-center

State Implementation and Scaling-Up of Evidence-Based Practices (SISEP) Center. This center is a national technical assistance center established to help

> state, regional, and district capacity to provide the critical content and foundation for establishing large-scale, sustainable, high-fidelity implementation of effective education practices to maximize academic and social outcomes of all students, especially those students with disabilities. This work is accomplished through the use of the science of implementation and strategies for organization change.

The site includes a keyword search engine for a variety of resources including briefs, presentations, tools, and videos.

* http://sisep.fpg.unc.edu

* http://implementation.fpg.unc.edu/?o=sisep

National Implementation Research Network (NIRN). Research and evaluation are the main foci of NIRN and their mission is to ultimately improve upon human services by contributing to the science of implementation, organization changes and system reinvention.

* http://nirn.fpg.unc.edu

Concerns-Based Adoption Model (CBAM) is an organizing framework and one of the most widely used perspectives for understanding, facilitating, and evaluating change processes. More than 40 years of research supports CBAM constructs and tools.

* http://www.sedl.org/cbam

Index

Forms, tables, and figures are indicated by *b, t,* and *f,* respectively.

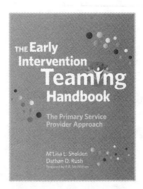
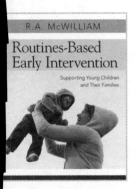